DVD PLAYER
FUNDAMENTALS

DVD PLAYER
FUNDAMENTALS

by John Ross

PROMPT® PUBLICATIONS

PROMPT© Publications is an imprint of Sams Technical Publishing, 5436 W. 78th St., Indianapolis, IN 46268.

International Standard Book Number: 0-7906-1194-5
Library of Congress Catalog Card Number: 00-108429

Acquisitions Editor: Alice J. Tripp
Editor: Will Gurdian
Assistant Editor: Kim Heusel
Typesetting: Will Gurdian
Proofreader: Kim Heusel
Cover Design: Christy Pierce
Graphics Conversion: Christy Pierce, Phil Velikan
Illustrations: Courtesy the author and Burr-Brown Corp., C-Cube Microsystems, Inc., Hitachi Limited, Philips Electronics N.V., ROHM Electronics LLC, Toshiba Corp., and Zenith Electronics Corp.

PRINTED IN THE UNITED STATES OF AMERICA

9 8 7 6 5 4 3 2 1

Dedication

I thank God for giving me the talent, knowledge, patience, and perseverance needed to complete this project. Without Him, the task would have been impossible. In addition, I dedicate this book to my parents—John C. and Lorraine N. Ross—for their ever-present support and priceless encouragement. My mother assisted with the preparation of the figure drawings and research. The staff of Forsyth Library at Fort Hays State University also provided assistance with the procurement of research materials. Finally, I wish to express my appreciation to Alice Tripp, Will Gurdian, and Christy Pierce of Sams Technical Publishing for their assistance and positive attitude.

Acknowledgments

I would like to thank the following companies and manufacturers for allowing me to use these images. The following companies and manufacturers do not state or imply any certification or approval of the material covered in this book.

Zenith Electronics Corporation: Figures 8-1B, 8-1C, 8-10, 8-11, 9-11, 10-6, 10-7, 11-4, 11-5, 12-10, 12-11, 12-12, 12-13, 12-15, 12-19, 12-20.

Philips Electronics N.V.: Figures 10-9, 11-7.

ROHM Electronics LLC: Figures 10-8, 11-10.

C-Cube Microsystems, Inc.: Figure 11-6.

Fairchild Semiconductor Corporation: Figure 9-12.

Burr-Brown Corporation: Figures 11-8, 11-9.

Hitachi Limited: Figures 1-2, 2-2, 2-3, 2-4, 12-1, 12-3, 12-4, 12-5, 12-6.

Toshiba Corporation: Figures 13-5A, 13-5B, 13-6, 13-7, 13-8.

Contents

Preface

Within a fairly short time, optical disc technologies such as compact discs, CD-ROMs, laser discs, and digital video discs (DVDs) have grown from a wish-list item to a technology that we almost take for granted. Prices for optical disc technologies have dropped to the point that most CD-ROM players found in personal computers are considered throwaway items. As disc technology has become commonplace, it has revolutionized the way we store information and play back music, and has allowed everyone access to multimedia technologies.

According to the Consumer Electronics Association, consumers purchased nearly 4 million DVD video players in 1999. Industry projections forecast that DVD player sales will double in 2000. Along with capacity and ease of use, the growing availability of DVD titles has pushed sales to higher levels. Market research firms show the availability of more than 5,000 DVD video titles and predict that sales of DVD titles will surpass sales of CD-ROM titles by 2002. With this, industry experts believe sales of DVD devices and titles will exhibit a growth pattern similar to the one experienced by CD-ROMs.

When considering recordable disc technologies, market projections show that shipments of DVD-ROM drives will surpass those of CD-ROM drives in 2001. Predictions point to healthy growth in the DVD-ROM drive market and indicate that sales will grow to more than 60 million units. Indeed, sales of DVD-Video, DVD-Audio, and DVD-ROM devices should show exponential growth during the next five years. Within the decade, DVD technologies will replace audio CD, videotape, laser disc, and CD-ROM technology and become the standard for home entertainment and desktop computing.

The popularity of disc technologies has grown due to several significant factors. While a compact disc can hold up to 650 megabytes of data, a digital video disc may contain as much as 10 gigabytes of data. Moreover, the DVD format supports future digital standards. With the introduction of new technologies such as blue lasers, DVD-ROM capacities will increase well beyond 2.6 gigabytes per side. By 2005, DVD-RAM discs will offer 50 gigabytes of storage space per side.

Despite this capacity to store immense amounts of textual, graphic, audio, or other digital information, disc readers and recorders remain available at low costs. Furthermore, the disc offers the consumer a very robust, removable multimedia storage medium that has a long lifetime. DVD-Video covers the disc technologies that play full-length movies and interface with a television. A close cousin, DVD-Audio, reproduces studio- quality audio and works like the common compact disc audio systems that have become widely popular. While DVD-ROM describes the read-only disc that functions with a computer system, DVD-RAM is a writeable version of the same technology.

As a result, the introduction of DVD technology has taken disc technologies to a new level. Since DVD technology operates with digital media, it offers interactivity within movies or other formats, real-time simultaneous support of multiple languages, and the use of multiple camera angles—not to mention parental control and other functions. The storage capability of a DVD allows the running of up to nine hours of Dolby AC-3 audio and MPEG-2 video programming.

Scope and Purpose of This Book

Although steady price decreases have accompanied the popularity of disc technologies, service opportunities remain. Many problems that occur with disc technologies have fairly easy solutions. As with VCRs, the disc players and recorders contain a mix of mechanical and electronic subsystems. Mechanical problems involve common issues such as dirty or misadjusted assemblies or dirty lenses. Electronic problems include tracking adjustments, servo adjustments, failed laser diodes, or bad connections.

While carefully considering the theory and characteristics of digital video disc technologies, *DVD Player Fundamentals* also takes a close look at the assemblies and circuits that allow CD-ROM and DVD players to function. This book discusses the physical construction of the discs, the information-encoding process, and the use of Dolby AC-3 audio and MPEG-2 video programming. In addition, this book covers the application of electronic systems such as digital signal processors, optical pickup units, microcontrollers, and audio-video decoders.

The first three chapters lay the groundwork for the remainder of the book with a comprehensive overview of optical disc, compact disc, and DVD fundamentals. While Chapter 4 details DVD-Video specifications and provides an overview of DVD video player functions, Chapter 5 considers copy protection for all DVD formats. Chapter 6 continues with discussions introduced in Chapters 4 and 5 with a detailed look at compression technologies. Chapter 6 emphasizes MPEG-2 and Dolby AC-3 video and audio compression.

Chapter 7 moves away from the concentration on DVD-Video and DVD-Audio technologies with a study of recordable DVD technologies. The chapter considers DVD-ROM, DVD-RAM, DVD-R, DVD-RW, and DVD+RW formats.

Chapter 8 begins a five-chapter focus on DVD video player circuitry with an analysis of power supplies found in the players. Each chapter in this series uses block and schematic diagrams of the Zenith DVC2200 DVD video player as a basis for the analysis. While Chapter 8 defines the purpose of electronic systems and provides an overview of common power supply designs used within DVD players, Chapter 9 continues the discussion with a look at the optical pickup unit, motor controls, signal processors, and microcontrollers.

Chapter 10 begins with an overview of frequency and signal characteristics and the factors that affect those characteristics, such as gain and amplification. The chapter continues with a look at basic circuits that process rf, if, and agc signals, moving then to an overview of digital signal processors.

Chapter 11 explains the characteristics of the video and audio signals through block diagrams and waveforms. After providing that basis, the chapter defines typical circuits that process video and audio circuits and then progresses to circuits used in the Zenith video player. Along with video and audio signal processing, Chapter 11 also covers the circuits that provide the MPEG, NTSC, and PAL encoding and encoding.

Chapter 12 continues with the analysis of DVD player circuits by examining the operation of the system microcontroller, as well as the customer control, customer display, and remote control circuits. In addition, the chapter shows the integration involved with typical DVD video player operations. By closing with a look at customer controls and displays, the chapter shows how circuit functions interface with the needs of the customer.

Chapter 13 concludes the discussion of DVD support circuitry by making another transition to computer systems and DVD readers. The chapter discusses software and hardware support for DVD-ROM and DVD-RAM devices.

About the Author

John Ross has authored three books on electronics and communications technologies, including *Guide to Satellite TV Technology* from Prompt®. In addition, he has served Fort Hays State University in a variety of capacities since 1989. Past responsibilities for FHSU include working as the manager of microcomputer services, director of the University Card Center, and director of special academic projects. In his current role as assistant to the provost, Ross has worked with university accreditation and assessment issues, while providing  project management for an initiative to offer distance-education courses to the military. In 1999, he was appointed director of Forsyth Library. Ross holds a bachelor's degree in English and a master's in political science from FHSU.

Optical Disc Technologies

Introduction

The term "optical disc technology" covers a wide range of applications, including laser discs, compact discs (CDs), and digital versatile discs (DVDs). Each type of optical technology involves the use of special materials and processes for the construction of the disc, electronic systems for data conversion, and lasers for reading and writing digital data to and from the disc. While optical discs receive data through an encoding process that involves the use of a high-power laser, the reading of data from the disc involves the use of a low-power laser. Manufacturing processes include mastering and mass production, as well as the use of a drive to write data to an individual disc.

This book emphasizes the most recent and most versatile optical disc technology: DVD. Although digital versatile discs have familial roots that extend back to older compact disc technologies, DVD technologies have distinctive characteristics that allow for a vast array of uses. Chapters 1, 2, and 3 lay the groundwork for the remainder of the book with a comprehensive overview of optical disc, compact disc, and DVD fundamentals.

Premastering and Mastering

Premastering involves the preparation of data for recording to the optical disc. During this process, electronic systems index, organize, and reformat the data. In addition, the premastering process applies error correction to the data.

Mastering physically transfers the data into indentations and spaces pressed into the disc material.

The premastering and mastering processes begin with the spin coating of a layer of light-sensitive photoresist onto the clean glass master disc from a solvent solution. From there, the photoresist becomes exposed to a modulated beam of a short-wavelength light that carries encoded data. Developing involves the use of a wet process to etch away exposed areas and to leave a pattern of tracks, grooves, pits, and lands on the master disc. Next, an electroplating technique coats the master disc with a 300 μm-thick metal layer and forms a stamper, or negative replica, of the disc. The forming of the stamper destroys the photoresist layer. Injection molding of the polycarbonate material produces the surface of the disc.

Compact discs, digital versatile discs, and laser discs carry data that may take the form of audio and video information, parity bits for error detection, control symbols, display information, and software applications. The placement of data on the disc begins with the bonding of two plastic substrates that may carry one or two layers of data. With usage depending on the disc manufacturer, three different bonding processes exist for DVD discs.

Data encodes onto the disc as indentations (called pits) and spaces (called lands) through a stamping process. Aligned into spiral tracks, each transition from a pit to a land or a land to a pit represents a binary 1, while each constant land or constant pit represents a binary 0. As a combination, the pits and lands represent the signal pattern given through a modulation process. Because of the precise nature of the data encoding and the small size of the pits and lands, the manufacturing process must ensure that no pinholes occur in the reflective layer. Even the smallest pinhole can cause a data dropout, resulting in errors during playback.

Archimedes Spiral

Optical discs use the Archimedes spiral as a data-formatting pattern. First studied by the Greek mathematician and inventor Archimedes in 225 B.C., the spiral has linear increases in diameter as the radius increases. As shown in

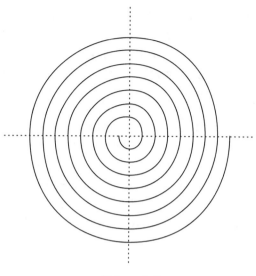

Figure 1-1

Figure 1-1, every interval between the turns of the spiral forms a track pitch and remains constant for optical disc formats. The curve created by the spiral can work as a cam for converting uniform angular motion into uniform linear motion. In turn, the cam consists of one arch of the spiral above the y-axis together with its reflection from the x-axis. Rotating the cam with uniform angular velocity about the center will result in uniform linear motion at the point where the cam crosses the y-axis.

Substrate Materials and Characteristics

Construction of optical discs utilizes substrate material that, in raw form, consists of a slab of plastic or glass. Focusing a beam of laser light through the substrate causes the development of an aberration called a coma. This occurs because of the relationship between the tilt of the disc and the optical axis of the objective lens found in the laser assembly.

New optical disc technologies such as DVD rely on polycarbonate—an inexpensive, moldable plastic also used for bulletproof windows—as the substrate material. Along with providing an inexpensive, moldable material, polycarbonate also offers optical characteristics that make the material valuable for disc applications. Polycarbonate remains transparent at infrared, red, and blue wavelengths. The transparent characteristics allow a focused beam of light to reach the data-storage layers of the disc.

In technical terms, polycarbonate classifies as a birefringent plastic. For some applications such as magnetic-optical disc technologies, birefringence becomes more of a problem than a solution. Birefringence refers to an optical characteristic that negatively affects the polarization state of a beam as it travels through the substrate material. Substrate material has refractive indices along the radial, azimuthal, and vertical directions, represented by n_r, n_ϕ, and n_z. As a combination, the in-plane birefringence has the characteristics of $n_r \cong n_\phi$ while the vertical birefringence has the characteristics of $n_r \cong n_z$.

The different levels of thermal heating that occur as the laser beam encodes data onto the disc change the reflectivity of the data layer and also affect the birefringence of the material. During the construction process, balancing techniques reduce the birefringence to a low level and reduce any optical losses that may occur. Other materials such as amorphous polyolefin have almost no birefringence and may take the place of polycarbonate in future optical disc applications.

Optical Encoding Methods

Encoding data onto an optical disc involves coating the substrate material with a photoresistive, reflective metal material, embossing a pattern of grooves and pits onto the substrate during an injection-molding process, converting and writing the data to the disc, and creating a special glass master disc. While compact discs rely on a single data-storage layer, discs used for DVD technologies may have multiple layers. While the storage layer sandwiches between two dielectric layers, a gold or aluminum reflective layer protected by a lacquer layer caps the storage level.

The dielectric and reflective layers create an optically tuned structure that has specific reflective and absorptive qualities. Encoding data to the disc with a laser beam takes advantage of those qualities, as well as the thermal characteristics of the materials.

Bonding Processes

Hot-melt bonding uses an adhesive to glue two substrates together for either single-sided or double-sided discs. Radical UV-cured bonding coats one or both of the substrates with a UV-cured resin that has the consistency of lacquer and then spins the disc for a consistent coating. The resin provides the optical and mechanical characteristics required for single-layer and dual-layer DVD performance. Cationic UV-bonding screen prints the resin over both substrates before bonding occurs, but uses an opaque resin not suitable for dual-layer discs. Each method uses ultraviolet light to harden the resin.

For single-layer discs, the bonding process places layer 0 closest to the readout side of the disc and layer 1 farther from the readout side. As shown in Figure 1-2, the optical pickup unit found in either a DVD player or DVD reader will read layer 0 first. Single-layer construction then uses either a vacuum-coating or ion-sputtering process to apply a reflective coating of either aluminum or silver over the plastic substrates.

For CD, CD-ROM, and DVD 5 format disks, the manufacturing process sputters a 55 nm-thick aluminum film on the polycarbonate substrate to ensure that the phase contrast generated by the pits during readout complies with the media specifications for the signal levels.

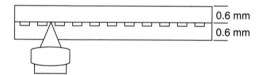

(a) Single-sided single-layer (4.7 GB)

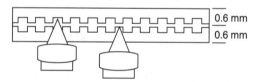

(b) Single-sided dual-layer (8.5 GB)

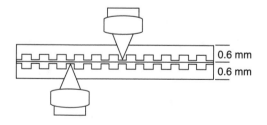

(c) Double-sided single-layer (9.5 GB)

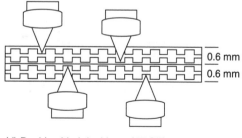

(d) Double-sided dual-layer (17 GB)

Figure 1-2

Application of the reflective coating establishes a semitransparent coating over layer 0, allowing the laser to reflect from the layer during a read. Because the laser must focus through layer 0 to read layer 1, the second layer has much greater reflectivity than the first.

Construction methods for dual-layer discs differ for single-sided, dual-layer discs and double-sided, dual-layer discs. For the former, the construction process involves stamping the data layer onto the plastic substrate and adding a semireflective coating. An upside-down inner data layer then stamps onto the second substrate before the addition of a fully reflective coating. The bonding process concludes with the gluing of the second substrate to the first.

Double-sided, dual-layer discs follow a nearly identical bonding process. But an application of thin molten transparent UV resin covers the outer layer after the addition of the semireflective layer. A final layer of acrylic resin protects the reflective and data layers on single-layer and dual-layer discs.

Data Conversion for Optical Discs

When used for reproduction of video and audio signals, the construction of a master disc requires the conversion of information from an analog to a digital format. As Figure 1-3 shows, this conversion process includes several substeps that establish consistent reading and writing of data from the disc. Electronic circuitry measures the analog signal and divides the signal into parts that eventually translate into digital information.

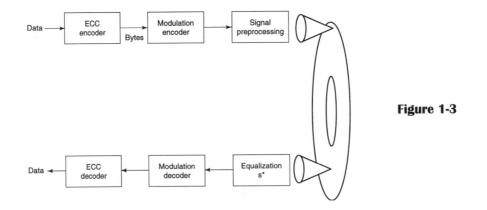

Figure 1-3

Binary Numbers

Computer systems work with the binary number system or a numbering system that allows only two values—0 and 1. The use of binary numbers in those systems breaks information down into elementary levels. In addition, since the binary number system relies only on 0s and 1s, it provides a very basic method for counting and accumulating values.

If we look at the digits of a binary number, each value in the columns equals a value based on the powers of 2. For example, a binary number represented by 111 has $2^0 = 1$ (or 1x1) for the rightmost column, $2^1 = 4$ (or 2x1) for the middle column, and $2^2 = 8$ (or 4 x 1) for the leftmost column. In the decimal system, this value would equal 1x1+1x2+1x4 (or 7). A binary number of 1101 equals 1x1+0x2+1x4+1x8 (or a decimal equivalent of 13). An electronic system uses high and low signals to represent binary numbers. Each high and low signal is separated by an area of voltage that has no binary meaning. While a high signal has a value of 3V dc to 5V dc, a low signal has a value of 0V dc to 1V dc.

Bytes and Bits

The simplicity of the binary system allows computer systems to move numbers from one part of a system to another and to work with large numbers. Each binary position is called a bit, while a group of eight bits equals one byte. The sum of bits provides a method for assigning a value. As a result, the number of bits required to complete a task depends on the magnitude of the number. With each bit existing as either a 1 or 0, the value of each successive bit can increase by a maximum value of 2. As a result, the individual bits of a binary number translate to the following decimal values.

32	16	8	4	2	1	1/2	1/4	1/8	1/16
2^5	2^4	2^3	2^2	2^1	2^0	2^{-1}	2^{-2}	2^{-3}	2^{-4}

Going back to the addition of binary numbers, the sum of true values in a byte equals a decimal value—that is, a byte that appears as 11001101 has an equivalent decimal value of 206.

Placing Digital Information on the Disc

Digital information has certain discrete values held either in a low or a high state. In contrast to analog information, the digital information shown in Figure 1-4 offers precise values at specific times and changes step-by-step. When considering optical discs, this preciseness translates into immunity against electrical noise distortion and variations in component values. Noise and component variations do not cause the low and high states of a digital signal to appear as opposite values.

With audio and video signals, the placement of data on the disc in-volves converting the original signals from an analog format into a digital format. By definition, analog information represents a quantity that may vary over a continuous range of values. Examples of analog signal waveforms include the sine wave, rectangular wave, triangle wave, and sawtooth wave shown in Figure 1-5. The square waves and pulses shown in Figure 1-6 pro-vide the basis for the digital information depicted in Figure 1-4.

An analog-to-digital conversion (adc) circuit converts the analog signal to a digital number that corresponds to the value of the analog signal. The adc circuit uses a sampling rate that represents the number of conversions per second for the conversion process. The digital number provided by the adc circuit may take the form of a regular binary number, a binary number with a sign bit, or a special format.

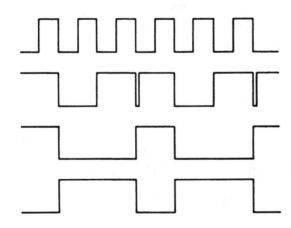

Figure 1-4

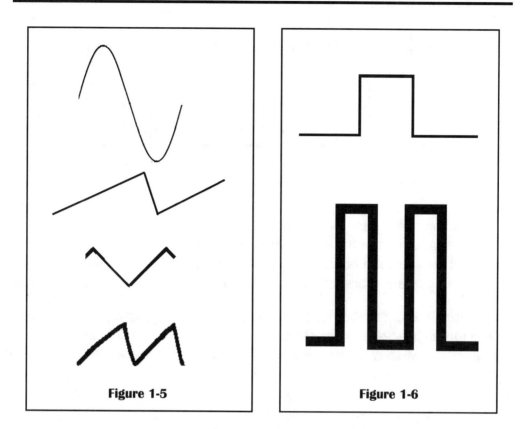

Figure 1-5   Figure 1-6

Sampling Audio and Video Data

Established through Nyquist's theorem, sampling begins the process of converting an analog audio signal to a digital format. Nyquist's sampling theorem states a sampling rate for the accurate reproduction of the analog signal. In mathematical terms, the sampling theorem shows that the sampling frequency must equal or have a greater value than the highest frequency found in the original signal.

Although the sampling theorem provides simplicity, two constraints affect the use of sampling in a digital audio system. With the first constraint, passing the original signal through an ideal low-pass filter limits the bandwidth of the signal to half the sampling frequency. A second constraint again passes the signal through an ideal low-pass filter for the reproduction of the analog signal.

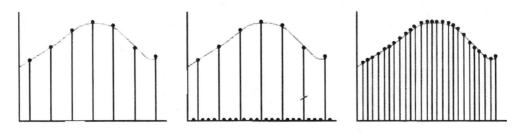

Figure 1-7

As shown in Figure 1-7, sampling measures audio and video data in intervals that equal tenths of millivolts. Each change in signal strength and polarity at the intervals becomes an expression of a decimal number. In addition, the sampling rate establishes the accurate reproduction of the original signal.

During the digitization of an analog-video signal, sampling of the luminance (or brightness) component occurs 13.5 million times per second, or at a rate of 13.5 MHz. With the sampling of the luminance signal, the digitization of the video signal provides an accurate reproduction of any activity found within a monochrome image. Sampling of the chrominance (or color) signals occurs 3.375 million times per second, or at a rate of 3.375 MHz. The difference in the sampling rates of luminance and chrominance signals is due to the fact that luminance signals contain brightness, contrast, and green signal information, while chrominance signals provide the red and blue color components for the complete image.

As the analog-to-digital conversion process occurs, the adc circuitry samples the signal during a given number of times per second and establishes a sampling rate. The sampling depth represents a given number of bits per sample. With more bits per sample, each sample may have more possible values.

For example, a one-bit sample depth represents either an on or an off condition, while a two-bit sample will have an on, off, and two intermediate values. An eight-bit sample depth will have 256 possible values. The minimum sampling depth required for accurate video representation is 24 bits (or 3 bytes), and provides for a maximum of 16 million colors.

Sampling Audio Data

For audio, each sound frequency found in the sample corresponds to a digital value. Conversion of music into a digital format requires a sampling rate of 44,000 samples per second and a sampling depth of 16 bits. With each sample equaling two bytes of information and 44,000 samples per second, every second of music results in 88 kilobytes of digital information.

Aliasing

Aliasing occurs when the sampling constraints do not remain in place. Without the constraints, the system responds with sampling errors that modulate the input signal and cause distortion. Frequencies generated through the errors image, or alias, back into the audible band.

Quantization

Quantization assigns numeric values to sampled data. The quantization divides a sampled data element into separate, distinct units (or quanta). Then, the process assigns numeric values to each unit. For example, the quantization for video signals assigns values to the intensity of the electron beam needed to accurately reproduce a televised image.

Typically, the quantization process allocates eight bits for each green, red, and blue image component. In turn, this yields 256 discrete values for each image component. Thus, one string of numbers represents the green signal, a second string of numbers represents the red signal, and a third string of numbers the blue signal. The three number strings combine to represent the video signal.

Going back to sampling rates, the green signal includes luminance values and has numbers appearing 13.5 million times per second, while the red and blue signals each have numbers appearing 3.375 million times per second. Each time a number appears, it has a value between 0 and 255. All possible combinations of these three values yield 16,777,216 different colors.

Oversampling

Oversampling yields tremendous performance through the use of a sampling frequency greater than the sampling frequency given through Nyquist's theorem. By interleaving zeroes between each sample with additional samples, oversampling boosts the signal-to-noise ratio and reduces quantization noise in the audio band. When used with oversampling circuits, digital signal processors operate as digital filters and offer precise, repeatable functions that have lower noise and distortion.

Modulating the Data

Modulation involves encoding a carrier wave with another signal or signals that represent some type of intelligence. For example, an audio frequency signal affects the frequency or amplitude of radio frequency (rf) waves, so that the waves represent communicated information. The carrier wave is the sinusoidal component of a modulated wave and has a frequency independent of the modulating wave.

As the name suggests, the carrier wave carries the transmitted signal. Modulating methods for optical discs include polarization rotation and reflectance of light. Most optical disc manufacturers use reflectance modulation for compact discs.

Digital communication systems use pulse modulation to convert the intelligence held within the modulating signal into a pulse. After the conversion occurs, the system pulses the rf signal for the type of pulse modulation used. The modulating pulses may control the amplitude, frequency, on-time, or phase of the carrier. Pulse-modulation methods include pulse-amplitude modulation, frequency shift keying, pulse-width modulation, and pulse-phase modulation.

Pulse Code Modulation

Invented in 1939, pulse code modulation (pcm) uses 0 and 1 pulse values to generate a 16-pulse train that indicates a sampled value. A linear pcm system encapsulates the following processes.

- Uniform sampling
- Uniform quantization
- Optimal dither
- Nondynamic psychoacoustic noise shaping
- Transparent data compression

Adaptive differential pcm varies the number of bits that represent a difference between consecutive 16-bit samples according to the signal.

Encoding the Data

Although programmers work with higher-level languages, and although customers see or hear information in an appropriate format, processors operate with machine languages and binary code. Optical technology uses an encoding scheme to produce eight-bit computer bytes. The binary 1s found in the data represent the transitions between the imprinted areas of the disc. Binary 0s represent the run-length of the data. At a rate of 1 million bits per second, a 16-bit number consisting of 1s and 0s can represent as many as 65,536 values.

As the process continues, encoding circuitry transforms the digital data into a usable form for placement on the disc. Each 16-bit binary word generated during the conversion process divides into two eight-bit symbols. Then, the encoding circuitry arranges the eight-bit symbols into frames that contain 24 bytes of data, adding eight bytes of error-correction data, a three-byte synchronization pattern, and one byte of subcode information. The addition of this information establishes an addressing scheme for the optical disc that shows the location of the data.

Disc Layout

CDs and DVDs divide into sections that support error-correction data, addressing information, and user data (see Figure 1-8 and Table 1-1 on Page 14). The lead-in contains information about the track layout of the current session. Written with the lead-in, the lead-out indicates the physical end of a session but does not contain data. While each lead-in uses 4,500 sectors

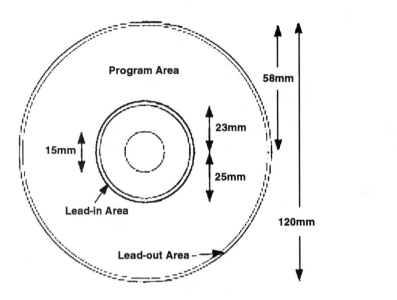

Figure 1-8

Table 1-1: Compact Disc and DVD Layout Dimensions

	Compact Disc	DVD
Outer Lead-in Width	117 mm	117 mm
Inner Lead-in Width	46 mm	45 mm
Outer Data Width	116 mm	116 mm
Inner Data Width	50 mm	48 mm
Center Hole Diameter	15 mm	15 mm

(or approximately nine megabytes of available disc space), the first lead-out uses 6,750 sectors (or 13 megabytes of space). Subsequent lead-out areas use 2,250 sectors (or four megabytes of space).

Moreover, CDs and DVDs have a diameter of 12 centimeters and a 15-millimeter center hole. For a compact disc, the lead-in contains digital silence in the main channel and places a table of contents in the subcode Q channel. The table of contents allows the laser pickup head to follow the pits and synchronize to the audio data before the start of the program area. The program area for CDs contains up to about 76 minutes of data, divided into a maximum of 99 tracks.

Forward-Error Correction (FEC)

Errors during the reproduction of audio information, video information, or data from an optical disc can occur because of scratches on the disc or problems within the playback circuitry. After the Verbiti error-correction code has been removed and used as needed, optical disc technology uses a second form of error correction called the Reed-Solomon code. A Reed-Solomon decoder processes each block of data and attempts to correct errors and recover the original data. The characteristics of the Reed-Solomon code dictate the number and type of correctable errors.

With the Reed-Solomon method, 188 bytes out of every 204 bytes are received as data, and the remainder are used as parity bits to help correct any remaining errors. Additionally, the forward-error correction (FEC) scheme also uses data-stream interleaving to prevent noise bursts from interrupting the flow of data in the same way that CDs use it to prevent dropouts caused by scratches.

These error-correction routines make the probability of an undetected error to be less than one in 1,025. In more physical terms, this means that there would be only one undetected error in 2 quadrillion discs. The error-correction data alone requires 288 bytes for every 2,048 bytes of informational content on the disc. This allows for the correction of numerous bad bits, including bursts of bad data more than 1,000 bits long.

Using linear block-based error-correcting codes that have a wide range of applications in digital communications and storage, Reed-Solomon codes operate as a subset of nonbinary codes. Specified as RS(n,k) with s-bit symbols, the Reed-Solomon code uses k to represent data, n to represent a parity code, and s to represent a quantity. During encoding, the Reed-Solomon encoder takes k data symbols of each s-bit and adds parity symbols to generate an n symbol codeword that has n-k parity symbols of each s-bit. Figure 1-9 (on Page 16) shows a typical Reed-Solomon codeword. The amount of processing required to encode and decode Reed-Solomon codes corresponds with the number of parity symbols per codeword. During decoding, a Reed-Solomon decoder can correct up to t symbols that contain errors. In this case, t (or the total number of symbols) has a relationship with the parity and data symbols

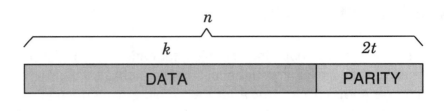

Figure 1-9

where $2t = n-k$. Although a Reed-Solomon decoder can correct a large number of errors, that capability requires additional processing power.

Cyclic Redundancy Check (CRC)

A cyclic redundancy check (CRC) detects errors in data transfer through the use of a mathematical algorithm. During operation, a special polynomial algorithm produces and uses a coefficient and a remainder that have a length of either 16 or 32 bits to verify the accuracy of the data transmission. CRC values change with the changing of any one bit in the file and occur as a reliable check of data integrity.

Cross-Interleaved Reed-Solomon Code (CIRC)

The cross-interleaved Reed-Solomon code (CIRC) automatically inserts any lost or damaged information through mathematical calculations. A cross-interleaved Reed-Solomon code encoder adds two bits of parity information to correct errors and interleaves the data on the disc to protect from burst errors. Compensating for even minor scratches, CIRC corrects error bursts of a maximum 3,500 bits (or 2.4 millimeters in length) and error bursts of a maximum 12,000 bits (or 8.5 millimeters in length).

Synchronization

DVD relies on a synchronization pattern in the pit structure to regulate the digital stream of information at a constant bit rate. The synchronization pattern supplies the readout system in a DVD reader or player with information needed to identify the location of specific data. For example, the sync bytes synchronize the read head onto the coding in the block and allow the reading of data to begin at the right place. DVD products use a combination of coding and firmware to synchronize video and audio output.

Subcode Information

Compact disc technologies rely on subcode information, or an addressing scheme represented as a time code. In practice, the subcode information travels in parallel with the main digital data stream. The time code represents the play time of the disc. As a result, the subcode-addressing scheme counts in units of minutes and seconds. Seventy-five data frames occur each second.

Sectors

The implementation of CD-ROM (compact disc read-only memory) technologies as a data-carrying optical disc technology required the use of an additional addressing scheme involving sectors and sector addresses. While sector refers to a block of data in a data media, a sector address uses a unique numeric label to identify sectors in databased optical disc formats. CD-ROM and DVD-ROM sectors typically comprise 2,048 bytes, although a variety of other sizes are possible. A player will access data on a sector-by-sector basis, and each sector has an associated sector address.

Although sectors are the smallest, independently addressable and accessible portion of the CD-ROM or DVD-ROM, each sector also allows access to smaller logical blocks. Using the ISO-9660 file format, a physical sector consisting of a 2,048-byte user-data area subdivides into logical blocks of 512, 1,024, or 2,048 bytes. With the address of the header bytes indicating minutes, seconds, and additional information for the blocks, the information also identifies the logical block number (LBN).

For example, the first accessible physical sector occurs at 00:02:00 and contains the LBN 0. With blocks occurring every 512 bytes, 18,000 blocks equal one minute, while 300 blocks equal one second and four logical blocks create a sector.

File Systems

A file system facilitates the storage and retrieval of files. In the computer industry, operating systems use a logical structure for data storage. For example, all files have a unique name. The file system also assigns files to hierarchically organized directories and permits files to have associated attributes. Specific to media types, the physical format establishes layout of data, data modes, error detection and correction, physical sector addressing, and other management techniques for data.

Recovering the Data During Playback

The data is played back with an optical pickup, which measures the intensity of the reflection from a laser beam directed at the track of data. As the playback spot size is wider than the pits on the disc, when reading a pit some light is reflected from the bottom of the pit and some light is reflected from the areas between the tracks. As pits are a quarter wavelength deep, the light reflected from the bottom of the pit is out of phase with the light reflected from the top surface, resulting in destructive interference of the light. This effect produces a detectable optical contrast that the player uses to recover the data from the disc.

Spinning the disc at a constant speed and then directing a laser beam onto the surface of the disc results in modulation. The pits cause optical contrast either "on" or "off" in the beam that is reflected from the surface of the disc. In turn, this beam is "read" by a sensor that translates the variations into an electrical signal processed through analog or digital electronic circuitry. It then emerges as pure data, sound, visual images, or a combination of signals.

Constant Linear Velocity (CLV) and Constant Angular Velocity (CAV)

Optical technology uses constant linear velocity (CLV) rotation, which relies on a spiral track of coding that begins near the center of the disc. With this approach, data reads from the CD-ROM at a constant speed, because the disc-rotation speed corresponds with the position of the read head. Data passes under the read head at the same rate regardless of the location in either the inner or outer parts of the track.

As the speed of a CLV drive increases, access times increase, due to the difficulty of abruptly changing the spindle velocity needed to maintain a constant high data-transfer rate. In comparison to CLV, the constant angular velocity (CAV) mode transfers data at a variable rate, while the drive spins at a constant rate. CAV maintains a steady spin speed, resulting in increased data-transfer rates and reduced seek times as the read head moves toward its outside edge. While early CLV drives had average access times greater than 500 ms, modern CAV drives typically have average access times less than 100 ms.

2

CD Standards and Technologies

Introduction

First introduced as an audio CD in 1982 and then as a CD-ROM in 1985, compact disc technology has served as a carrier for music, data, and multimedia information. Within a relatively short time, compact disc technology has become the most popular media for entertainment and computer applications. The combination of large storage capacity, small size, recordable media, and the availability of low-cost players and drives firmly established compact disc technology in many households and businesses.

Red Book Standards: CD-DA and CD-Extra

Established in 1982 as the first defined standard for a compact disc, the Red Book defines compact disc standards and the format of a digital audio CD (CD-DA). Along with the size and mass of the disc, these standards also cover rotational speed, pit depth and length, and track pitch. The Red Book Plus standard contains extensions of the Red Book standards, such as CD-Extra.

With the digital audio format, a producer can store a maximum of 74 minutes of uncompressed digital audio data at a fixed frequency of 44.1 kHz. A CD-DA disc consists of several audio tracks, with each track representing a song, and sectors that have 2,352 bytes of user data. While each sector has an address designated in minutes, seconds, and sectors, each track must contain a minimum of four seconds (or 300 sectors). Address information stores in subchannel Q. Absolute time (or Atime) addressing measures from the start of the disc, while track-relative time measures from the start of the track. With all of the 2,352 bytes of a sector allocated as user data, the CD-DA transfers data at a rate of 1.41 Mbps. The disc format has a sampling rate of 44.1 kHz, with 16-bit samples for two stereo channels.

For each sector, 882 additional bytes store on the disc and provide 784 bytes of CIRC and 98 control bytes of error detection and correction code. Each sequential bit of the control byte receives a designation letter ranging from "P" to "W." The data stream resulting from all first bits of the 98 control bytes establishes the "P" subchannel, while the stream of all second bits establishes the "Q" subchannel.

A third subchannel combines the bits "R", "S", "T", "U", "V," and "W" into a six-bit word and produces the "R through W" subchannel. The "P" subchannel flags the beginning of the audio data in a track, while the "Q" subchannel provides the time code. In the lead-in of the disc, this subchannel contains the table of contents. Beside sync, control, and error-correction bits, the "R through W" subchannel may also include graphic or MIDI data.

Table of Contents

Referring back to Chapter 1, the table of contents lists the files and addresses of a CD-ROM application (also see Figure 2-1). In current multisession applications, each session has an individual table of contents. During operation,

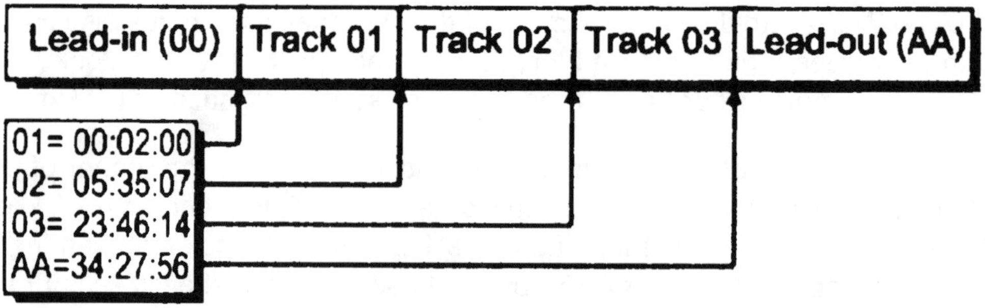

Lead-in (00)	Track 01	Track 02	Track 03	Lead-out (AA)

01= 00:02:00
02= 05:35:07
03= 23:46:14
AA=34:27:56

Figure 2-1

an application scans the disc and begins to read the last table of contents first. Since file sizes can change and be broken into parts with magneto-optical discs, the file-allocation table doubles as the table of contents. The file-allocation table has an updateable table of file locations for the logical partition.

CD-Extra

As mentioned, each writing of data to a compact disc creates a session. Because some file formats require the writing of data in one session, the number of sessions becomes important for many applications. Formats that support multisession capabilities allow the addition of new data after the initial creation of the disc. CD-Extra combines normal compact disc audio tracks with CD-ROM/XA (Compact Disc Read-only Memory/eXtended Architecture) data tracks on the traditional disc and provides multisession capabilities.

While compact disc audio players can access only the first session including the audio tracks, multisession CD-ROM drives can read the information in the second session located in the outer perimeter of the disc. The second session could include video clips, lyrics, liner notes, photographs, animation, text, and multimedia applications. In addition, CD-Extra discs may contain a file that gives information about various computer platforms that can execute the applications on the disc. Designed to start the CD title when the disc inserts in the CD-ROM drive, the CD-Extra format operates with Microsoft Windows and Apple Macintosh OS.

Orange Book Standards: Magneto-Optical, Write-Once, Rewritable

During the implementation of optical disc technologies, manufacturers have developed several methods of writing to the media. With write-once, read-many (WORM) discs, a drive can write information once. Replacing the data written to the disc requires the erasure of the disc. Magneto-optical discs allow writing, erasing, and rewriting of information placed on a disc. Originally published by Philips in 1990, the Orange Book standard defines magneto-optical and write-once technologies. In addition, the Orange Book sets standards for Compact Disc-Rewritable (CD-R) products that use phase change methods for writing data.

Magneto-Optical Discs

Magneto-optical (CD-MO) drives implement magneto-optical recording technology on standard size discs that have a rating for millions of rewrites. Constructed from an alloy of terbium ferrite and cobalt, the reflective layer of the magneto-optical disc has different reflective characteristics when struck by a reading laser beam.

Since CD-MO drives use two optical heads, slower access and seek times occur. One head erases data while the other head writes data in a double-pass process. The read-only area of a CD-MO disc contains system and other information that allows reading of the CD-MO disc by a CD-ROM drive. The remainder of the disc space establishes a recordable-user area that provides an accessible area for recording data.

CD-WO and CD-R

CD-Write-Once (CD-WO) defines the technology for writing data to the tracks of a recordable disc. But a CD-WO will not accept the erasing and rewriting of data. The initial tracks of a CD-WO include the program-calibration area, the lead-in area, and the program area set aside for the user data. The recording session finishes with the lead out. A CD-WO hybrid disc establishes an area for the placement of read-only files. The remainder of the disc provides for the write-once data.

Due to standardization given through the Orange Book, a CD-ROM drive or audio CD player can read a CD-R or CD-WO. In addition, the Orange Book permits the presence of multiple sessions on the CD-R, with each session having an individual lead-in, program area, and lead-out. After storing the data and finishing the first session, another session with other data can record at a later time. Within each lead-in, a table of contents (TOC) also writes to the disc. The last lead-in contains the updates for the entire disc.

The construction of a CD-WO or CD-R applies a thin layer of cyanide or phthalocyanine organic dye to the polycarbonate substrate. Applying a laser beam causes the light-absorption characteristics of the dye to change. Since the rotation speed of the disc depends on the laser-writing location, the disc also contains information about the velocity of the CLV disc. The information becomes accessible through defined waveforms that have a frequency maintained at 22.05 kHz during recording.

Frequency modulation indicates the position of the laser and provides time-code information called absolute time in pregroove (ATIP). At the beginning of the disc and just preceding the lead-in, a zone called the power-calibration area (PCA) provides alignment information. Used for partially recorded discs, the program-memory area (PMA) contains the track numbers of the recorded titles and includes absolute start and stop times for data recorded to the tracks.

Virtual Partitions

CDR is a write-once, sequentially written medium. To provide the appearance of a read-write disc, it uses a virtual allocation table (VAT). Essentially everything uses a virtual sector number, which is mapped via the VAT to the physical sector. In that way, files can be rewritten simply by rewriting the VAT (which is always the last thing written on the disc). Thus, it provides a way to effectively provide for the appearance of a rewritable disc on a write-once medium.

Spared Partitions

Spared partitions are intended for use on CD-Rewritable (CD-RW) discs, to handle the fact that unlike optical discs or DVD-RAM, there is no automatic bad block handling. A spared partition table is put on the disc, which contains details of any blocks remapped because they are bad.

Phase-Change Technology

CD-RW discs use phase-change technology and the universal disk format (UDF) file system for the rewriting of data in one pass. Phase-change technology uses an information layer based on an alloy of silver, indium, antimony, and tellurium. In the initial phase, the alloy remains in an amorphous state. Heating small zones of the surface with a high-energy laser causes the amorphous material to change into a crystalline state.

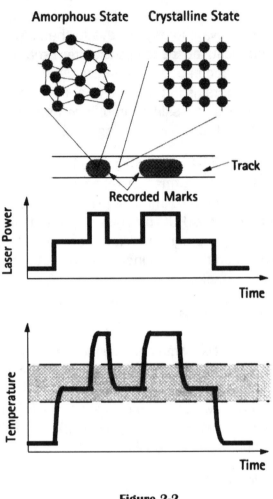

Figure 2-2

As shown in Figure 2-2, the use of a different power laser during the recording process causes the material contained within the active layer of the disc to change between an amorphous and a crystalline state. The distinct states have different levels of reflectivity detectable by the optical readers found in DVD drives and allow the reading of data.

Before recording begins, the phase-change material remains in a crystalline state and has high reflectivity. Modulating the light intensity of the laser beam writes data marks to the surface of the disc. To do this, the 10 mW-laser spot melts the reflective recording layer. Increasing the temperature of the laser beam and then rapidly decreasing the laser power to 5 mW causes rapid cooling of the disc surface. Phase-change material in the area affected by the laser pulse remains in a low-reflective amorphous state and becomes a recorded data mark.

As the energy of the laser beam strikes the disc surface again, the surface temperature reaches the crystallization point and causes the material to revert to the highly reflective state and erases the data mark. The emission of a low-power spot onto a layer and the subsequent doubling of the power spot deletes previously stored data and writes new data. This is called direct overwriting.

Figure 2-2 also shows the crystal state change and the relationship of the change to the laser power, temperature, and time. The multipulse, waveform-write strategy forms recording marks reliably. Varying the duration of laser pulses establishes different marks.

Land-groove Recording

As shown in Figure 2-3, land-groove recording complements the phase-change technology. Setting the land and groove to an equal width and recording data on both lands and grooves attenuates crosstalk that occurs through the pattern of marks recorded on adjacent tracks. Figure 2-4 shows a typical pattern of recorded data on both lands and grooves.

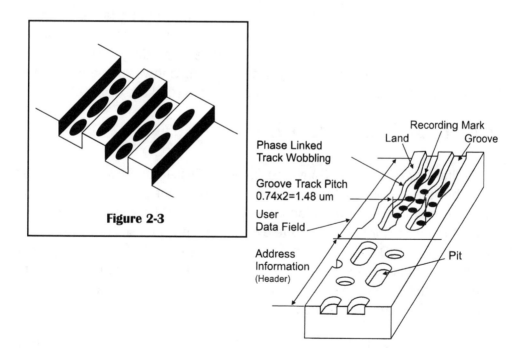

Figure 2-3

Phase Linked Track Wobbling

Groove Track Pitch 0.74x2=1.48 um

User Data Field

Address Information (Header)

Land

Recording Mark

Groove

Pit

Figure 2-4

Disc-at-Once Recording

Disc-at-once (DAO) recording writes all blocks of a compact disc in a single pass without any interruption of the laser head. Writing in the DAO mode controls the length of pauses between individual tracks. As a result, the recording doesn't require link blocks, or forced short pauses, between the tracks and promotes the writing of text to the disc. Disc-at-once recording works well for the recording of a master disc.

Track-at-Once Recording

Track-at-once (TAO) recording writes each track individually and forces two link blocks between two tracks. With this, little or no control exists for the pause length. Most multisession compact discs rely on track-at-once recording.

Sector-by-Sector Recording

Sector-by-sector, or incremental packet, recording supports the writing of data packets with fixed or variable lengths. Since only more recent CD-R drives support incremental packet writing, the writing and reading of the data can occur only by the newer devices and accompanying software. In addition, the playback system requires the use of a redirector to read the disc.

Green Book Standards: CD-i

Defined by Philips and Sony, the Compact Disc-Interactive (CD-i) format sets within the Green Book and provides an excellent platform for creating interactive multimedia applications. Playback of a CD-i disc requires special devices that allow connection to a television. Since CD-i discs have the same sector format as CD-ROM/XA, the format permits the interleaving of sectors and files. In addition to describing the format of the sectors, the CD-i standard also defines the CD-RTOS operating system. CD-i players run on a minimum of a Motorola 68070 microprocessor.

CD-i players connect to a television and amplifier. With the CD-i standard specifying video and audio formats, a CD-i disc player can play CD-DA discs as well as PhotoCDs and CD-i titles that utilize an interactive structure and a combination of text, audio, graphics, animated cartoons, still video, and full-motion video. The CD-i format accommodates three levels of audio playback and normal-, double-, and high-video resolutions.

Pixels and Refresh Rates

All this leads us to some basic discussions. When we talk about video displays, the ability of the display to show a clear image is defined through a constant called dot pitch. In any display, a pixel consists of three individual red, blue, and green dots. Dot pitch is the distance between the center points of adjacent horizontal pixels on the cathode-ray tube (crt) screen. Most advertisements for video-display monitors will list the dot-pitch measurement in millimeters. Any video display that has a smaller distance between pixels will have a higher possible resolution. A lower dot pitch number—such as .28—shows that the dots are closer together than those seen with a .31 dot pitch.

Each line that results from the vertical and horizontal scanning of the crt electron beam yields a set number of pixels. The longer horizontal lines will have more pixels than the shorter vertical lines. If the specifications of a monitor list a resolution of 640 x 480 pixels, the horizontal scan lines show 640 pixels, while the vertical line shows 480 pixels. Multiplying the two figures gives us the total amount of pixels that the raster will display. In this case, the total number of pixels is 307,200. Since the number of pixels depends on the deflection signals, varying the horizontal scan rate also varies the number of displayable pixels. Televisions and older computer-monitor designs have a horizontal frequency of 15,734 kHz. Newer computer-monitor standards and the new high-definition television standard use horizontal sync signals of 21.80 kHz, 31.50 kHz, and 35 kHz. By retaining the 60 Hz vertical scan rate and increasing the horizontal scan rate, more horizontal lines become squeezed into the vertical cycle.

An increased number of horizontal lines further improves the clarity produced by the video monitor. Information-display monitors also use higher picture bandwidths than television receivers. In other words, the monitor turns its display pixels off and on quicker than a television receiver. We know that television receivers have a bandwidth of 4.5 Mhz. Information-display monitors have a bandwidth of 35 Mhz or higher. The higher bandwidth allows the monitor to display more pixels during one horizontal scan. Without the needed bandwidth, a monitor is limited in the resolution that it can provide.

Refresh rate defines the rate at which a screen image is redrawn. Also, refresh rate shows how many frames are scanned per second, and it's also the vertical scanning rate. Since cathode-ray tubes form images in frames, the amount of refresh rate coincides with the amount of flickering seen on the screen. A refresh rate between 60 Hz and 75 Hz with a refresh rate of 75 Hz is becoming commonplace. Table 2-1 lists bandwidth measurements in combination with resolution, the number of pixels, and horizontal sync rates.

Table 2-1: Pixels, Bandwidth, and Horizontal Sync Rates

60 Hz Refresh Rate			
Resolution	# of Pixels per Screen	Bandwidth	Horizontal Sync Rate
800 x 600	480000	28.8 MH	36 kHz
1024 x 768	786432	47.2 MHz	46.1 kHz
1152 x 900	103680	62.2 MH	54 kHz
1280 x 1024	1310720	78.6 MHz	61.4 kHz
66 Hz Refresh Rate			
800 x 600	480000	31.7 MHz	39 kHz
1024 x 768	786432	51.9 MHz	50.7 kHz
1152 x 900	1036800	68.4 MHz	59.4 kHz
1280 x 1024	1310720	86.5 MHz	67.6 kHz
72 Hz Refresh Rate			
800 x 600	480000	34.6 MHz	43.2 kHz
1024 x 768	786432	56.6 MHz	55.3 kHz
1152 x 900	1036800	74.7 MHz	64.8 kHz
1280 x 1024	1310720	94.4 Mhz	73.7 kHz

Interlaced Scanning

When television was first introduced, the NTSC, or National Television System Committee, selected interlaced scanning as a standard for broadcast signals, because of the limited bandwidth available for delivering picture information. Interlaced scanning is a process in which electron guns draw only half the horizontal lines with each pass. With one pass, the guns draw all odd lines, while the next pass draws all even lines.

As a result, one complete frame of information is created for every two fields scanned. With fields generated every 1/60th of a second, the human eye cannot discern the scanning motion. To compensate for any possible flicker, manufacturers of interlaced scanning displays choose phosphors that have a higher decay time.

Because interlaced scanning refreshes only half the lines at one time, it can display twice as many lines per cycle. Thus, the display technique provides an inexpensive method for yielding more resolution. Interlaced scanning has a relatively slow trace and retrace time that affects the ability of a display to show animations and video graphics.

Noninterlaced Scanning

Interlaced scanning has two problems. Due to the higher resolution, any amount of flicker caused by screen-phosphor decay would be noticeable and distracting. With all the individual dots displayed, some will dim as others become illuminated. In addition, the scanning lines in an interlaced-scanning display are visible. If a person stands too close to a display device, each line of information can be seen as it displays on the screen. For that reason, the optimal viewing distance for an interlaced display is always listed as 4.5 or 6 times the height of the display screen. At this distance, scanning lines seem to merge together and create the illusion that one complete image is displayed. With larger display devices such as projection televisions, however, the scanning lines are more noticeable.

To counter the flicker and scanning-line problems, computer displays and the new HDTV standard use noninterlaced refresh or progressive scanning. With progressive scanning, every line of information on the display is scanned by the electron gun at each pass across the panel. This technique enhances the vertical resolution of the display, while allowing the viewer to sit closer to the display. Viewing distances with progressive scanning shorten to 2.5 times the height of the display.

CD-i, NTSC, and PAL

The NTSC established the current television broadcasting and reception standard in 1940. That standard utilizes 525 horizontal scanning lines, interlaced scanning, the transmission of separate luminance and chrominance signals, and relies on a 60 Hz frame rate. Of the 525 scanning lines, only 483 are visible, while the remaining lines are used for interval timing or other functions. The bandwidth for those signals covers 4.2 MHz.

Although many nations use the NTSC standard, most European nations rely on another standard called phase-alternation line (PAL). This signal relies on a 50 Hz frame rate, uses a color subcarrier frequency of 4.43 MHz, and has 625 scanning lines. The PAL standard arose because of detectable shifts in the color subcarrier phase of the NTSC. Due to a difference in frame frequencies, NTSC systems cannot display PAL broadcasts.

At the normal resolution level, CD-i matches the horizontal and vertical resolution of either the NTSC or the PAL standards. The NTSC standard provides a resolution of 384 pixels x 240 pixels, while the PAL system offers 384 pixels by 280 pixels. CD-i double resolution provides 768 horizontal pixels and either 240 or 280 vertical pixels. The high-resolution mode for CD-i doubles both the horizontal and vertical resolutions and yields either 768 horizontal pixels by 480 vertical pixels or 780 horizontal pixels by 560 pixels. Each of the different video formats supports different image contents.

White Book Standards: Video-CD and Bridge Discs

Established in 1993 in the White Book, the video-CD standard allows the use of MPEG full-motion video sequences. The first track provides a CD-i-playback program for the video-CD, while other tracks contain CD-i, MPEG, and vcd directories based on the ISO-9660 file system. CD-i players, special video CD players, and CD-ROM drives that include CD-ROM/XA support and an MPEG decoder can accommodate the video-CD standard.

Bridge Discs

Bridge discs contain information read by computer systems using either CD-ROM/XA drives or CD-i players. Due to the identical character of the sectors and nearly identical audio and video formats, bridge discs can store data accessible by both systems. Created in 1991, bridge discs use a Mode 2 format for all data tracks and require special software tools for production.

Kodak's Photo CD runs on either a CD-i player, an XA system, or a Photo-CD player. In addition, the Kodak Photo CD has multisession capabilities and allows the appending of new data at different points in time. Each session has an individual lead-in, program area, and lead-out. All addressing of data occurs during all sessions.

Yellow Book Standards: CD-ROM and CD-ROM/XA

Formed in 1984, the Yellow Book established a compact disc standard that accepts computer data. Representing compact disc read-only memory, the CD-ROM has become a mainstay in the computing industry. Although DVD-ROM and DVD-RAM technologies seem ready to supplant CD-ROM, CD-R, and CD-RW technologies, the combination of low-cost and acceptable storage capabilities have created a niche for recordable compact disc technologies. A CD-ROM can store a maximum of 640 megabytes of data.

Mode 1 and Mode 2 Sectors

To accomplish this, the Yellow Book defined two new types of sectors. As shown in Figures 2-5 and 2-6, Mode 1 sectors store computer data and Mode 2 sectors store compressed audio or video/graphic data. Due to the need for precise access to computer data stored on tracks, both sector formats use bytes at the beginning of the sector for precise addressing. The first 12 bytes

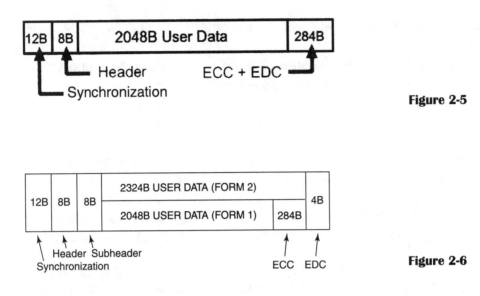

Figure 2-5

Figure 2-6

provide synchronization and sector separation through a combination of the byte content and length of the sector. Three of the following header bytes provide addressing, while the fourth header byte marks the mode used by the sectors of the track. With each sector divided into logical blocks that may have lengths of 512, 1,024, or 2,048 bytes, Mode 1 sectors have 2,048 bytes of user data.

Mode 1 sectors include the CIRC error-detection and correction scheme seen with an audio CD. Since computer data requires a higher level of data integrity, however, the sectors also contain an error-detection and correction level called layered EDC/ECC (layered error-detection and correction code). This additional error-detection and correction level uses four bytes for error detection and 276 bytes for error correction. Eight unused bytes separate the error-detection and error correction bytes.

Mode 2 sectors don't contain any additional error-detection and correction data. As a result, the 2,336 bytes that follow the sync and header bytes remain classified as user bytes. Due to the difference in sector formatting, different data-transmission rates exist for Mode 1 and Mode 2 at approximately 1.22 megabits for Mode 1 and 1.4 megabits for Mode 2. Although Mode 2 provides a higher data rate and increased space for data, only applications using the CD-ROM/XA and CD-i formats used Mode 2 sectors.

CD-ROM/XA

Compact Disc Read-only Memory/eXtended Architecture (CD-ROM/XA) supports CD-i audio and video formats and integrates MPEG full-motion video. CD-ROM/XA extensions correspond with the Green Book specifications for the CD-i standard. With disc tracks containing binary code as well as video, graphic, text, and compressed audio data, the CD-ROM/XA format interleaves two different sector formats in a track. As a result, one sector format (called Form 1) may precede a different sector format (called Form 2).

Form 1 sectors contain computer data and additional layered error-detection and correction code (layered EDC/ECC). Like CD-ROM Mode 1 sectors, Form 1 sectors also use the first 12 bytes for a sync pattern, use the following four bytes for header data, and contain 2,048 user bytes. But Form 1 sectors also add a subheader behind the header bytes. In addition, Form 1 sectors have no unused bytes between the error-detection and the error-correction code bytes. Form 2 sectors have the same arrangement as Form 1 sectors, without the additional ECC information. At the end of the user-data sector, a reserved four-byte field may provide a quality-control function during the disc-production process. While Form 1 sectors have a data rate of 1.2 megabits per second, Form 2 sectors have a data rate of 1.4 megabits per second.

Since different sectors with different contents can store in interleaved fashion, the first byte of the subheader provides a file number for identifying the interleaved sectors belonging to the same file. Because an interleaved file may contain different pieces of information that can play back in combination or as separate files, the second byte establishes a channel number for the real-time selection of this information. The next byte, called the submode byte, defines global attributes of a sector. Each bit can represent a flag to indicate information type, mark the last sector of a file or a record, or set a real-time mode. The use of real-time sectors establishes the timing of the data reading as a priority over data integrity. As a result, error correction occurs only when the correct timing of the data remains unaffected. The coding-information byte follows the submode byte and defines the type of data located in the user area of the sector.

File Formats

ISO-9660

Seen as an international file system, the ISO-9660 standard specifies a standard volume and file format that serves various computer platforms or operating systems. Although UNIX, Macintosh, and Windows operating systems require specific executable programs, the ISO-9660 standard establishes compatibility between the optical disc and the operating system and provides cross-platform access to the same data files. For example, the file-management standard allows the storage and sharing of TIFF, JPEG, and MPEG files between different operating systems. As a result, ISO-9660 allows CD-ROM drives and discs to operate with text, graphics, audio, and video for a wide variety of applications.

As a hierarchical file system, ISO-9660 defines directories, subdirectories, and paths. Using Interchange Level 1 as a limiting factor for File and Directory Identifiers, a file name may have an eight-character length, while a file extension may use 3 letters. Interchange Level 1 also specifies the use of capital letters from "A" to "Z", digits from "0" to 9", and the underscore "_". Because more recent versions of operating systems rely on file systems that allow long file names, the ISO-9960 standard also uses the Joliet File System by Microsoft. The enhancement allows ISO-9960 to use file names with a maximum length of 64 characters and accommodate any language.

ECMA 168

Approved as a European standard by the European Computer Manufacturers Association, ECMA 168 establishes the volume and file format standard for write-once disc technologies. Because the standard allows full Orange Book functionality such as multisession recording, track-at-once recording, and packet recording, it allows a write-once disc to serve as a general-purpose storage peripheral. ECMA 168 incorporates the capability to use UNIX-style file names, UNIX permissions, and deep directory hierarchies and accommodates multiple-byte character sets.

Macintosh HFS

The Hierarchical Filing System (HFS) format used for Macintosh-based CD-ROMs supports the Macintosh resource, data forks, and file information. While supporting a folder-based operating-system environment, HFS also supports file names that have a maximum of 31 characters and volume names that have a maximum of 27 characters. HFS files feature a resource fork that contains Macintosh resources used by applications to identify file types, as well as a data fork used by applications to store the contents of a document.

Joliet Specification

The Joliet specification uses the supplementary volume descriptor (SVD) feature of ISO-9660 to solve limitations seen with the original ISO-9660 file structure. The limitations include:

- A character set using only upper case characters, numbers and an underscore.
- A maximum of eight characters and a three-character extension in the file name.
- Shallow directory tree depth.
- Directory name format limitations.

To maintain compatibility with Microsoft Windows, SVD features a second path table with long file names.

Rockridge Group

The Rockridge Group developed extensions to ISO-9660 so that ISO-compliant applications could function with multiple operating systems such as UNIX. The System Use Shared Protocol (SUSP) and Rockridge Interchange Protocol (RRIP) support multiplatform formats, tables of contents with deeper levels of hierarchy, and the use of file names larger than those allowed by MS-DOS. In practice, the extensions make the ISO-compliant contents of the disc appear like a UNIX File System to UNIX machines configured to support Rockridge extensions.

Universal Disk Format (UDF)

Universal Disk Format, developed by the Optical Storage Technology Association (OSTA), is a standard file system providing compatibility across all platforms for DVD. While preserving the data-interchange benefits of the ISO-9660 format, UDF adds rewritable file-system features such as the ability to create, extend, modify, or delete a single file. UDF supports files and directories, soft links, hard links, and special file types. With no name-length restrictions, file storage begins with a basic set of attributes that seem similar to UNIX-style attributes. UDF also allows the storage of extended attributes to accommodate the requirements of operating systems such as Windows NT, OS/2, and the Macintosh operating system.

With the implementation of UDF version 1.50, the file system operates with sequentially recorded media (such as CD-R) and packet-written erasable media (such as CD-RW). The Micro UDF format provides a bridge format for DVD-ROM discs. By placing the UDF and an ISO-9660 file systems on the disc, Micro UDF supports compact disc and DVD technologies.

El Torito

A relatively new standard, called El Torito, also supports bootable compact discs and allows the developer of CD-ROM titles to package the application and the environment of the operating system onto the disc. With this approach, the software can run while using all necessary information from the disc. Figure 2-7 compares the configuration of a standard CD-ROM with the single boot-image and multiple boot-image configuration of an El Torito CD-ROM.

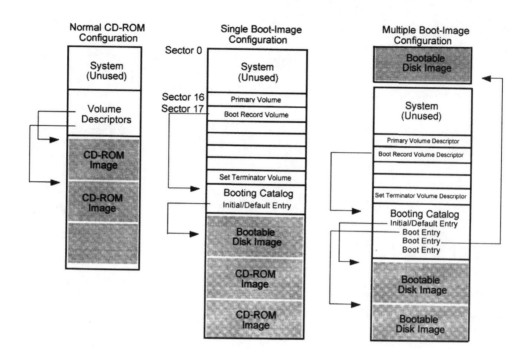

Figure 2-7

3

DVD Basics

Introduction

Despite the popularity of the compact disc media, manufacturing and production companies such as Toshiba, Time Warner, Philips, and Sony have sought methods for increasing the capabilities of the standard 74-minute, 650-megabyte disc since the early 1990s. The buying public's desire for greater storage capacity and the capability to play back full-length movies in the digital format pushed companies to explore new technologies.

In 1993, Nimbus Technology and Engineering introduced the first double-density CD format with two hours of MPEG-1 video playback as a demonstration that small-disk technology could carry high-quality video as well as audio. With the possibility of a new storage technology rapidly becoming a reality, manufacturers and producers began to explore options for standards. With this, Toshiba and Time Warner showcased the Super Density (SD) disc, while Philips, Sony, and 3M offered the MultiMedia CD (MMCD).

DVD Forum

In 1995, after forming the DVD Consortium, Hitachi, JVC, Matsushita, Mitsubishi, Philips, Sony, Thomson Electronics, Time Warner, and Toshiba agreed that a single high-density compact disc standard called Digital Video Disc (DVD) should exist, rather than several standards. Although the initial makeup of the DVD Consortium consisted of only 10 corporations, it also involved working groups that represented other companies from the manufacturing, electronics, computing, and entertainment industries. By mid-1997, the 10-member DVD Consortium had evolved into the DVD Forum, which now has a membership that includes more than 100 companies.

The DVD Forum specifies and controls all formats developed as DVD technologies and has published a book outlining specifications and applications for each format. In a general sense, the DVD Consortium and DVD Forum recommendations for all the formats cover video resolution, video and audio recording capacity, support for different languages, copy protection, support for titles and subtitles, and support for various aspect ratios. The DVD Forum has published a number of books on various topics, including books on:

- DVD-ROM
- DVD-Video
- DVD-Audio
- DVD-Recordable
- DVD-RAM

Comparing CD and DVD

As we saw in Chapter 2, the original compact disc format relied on a 12-centimeter disc and offered a typical capacity of 650 megabytes, an access time in the 300-microsecond range, and a 100-kilobit-per-second data-transfer rate. Compact discs provided a storage medium for audio and video information as well as computer data. In comparison, the DVD format offers a minimum 4.7-gigabyte capacity, an access time in the 100-millisecond range, and a 10-megabit-per-second data-transfer rate. Depending on the disc format, 4.7 to 17 billion bytes of digital data can be stored on DVD media. Increasing the storage capacity on the DVD media more than eight times the storage capacity seen with compact disc technologies occurred through the use of:

- Shorter wavelength lasers.
- Higher quality optical systems.
- Additional data layers.
- Greater pit density.
- Narrowed track spacing.
- Faster rotation speeds.
- Enhanced error-correction codes.
- Faster servo systems.

Storage Capacity

Along with the data-transfer rate and access time, storage capacity defines any type of storage medium, including optical disc technologies. With compact discs and DVD technologies, storage capacity becomes a function of laser-spot size and the dimensions of the disc. Laser-spot size establishes the minimum dimensions of a stored bit.

Given these two factors, the areal density of a disc measures the storage efficiency of the medium with a ratio of gigabytes to inches squared. (Areal density represents the number of bits stored per square inch or square centimeter.) Breaking this down even further, the areal density shows the amount of data that can store per square inch on a disc. As a result, areal density also equals the number of tracks per inch multiplied by the number of bits per inch along each track.

Media resolution, numerical aperture of the optics, the wavelength of the laser, and the positioning of the optical head over the tracks can limit areal density. In turn, the track density, or the number of tracks per inch, works as a metric for the positioning of the optical head. Finally, the linear bit density, or the spacing of optical transitions measured in bits per inch, also may limit areal density. For red light emitted at approximately 600 nanometers, the data density reaches approximately 1.2 gigabits per second/cm^2 or 33 Mb/cm^2.

Optics

The optics reading of data packed onto the DVD media requires a laser that can produce a shorter wavelength beam. Measured in nanometers, a shorter laser wavelength provides more precision. In addition, reading media placed in two different data layers also makes the use of more accurate aiming and focusing mechanisms a necessity. As the reader moves to the data located in the second layer, it focuses the laser deeper. In addition, the laser beam has the capability to switch between intensities, with the strongest intensity used for reading the second layer.

Wavelength

Generally, electronic equipment used for communications operates with electrical energy that takes the form of electromagnetic waves. That energy may take the form of radio waves, infrared light, visible light, ultra-violet light, X-rays, and other forms. Magnetic and electric fields—placed at right angles to each other and to their direction of travel—make up electro-magnetic waves. The wave-like nature of those fields becomes apparent as the magnetic and electric fields vary continually in intensity and periodi-cally in direction at any given point.

Each complete series of variations forms a wave. As one wave travels through space, another wave immediately follows. While the term "frequency" describes the number of waves that passes a point each second and the rate of polarity change, frequency is measured in hertz. The distance in space from any given point or condition in one wave to the corresponding point of the next wave is defined as wavelength. Mathematically, wavelength, or λ, appears as

$$\lambda = c / f$$

where c = the speed of light (2.998×10^8 meters per second), and f = frequency. Since radio waves travel through space at the speed of light, or 300,000,000 meters per second, the velocity always equals either 300,000,000 meters per second or 984,000,000 feet per second. As a result, we can measure wavelength either in meters or feet per second. Over time, we have gained the ability to produce and use radio waves for the purpose of communicating over long distances.

Reflectivity

In optical technology, baseline reflectivity refers to the reflectivity of the lands. Comparatively, pits always have reflectivity characteristics that measure lower than baseline reflectivity. During the reading of data, circuitry detects and decodes the changes in reflectivity. As Table 3-1 shows, substantial differences in base reflectivity may exist when comparing disc formats and types. As an example of the operational impact of reflectivity, some CD-ROM readers cannot read CD-RW media. In addition, DVD video players have wavelength problems when attempting to read CD-R discs, because the CD-R media does not completely reflect the DVD laser beam.

Table 3-1: Comparison of Compact Disc and DVD Optical Characteristics

	Compact Disc	DVD
Laser Wavelength	790 nanometers	630 to 650 nanometers
Objective Lens Numerical Aperture	0.60	0.45
Spot Size	1	0.63
Refractive Index	1.55	1.55
Focus Depth	1	0.47
Chromatic Aberration	1	0.35
Spherical Aberration	1	0.26
Reflectivity Percentage	70	70 Single-layer 25 to 40 Dual-layer

Mass

As Table 3-2 illustrates, DVD media operate with a data layer one-half the thickness of the data layer of a compact disc. Combined with the use of better optics, the thinner data layer allows the writing of data to and the reading of data from both layers of a dual-layer disc. Moreover, the adjacent surfaces must have enough size to reduce crosstalk. With a 0.5-NA objective lens, a separation of 40 or 50 microns ensures acceptable levels of crosstalk from these other surfaces.

Table 3-2: Comparison of Compact Disc and DVD Physical Characteristics

	Compact Disc	DVD
Substrate Thickness	1.2 millimicrons	0.6 millimicrons
Disc Thickness	1.2 millimicrons	1.2 millimicrons
Spacing Layer Thickness	N/A	40 to 70 microns
Disc Mass	13 to 20 grams	6 to 9 grams (single-layer) 14 grams (dual-layer)

Pits

While compact discs and DVDs share the same basic pit design—with data placed onto pits embossed on the disc surface—a DVD has a pit density four and a half times the density seen with a compact disc. The combination of pit density, more efficient data modulation, and better error-correction methods allows the pits found on the DVD to store nearly seven times as much user data per side. As shown in Table 3-3, the pits have sufficient size to remain discernible by the laser optics. The depth of the pits on the DVD nearly matches a quarter of the effective laser wavelength.

While increased pit density increases the number of available bits for data storage, different pit lengths on the DVD generate different frequency rates. Designated as the 3T pit, the smallest pit has a length that ranges from

Table 3-3: Comparison of Pits, Tracks, and Layers for Compact Disc and DVD Technologies

PITS	COMPACT DISC	DVD
Pit Width	0.5 microns	0.4 microns
Minimum Pit Length	0.833 to 0.972 microns Pit 2T	1.6 microns Pit 3T
Maximum Pit Length	3.054 to 3.560 microns Pit 10T	1.87 microns for Single-layer 2.13 microns for Dual-layer Pit 14T
TRACKS		
Track Pitch	1.6 microns	0.74 microns
LAYERS		
Number of Layers	1	1 or 2
STORAGE CAPACITY		
Maximum Payload (Gigabytes)	.065 Mode 1 0.742 Mode 2	4.7 Single-layer, Single-Side 8.54 Dual-layer, Single-Side 9.4 Single-layer, Double-Side 17 Dual-layer, Double-Side

0.394 millimicrons for single-layer discs to 0.441 millimicrons for dual-layer discs and generates a frequency of 4.386 MHz. The 14T pit has the largest pit length at 1.840 millimicrons for single-layer discs and 2.058 millimicrons for dual-layer discs and generates the slowest frequency at 940 kHz. But longer pits provide the highest signal quality.

Tracks

Table 3-3 also shows that DVD media has a much smaller track pitch at 0.74 microns than the 1.6-micron track pitch seen with compact discs. In a DVD player, the track buffer receives the fluctuating user bit stream and sends a smooth bit stream that uses a variable MPEG stream as a reference. Decreasing the track pitch produces higher data density or program time.

During the reading of data, the tracking signal combines with signals from adjacent tracks to produce crosstalk, or unwanted noise. Maximizing the track pitch produces lower crosstalk between the tracks. In addition, sufficient track spacing also prevents crosstalk.

Dual-Layer Discs

The bonding of two layers of polycarbonate substrate one-half the thickness of a standard CD has propelled DVD disc-storage capacity to a greater level. The DVD-9 and DVD-18 standards introduce the most complex application of multiple layers in the DVD format. With DVD-9 and DVD-18, the player can read one layer and then refocus the laser to read a second layer through the first one—without any need to turn the disc over. Prior to DVD-9 and DVD-18, the listener or viewer had to manually turn the disc over at the completion of the side-one or side-two programming.

With the construction of a DVD-9 or DVD-18 disc, the thin reflective metal layer on the layer of data nearest the optical pickup unit has enough transparency to become semitransparent. As a result, the optical pickup unit gains the ability to focus on the data contained within the first layer or the data contained within the second layer.

Producing DVD-9 and DVD-18 Discs

The manufacturing process for a DVD-9 disc involves the bonding of two substrates, with each containing back-to-back layers of data. With this, the second layer on the disc, or layer one, plays back from the opposite side. The mastering process for DVD-9 discs rotates the glass substrate in the opposite direction from the data layer and rotates in the correct direction.

The DVD-18 manufacturing process mimics the DVD-9 process, with the exception of placing two playable layers on the disc. To place the data layer properly, the process uses a different material for the substrate that will not adhere to aluminum. After pressing the layer, the process peels the substrate away and leaves the polycarbonate substrate of layer zero, the semireflective layer, the bonding layer, and the reflective aluminum layer one. From there, the same process occurs with a second data layer. Then, the two discs bond together to form the DVD-18 disc, with two layers of playable information on each side.

Movement and Data Rates

Although optical discs can achieve high transfer rates, the seek time across an optical disc to find a sector remains much higher than the seek time of a hard disk. Unlike hard disks that have a 512-bytes-per-sector size, optical discs typically use 512, 1024, or 2,048 bytes per sector. To acquire maximum capacity from a disc, the system requires media with larger sector sizes.

Data-transfer rates define the capability of a drive to read data from a disc as a large sequential stream and transfer the data to a host computer. The computer and telecommunications industries use kilobytes per second (Kbps) and megabytes per second (Mbps) to describe a data-transfer rate. But the data-transfer rate for an optical drive refers to the sustained reading of a sequential large file, rather than the accessing of data located across the disc.

The standard compact disc format dictates a data-transfer rate of 75 sectors of data per second for a single-speed drive. With each sector containing 2,048 bytes of data, the data-transfer rate equals exactly 150 Kbps. Since CDs record in a CLV format, the rotational speed of the disc varies to keep the track speed constant. Spinning the disc at a higher linear velocity will increase the data-transfer rate. Consequently, a double-speed drive simply attains a transfer rate of 300 kilobits per second. The linear density of the disc, the rotational speed of the drive, and the number of pickup heads combine to determine the data-transfer rate. Limiting factors for the data-transfer rate include the availability of optical power, the speed of the pickup-head servo controllers, and the tolerance of the media to high centrifugal forces.

Access time equals the delay between the drive receiving the command to read and the first actual reading of a bit of data. Recorded in milliseconds, the access time provides an average access rate. When the read mechanism moves to a portion of the disc close to the narrow center, the drive has a faster access rate than when the read mechanism moves to the outer perimeter of the disc. Tables 3-4 and 3-5 compare the movement and data rates of compact discs and DVDs.

Table 3-4: Direction and Velocity

	Compact Disc	DVD
Spiral Direction	Clockwise	Clockwise
Maximum Revolutions per Second (hertz)	8	25.5
Minimum Revolutions per Second (hertz)	3.5	10.5
Reference Scanning Velocity (microns per second)	1.2 to 1.4	3.49 Single-layer 3.84 Dual-layer

Table 3-5: Compact Disc and DVD Data-Transfer and Access-Time Comparisons (Megabits Per Second)

	Compact Disc	DVD
Channel Bit Rate (Actual Raw Data Rate)	4.32	26.2
Constant Bit Rate		
FEC Rate	0.47	3.00
User Rate	1.47	11.1
Actual Data Rate	1.41	10.1

Table 3-6 compares the disc sizes, layer formats, data-storage capacity in gigabytes, and video-storage capacity in hours for all DVD standards. As the table shows, a single-layer DVD stores two hours of video. While Table 3-6 compares storage capacity, it does not show the effect of bit rates on the

Table 3-6: Comparison of DVD Formats

DVD Standard	Disc Size	Layers	Data Storage Capacity	Video Storage Capacity (2 gigabytes = 1 hour of video)
DVD-1	3.1 inches	Single Side/Single Layer	1.4 Gigabytes	0.5 hours
DVD-2	3.1 inches	Single Side/Dual Layer	2.7 Gigabytes	1.3 hours
DVD-3	3.1 inches	Double Side/Single Layer	2.9 Gigabytes	1.4 hours
DVD-4	3.1 inches	Double Side/Dual Layer	5.3 Gigabytes	2.5 hours
DVD-5	4.7 inches	Single Side/Single Layer	4.7 Gigabytes	2 hours
DVD-9	4.7 inches	Single Side/Double Layer	8.5 Gigabytes	4.5 hours
DVD-10	4.7 inches	Double Side/Single Layer	12.33 Gigabytes	6.5 hours
DVD-14	4.7 inches	Double Side/Single Layer on One Side and Dual Layer on Other Side	13.24 Gigabytes	6.5 hours
DVD-18	4.7 inches	Double Side/Dual Layer	17 Gigabytes	8 hours
DVD-R	3.1 inches	Single Side/Single Layer	3.68 Gigabytes	n/a
DVD-R	3.1 inches	Double Side/Dual Layer	7.38 Gigabytes	n/a
DVD-R	3.1 inches	Single Side/Single Layer	1.23 Gigabytes	n/a
DVD-R	3.1 inches	Double Side/Dual Layer	2.46 Gigabytes	n/a
DVD-RAM	4.7 inches	Single Side/Single Layer	2.58 Gigabytes	n/a
DVD-RAM	4.7 inches	Double Side/Single Layer	5.16 Gigabytes	n/a

carrying capacity of the disc. As an example, constant bit-rate traffic requires guaranteed levels of service and throughput in delay-sensitive applications, such as digitized audio and video represented by a continuous bit stream.

When we consider bit rates, video requires 3.5 Mbps, while three soundtracks require 1.2 Mbps. On the average, a two-hour movie with three soundtracks requires a minimum of 5.2 Mbps. A dual-layer disc can hold a two-hour movie at an average of 9.5 Mbps. If we place mostly audio information on the same disc, we find that the disc can play for nearly 24 hours. If the audio information is compressed at a rate of 64 Kbps and is monophonic, the dual-layer disc can play for 295 hours.

DVD File Management Structure

With the UDF volume, video zone, title set, video object, and cell structure, DVD media remains compatible across set-top players and personal computers equipped with DVD-ROM readers. All the DVD physical media specifications share a basic set of parameters given through the UDF file system. The UDF file system limits the maximum number of titles on a DVD disc at 99 and the number of titles per set at 10. DVD files have a maximum size of one gigabyte.

Volume

As shown in Figure 3-1, the UDF file system places the volume as the top level of organization on a DVD. Volume contains the UDF bridge-file system, a

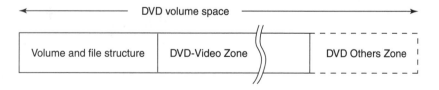

Figure 3-1

single DVD-video zone, and a DVD others-zone used for non-DVD-video data elements such as desktop-computer applications.

Video Zone

At the next level, the DVD video zone begins with a video manager, or a master directory for the data elements on the disc. The video manager includes an introductory clip of video and audio such as an opening logo and a title menu that allows navigation to the video-title sets (VTS). A range of one to 99 video-title sets that include the video and audio elements follows the video zone. Figure 3-2 shows a drawing of the DVD video zone.

Video-Title Sets (VTS)

The video-title sets usually take the most space on the DVD. While a DVD can contain multiple title sets, most DVD-Video discs have one VTS reserved

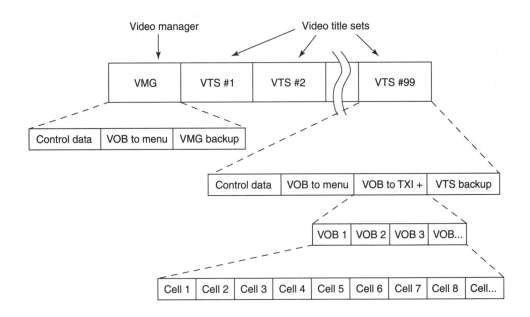

Figure 3-2

for the movie. A video-title set consists of a VTS menu and one or more video titles. In turn, the titles sometimes break down into parts of titles that have a format similar to a chapter.

Video Objects (VOB)

Data within the video title consists of video-object sets (VOBS). Each video-object set contains one or more video objects (VOB). Recognized as the fundamental media-file element of the DVD, a video object contains the video, audio, subpictures, and navigation data for a program. Figure 3-3 shows a drawing of the VOB data stream.

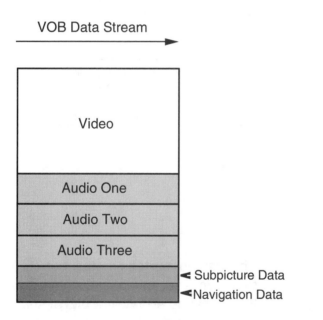

Figure 3-3

Cells

Cells occupy the lowest branch of the DVD structure. With each VOB breaking into one or more cells, a cell can vary in size from a movie length down to an MPEG instruction addressed by interactive playback.

Forward-Error Correction (FEC)

Reed-Solomon Product Code

The Reed-Solomon product code (RSPC) expands the functionality of the Reed-Solomon cyclic redundancy compression algorithm. More specifically, the RSPC provides 10 times the protection seen with the CIRC algorithm and compact disc technologies by expanding the Reed-Solomon cyclic redundancy compression algorithm. To provide this protection, the RSPC multiplies the number of rows times the number of columns and uses the product as a final code. Table 3-7 compares the compact disc and DVD error-correction methods.

Table 3-7: Compact Disc and DVD Error Correction

	Compact Disc	DVD
ECC Method	Reed-Solomon CIRC	Reed-Solomon Product Code
FEC Format (bytes)	(28/32) x (24/28)	(208, 192, 17) x (182, 172, 11)
Correctable Burst Length (millimicrons)	2.5	6.0 Single-layer 6.5 Dual-layer

Encoding Methods

Eight-to-Fourteen Modulation

Compact disc manufacturers use the eight-to-fourteen modulation (EFM) method for encoding source data into a form that reliably accommodates mastering, replication, and playback. EFM converts every eight bits of source data into a 14-bit code from a lookup table that has 256 possible combinations. In the resulting 14-bit code, the zeroes designate a land or pit, and the ones signal a transition between lands and pits. Since every compact disc has at least three and no more than 11 zeroes between transitions, pits and lands have nine discrete lengths.

Then, the 24 data bytes and eight error-correction bytes from each frame pass to the first Reed-Solomon decoder. During operation, the Reed-Solomon decoder uses four of the error-correction bytes and can correct one byte in error out of the 32. If no uncorrectable errors exist, the decoder passes the data along. If errors occur, the decoder marks the data as being in error at this stage of decoding.

Before going through the second Reed-Solomon decoder, the 24 data bytes and four remaining error-correction bytes pass through unequal delays. Passing through unequal delays causes an interleaving of the data that spreads long error bursts, and allows correction of error bursts up to 450 bytes long to occur. The second Reed-Solomon decoder uses the last four error-correction bytes to correct any remaining errors in the 24 data bytes. At this point, the data goes through a de-interleaving process that restores the correct byte order.

EFM+

EFM+ uses nearly the same technique for encoding data to a DVD disc. Rather than convert the eight-bit source code into 14 bits, EFM+ converts the eight-bit source code into a 16-bit code. Since the lookup tables for EFM+ have a format that doesn't require the merging of bits as seen with the EFM method, it provides a more efficient and reliable modulation technique.

4

DVD-Video

Introduction

Compared to all the DVD formats, DVD-Video has the largest, most detailed, and most restrictive specifications. The DVD-Video application layer defines data types, auxiliary files, MPEG 2 variable bit-rate video, camera angles, aspect ratios, interactive menus, parental control, and navigational controls. In addition, the DVD format includes Dolby AC-3, MPEG 2, or linear pcm audio and supports stereo or surround sound, a maximum of eight soundtracks, and 32 subpicture streams used for subtitles.

Interactivity

DVD-Video offers interactivity through the available range of controls for selecting data and through format structured to enable multiple story lines and interactive games. With its lineage going back to the video-CD (VCD) format, DVD-Video utilizes the VCD hierarchical branching-menu style of interactivity. As a result, a user can navigate through a disc by jumping from menu to menu or video to video. But most DVD movies limit interactivity through menu choices such as language, biographies of the actors, or a chapter menu that allows a jump into the disc at various points.

DVD-Video and Variable Bit-Rate Coding

DVD-Video movies rely on variable bit-rate MPEG-2 coding to maximize quality and playing time, meaning the bit rate varies according to the demands of the material. A typical 24-frames-per-second movie in the NTSC 525/60 format has an average bit rate of 3.5 megabits per second. Sections that feature a great deal of movement have a higher bit rate at 8 Mbps or 9 Mbps.

System Parameters and General Parameters

DVD video players have system and general memory parameters that cover default settings and memory locations. Set by either the consumer or the DVD title, system parameters control default settings for features such as language, aspect ratio, and parental rating level. Addressed only by the operating DVD video disc, general parameters determine sixteen 16-bit memory locations used for basic computations or the storage of values. As a combination, the established general parameters increase the interactivity of a DVD title. For example, the set of general parameters that control the storage of values might cover the previous direction of a story for interactive titles and games.

Menus

DVD video players and DVD titles use menu functions to give consumers the capability to interact with program content. The menus include full-motion video or 24-bit still-background image frames, a subpicture overlay, a button-highlight area, and options for audio cues. Depending on the supported aspect ratio, a DVD video player can support three different sets of buttons and the creation of highlights for each possible display mode.

Displayed menu choices can appear on-screen as part of the background image or as subpicture overlays. With either option, a button highlight represents the selection and action of a button. Also, a button highlight occurs as a rectangular region of the screen that can have a color and transparency for both a selection and an action. While the use of subpicture overlays provides the fastest navigation, the use of background images supports greater color depth and image variety. The highlight region also may key a highlight color over a predetermined color in a background image or subpicture.

For example, an unselected menu choice may appear as black and have letters that change to green when selected. This allows the highlight region to color complex shapes, even though the highlight area is limited to x and y coordinates that define a box.

Available Menus

The DVD-Video specification defines system menus available to the user through the press of a button on the remote control. Table 4-1 lists the system menus and functions.

Table 4-1: DVD-Video System Menus and Functions

Menu Type	Menu Location	Menu Function
Title	Video Manager	Access titles on the DVD video disc
Chapter	Video Title Set	Select particular chapter or scene at random
Angle	Video Title Set	Change video angle
Audio	Video Title Set	Change audio stream
Subpicture	Video Title Set	Change Subpicture stream

DVD video players use system memory to remember the location of a video stream during the accessing of the system memory. After the viewer has either finished looking at the menu or has made a selection for a language or subpicture-stream option, the video stream can return to the location where playback ended. Placing the menus in the video manager and video-title set allows the consumer to quickly jump from playback to menu or from menu to menu through the use of the remote control. Consequently, DVD-Video increases the possibilities for interaction with the movie.

For example, a subpicture may appear during the playback of a movie and indicate a series of choices that the viewer could make for the direction of the story. Clicking the left or right button on the remote control produces a highlight command that indicates the selection, while pressing "Enter" links the movie to a new program chain. In addition, the viewer can choose to associate specific times and changes for story options in the movie.

Subpicture Overlays

As shown in Figure 4-1, the DVD-Video standard supports the capability to enable the multilanguage subtitling required by the entertainment industry. Enabling of the subtitling occurs through the use of subpicture overlays, which are images generated by the DVD player on playback. A DVD video-player user can key the subpicture overlays over background video or still images. Subpictures may show text information or bitmap graphics that have maximum resolutions of 720 x 480 or 720 x 576.

Along with multilanguage subtitling, subpicture overlays have applications such as karaoke lyrics, buttons, and instructions. Menu options allow for the changing of subpicture overlays on a frame-by-frame basis. Menu options also support subpicture special effects such as fade in, fade out, wipe in color or transparency, scroll up, and scroll down. Subpicture overlays provide four single-bit color layers based on the 16-color palette that accompanies each program chain.

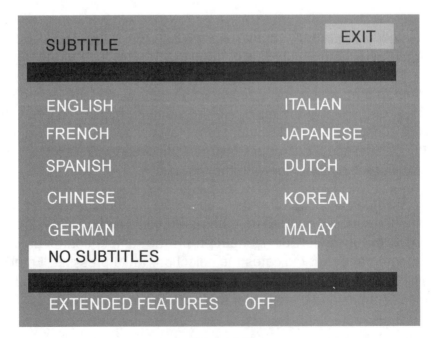

Figure 4-1

Presentation and Playback Program Chains

Program chains (PGC) direct the playback of a DVD video disc. With video objects representing the multiplexed audio, video, and subpicture overlay, a PGC instructs the DVD player about the playback method, conditions, and order of the video objects. With this in mind, we can consider program chains as maps used by the DVD video player to navigate through the data on the disc.

Each program chain includes a precommand, a group of programs, and a postcommand. The precommand establishes conditions for the VOB playback. For example, the precommand may designate an audio stream or list the viewing history of a program. The precommand also provides a list of cells within the VOB for playback. The list may include edit-decision lists (EDL), which show two different programs referencing the same video objects.

Navigation Commands

The 128 navigation commands available through program chains fall under categories such as jump and link, calculation, comparison, parameter setting, and program flow. When used either singly or as combinations, the navigation commands set up complex functions. For example, these functions could include keeping a game score, randomizing title playback, or ensuring the selection of a unique ending for a movie. Grouping together multiple commands or moving between video-title sets may require the use of dummy program chains, which do not contain video objects but offer precommand and postcommand areas.

Title Design

The flexibility of the DVD format presents a wide range of applications for title design. Once a viewer selects an option from a title menu, branching can occur to multiple points. For example, the selection of a menu option could initiate a chapter menu that branches to a language menu, which, in turn, branches to audio and subtitle menus. In addition, the title-menu selection could branch to a still image and biography of a performer enclosed within a VTS. All this combines to present the type of versatility needed to produce interactive training manuals, multilanguage course work, archival video and audio storage, interactive movies, games, and hybrid DVD-ROM and DVD-Video titles.

Still Images

The DVD-Video specification allows the delivery of single frames of video encoded in full color and full resolution as navigation tools for interactive elements. Along with providing menu backgrounds, still images may also work as manually advanced still shows or automatic slide shows. With either type of show, the use of still images may include associations with audio.

Aspect Ratio

In Chapter 2, we found that the currently used NTSC television standard offers a video resolution of 384 x 240 with 525 scanning lines. As shown in Figure 4-2, the NTSC standard also provides an aspect ratio—the ratio of picture width to picture height—of 4:3. Introduction of the HDTV standard established a larger aspect ratio of 16:9, as shown in Figure 4-3. Because of this, the viewer gains the capability to receive almost six times more information.

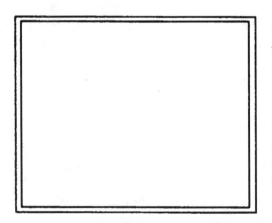

Figure 4-2

To match the capabilities of the HDTV standard, DVD-Video supports the 16 x 9 aspect ratio. Use of the larger aspect ratio also gives higher picture quality for home theater and large-screen television owners. As Figures 4-4 and 4-5 (on Page 64) show, some DVD video players provide an option for either the 4:3 or the 16:9 aspect ratio through "Display" and "TV Shape" menus.

Figure 4-3

DVD video players that don't have an option for the 16:9 aspect ratio provide other methods for displaying video formatted for the wide screen. The use of the pan-scan feature crops the sides of the wide-screen video so that the picture fits within the 4:3 display area. Although cropping occurs, pan-scan vectors embedded in the video stream allow the picture to represent the most important elements of the original video image. In effect, the viewable area pans and scans the video image.

Another option, called letterbox, displays the wide-screen image along with black bars at the top and bottom of the screen (see Figure 4-6). Letterboxing scales the original video image aspect ratio down to fit the 4:3 aspect ratio. If the DVD video player lacks the pan-scan feature, it automatically defaults to letterbox.

DISPLAY

SCREEN DISPLAYS	ENG
TV SHAPE	4:3
DISPLAY MODE	LB
ANGLE ICON	ON
SUBTITLE	---
DISC MENU	ENG

Figure 4-4

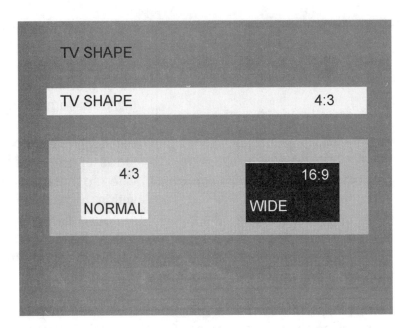

Figure 4-5

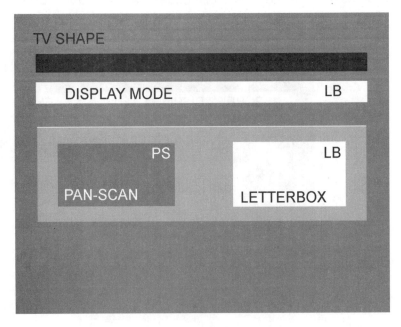

Figure 4-6

Angles

The DVD-Video format offers the capability to place as many as nine multiangle video streams on a disc. This feature provides selectable multiple points of view for sporting events, music videos, and movies. Given the use of this option, a viewer can change the viewing angle without changing the video or audio circuitry. Most DVD video-player manufacturers integrate an angle icon into the display to show that the source video takes advantage of multiple angle shots during production. Although the maximum bit rate of each video stream must drop slightly to accommodate the data interleaving required, the overall quality of each angle remains very high.

Audio

While DVD technologies initially emphasized the reproduction of video images, these technologies currently support high-quality, multichannel audio through the pcm, Dolby AC-3, and MPEG-2 formats. In addition, the DVD Forum has recently established a new DVD-Audio format that follows DVD-Video, DVD-ROM, DVD-RAM, and DVD-R. This new DVD-Audio format supports sampling frequencies as high as 192 kHz and as low as 44.1 kHz, and uses 16-bit, 20-bit, and 24-bit quantization bits.

During operating, DVD-Audio can store 192-kHz, 24-bit, two-channel sound for 74 minutes on single-sided, single-layer discs. By using standard linear pcm coding, single-sided, single-layer discs can store 74 minutes of 192-kHz, 24-bit, two-channel sound. The DVD Forum Working Group 4 also introduced a lossless coding method that allows the transmission of limited-transfer-rate, high-frequency audio signals without any loss of the original musical information. With this method, DVD-Audio enables the storage of 74 minutes of sound at the highest frequencies.

Most DVD video players provide options for choosing from the Dolby digital AC-3 audio, MPEG audio, or pcm formats. An "Audio Sel" option button found on the "Audio Setting Menu" provides a method for selecting any of the audio options. For countries using the NTSC standard and NTSC-based discs, pcm and Dolby digital operate with MPEG audio as an option. Countries using the PAL television standard use pcm and MPEG audio and have Dolby digital as an option. The DVD-Video specification also supports the Digital Theater Systems (DTS) and Sony Dynamic Digital Sound (SDDS) formats when used with a pcm, Dolby digital AC-3, or MPEG audio stream. In late 1999, the DVD Forum designated Dolby AC-3 encoding as the standard for video clips. In some instances, Dolby digital AC-3 remains an option, if the customer connects the player to an external digital surround-sound processor. Selection of the pcm option relies on the use of digital and analog input connectors, along with an onboard AC-3 decoder. While the connectors provide a method for attaching a preamplifier to the DVD video player, the decoder provides dynamic range control for quiet sounds. Selection of the pcm format also provides access to the karaoke vocal track on discs that support karaoke.

Independent Audio Streams

As shown in Figure 4-7, the "Audio Setup" menu selection found in DVD video players provides access to different soundtrack languages and to as many as eight independent audio streams on a single disc. Most DVD-Video discs include a selection of soundtrack languages and abbreviations (see Figure 4-8), and set English as the default soundtrack language. Use

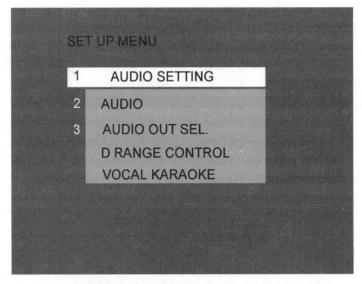

Figure 4-7

Abbreviation	Language	Abbreviation	Language	Abbreviation	Language	Abbreviation	Language
--	No alternate language	ET	Estonian	LO	Laotian	SM	Samoan
CHI	Chinese	EU	Basque	LT	Lithuanian	SN	Shona
DUT	Dutch	FA	Persian	LV	Latvian, Lettish	SO	Somali
ENG	English	FI	Finnish	MG	Malagasy	SQ	Albanian
FRE	French	FJ	Fiji	MI	Maori	SR	Serbian
GER	German	FO	Faroese	MK	Macedonian	SS	Siswati
ITA	Italian	FY	Frisian	ML	Malayalam	ST	Sesotho
JPN	Japanese	GA	Irish	MN	Mongolian	SU	Sundanese
KOR	Korean	GD	Scottish Gaelic	MO	Moldavian	SV	Swedish
MAY	Malay	GL	Galician	MR	Marathi	SW	Swahili
SPA	Spanish	GN	Guarani	MT	Maltese	TA	Tamil
AA	Afar	GU	Gujarati	MY	Burmese	TE	Telugu
AB	Abkhazian	HA	Hausa	NA	Nauru	TG	Tajik
AF	Afrikaans	HI	Hindi	NE	Nepali	TH	Thai
AM	Amharic	HR	Croatian	NO	Norwegian	TI	Tigrinya
AR	Arabic	HU	Hungarian	OC	Occitan	TK	Turkmen
AS	Assamese	HY	Armenian	OM	(Afan) Oromo	TL	Tagalog
AY	Aymara	IA	Interlingua	OR	Oriya	TN	Setswana
AZ	Azerbaijani	IE	Interlingue	PA	Panjabi	TO	Tongan
BA	Bashkir	IK	Inupiak	PL	Polish	TR	Turkish
BE	Belorussian	IN	Indonesian	PS	Pashto, Pushto	TS	Tsonga
BG	Bulgarian	IS	Icelandic	PT	Portuguese	TT	Tatar
BH	Bihari	IW	Hebrew	QU	Quechua	TW	Twi
BI	Bislama	JI	Yiddish	RM	Rhaeto-Romance	UK	Ukrainian
BN	Bengali, Bangla	JW	Javanese	RN	Kirundi	UR	Urdu
BO	Tibetan	KA	Georgian	RO	Rumanian	UZ	Uzbek
BR	Breton	KK	Kazakh	RU	Russian	VI	Vietnamese
CA	Catalan	KL	Greenlandic	RW	Kinyarwanda	VO	Volapük
CO	Corsican	KM	Cambodian	SA	Sanskrit	WO	Wolof
CS	Czech	KN	Kannada	SD	Sindhi	XH	Xhosa
CY	Welsh	KS	Kashmiri	SG	Sango	YO	Yoruba
DA	Danish	KU	Kurdish	SH	Serbo-Croatian	ZU	Zulu
DZ	Bhutani	KY	Kirghiz	SI	Singhalese		
EL	Greek	LA	Latin	SK	Slovak		
EO	Esperanto	LN	Lingala	SL	Slovenian		

Figure 4-8

of the "Language" menu shown in Figure 4-9 allows the selection of a different default language. Each stream may store in any of the available DVD audio formats.

Parental Control

Using the same features that allow the switching between a director's cut of a movie and the theatrical release, the DVD-Video format can assign a rating to a particular movie. Moreover, the video format can actively change the content through the selection of a specific movie rating. When the viewer places a DVD movie into a video player, circuitry within the player maps the original rating level of the movie against the rating levels set in the player. For example, a DVD video player set for the playback of only PG-rated movies will automatically switch to a PG-rated version of the movie. If an R-rated DVD does not offer a PG-rated version of the movie, the player will refuse to play the disc.

Figures 4-10 and 4-11 show screen shots of the "Parental Lock" and "Parent Lock Preset Security Code" menus. Both of these menus provide methods for locking designated movies or ratings away from general access. While

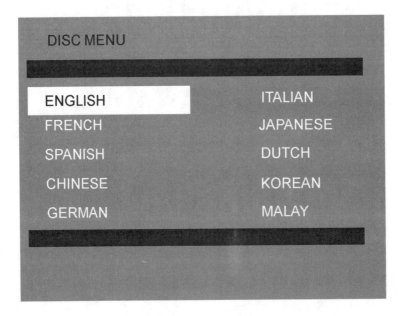

Figure 4-9

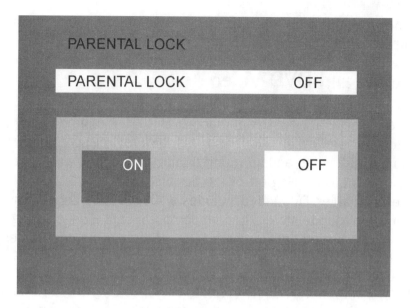

Figure 4-10

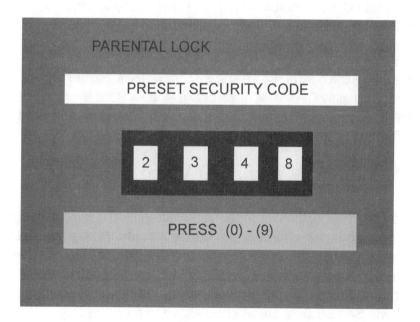

Figure 4-11

the parental lock menu switches locking on and off, the preset security code menu applies a specific four-digit code for access control.

DVD-ROM and DVD-Video

There are several ways to approach DVD-ROM. It can be thought of as a way to store general information, as a platform for reissuing older CD-ROM titles with MPEG-2 video and surround audio, or as a whole new medium for title development leveraging off of the flexibility of the DVD-Video format. As was discussed earlier, DVD-Video includes a "DVD Others Zone." This area of the disc may be used to store standard computer-data files, creating a hybrid DVD that can be played back on both DVD set-top players and PCs equipped with DVD-ROM readers.

This type of hybrid disc can have both set-top interactivity and video, while sharing files with an application written especially for a personal computer. An example of a DVD-hybrid title would be a feature film, which, when placed in a set-top DVD player, had simple interactivity, but when placed in a DVD-ROM-equipped PC, had additional games and links to the movie studio's web site. Such hybrid DVDs are already in production and will undoubtedly bring additional value to the format.

Since DVD-ROM operates as a super-set of DVD-Video, the players designed for DVD-Video will play DVD-ROM discs or DVD-Video/ROM hybrids. The creation of the DVD-ROM format also led to the development and standardization of recordable formats that include DVD-RAM, DVD-R, and DVD-RW.

High-Definition TV and DVD-Video

In the early 1990s, three competing high-definition television design teams agreed to combine their efforts and produce a standard, high-quality product. These three design teams—working under the direction of AT&T and Zenith Electronics; the General Instrument Corporation and the Massachusetts Institute of Technology; and Philips Consumer Electronics, Thomson Consumer Electronics and the David Sarnoff Research Center—have formed the Digital HDTV Grand Alliance. The high-definition television standard produced by the Grand Alliance establishes a technological framework for the merging of broadcast, cable, tele-communications, and computer technologies. Not surprisingly, the introduction of a high-definition television standard affects both the transmission system and the receiver design for modern video receivers.

With HDTV, the amount of luminance definition doubles both horizon-tally and vertically. An HDTV system provides four times as many pixels as the older NTSC system. In addition, the wider aspect ratio given by HDTV systems establishes more visual information for the viewer. Specifically, the high-definition system yields increased vertical definition through the use of 1,125 lines in the scanning pattern. The system provides additional video detail through the application of video bandwidth five times that seen with the conventional NTSC system.

HDTV 1125/60 Standard

During the planning and development of the HDTV system, the design team chose to use 1,125 scanning lines with a picture-refresh rate of 60 Hz. This 1125/60 standard compares with the type of resolution given by project-ing a 35-millimeter formatted film onto a large screen and establishes 1,035 scanning lines in the active picture display. Also, as an international standard, the 1125/60 system fits within the need to convert from older systems that have 525 and 625 scanning lines.

Thus, the 1125/60 standard allows existing television-signal distributors to convert from the NTSC 525/59.4 standard through readily available large-scale integrated circuits, as well as establishes a format for the global distribu-tion of video information. Currently, the HDTV broadcast system shares televi-sion bands with existing services and utilizes unused channels. With this, tele-vision-signal broadcasters are temporarily assigned a second channel to ac-complish the transition from the NTSC format to the HDTV format.

Other HDTV Standards

Along with the 16:9 aspect ratio and the 1125/60 scanning-refresh stan-dard, the HDTV design team also determined that the new system should have:

- 2:1 interlaced scanning combined with noninterlaced scanning.
- A luminance bandwidth of 30 Hz.
- Two color-difference signals with bandwidths of 15 MHz.
- An active horizontal picture duration of 29.63 microseconds.
- A horizontal blanking duration of 3.77 microseconds.
- A new sync waveform.

The HDTV standard assembled by the Grand Alliance takes advantage of the interlaced scanning used for television transmission and reception and the noninterlaced scanning commonly seen with computer monitors. With noninterlaced, or progressive scanning, the HDTV system provides a choice of 24-, 30-, and 60-frames-per-second scanning (with a 1280 x 720 pixel dot resolution) and a 24- and 30-frames-per-second scanning (with a 1920 x 1080 pixel dot resolution). As a whole, HDTV supports the following spatial formats.

1280 x 720	23.976/24 Hz	Progressive
	29.97/30 Hz	Progressive
	59.94/60 Hz	Progressive
1920 x 1080	23.976/24 Hz	Progressive
	29.97/30 Hz	Progressive
	59.94/60 Hz	Interlaced
	59.94/60 Hz	Interlaced

With this, the HDTV system provides direct compatibility with computing systems. In addition to the noninterlaced scanning formats, the system also offers 60-frames-per-second interlaced scanning at a resolution of 1920 x 1080. The use of interlaced scanning becomes necessary for the two 1920 x 1080 x 60 formats, because of the lack of a method for compressing the formats into a 6-MHz channel.

Each of the formats features square pixels, a 16:9 aspect ratio, and 4:2:0 chrominance sampling. When compared to the NTSC standard, the HDTV system provides a broader choice of colors that aligns with newer film technologies, computer graphics technologies, and print media. As may be expected, the capability of the HDTV standard to reproduce a broader spectrum of colors affects both camera and display technology.

The system achieves many of the improvements in resolution and color reproduction through the decision to establish a 30 MHz luminance bandwidth, as well as two color-difference signals with a bandwidth of 15 MHz each. In effect, the decision to use the 30-MHz and 15-MHz bandwidths depended on the decision to use 1,125 scanning lines. As a result of that decision, the system required a bandwidth of at least 25 MHz. From an overall perspective, the combining of increased horizontal and vertical resolution with wider luminance and chrominance bandwidths yielded a larger number of viewable pixels. Given 1,920 horizontal pixels, the HDTV system becomes a platform for several different applications of computer-display technologies ranging from computer-aided design and manufacturing to medical imaging.

The HDTV broadband, 20-megabit-per-second digital transmission system enables the convergence of the entertainment, industrial, medical, and educational technologies by using a packetized data-transport structure based on the MPEG-2 compression format. Each data packet is 188 bytes long, with four bytes designated as the header or descriptor and 184 bytes designated as an information payload. With this type of high-compression data transportation, the HDTV system can deliver a wide variety of video, audio, voice, data, or multimedia services and can interoperate with other delivery or imaging systems.

High-Definition DVD

Proposed during the latter part of 1999, the dual-layer, nine-gigabyte high-definition DVD can store 133 minutes of images at 1920 x 1080i resolution. Signals recorded in this proposed HD-DVD encode through MPEG-2 and modulate through the HDTV 8VSB-modulation scheme. Proprietary encryption technologies embed on the disc as recorded signals on top of the high-definition signals. A smart card located inside the HDTV receiver will decrypt the incoming signal.

5

DVD and Copy Protection

Introduction

With the introduction of DVD technologies, suggesting, approving, and implementing copy protection has become one of the most complex tasks for the industry. The complexity stems from policy-making that involves manufacturers, production houses, and content providers, as well as from the need to match technologies with the new policies. In part, the complexity also evolves from the broad approach to DVD technologies. As mentioned in previous chapters, DVD technologies cover the reproduction of video and audio content, as well as the capability to read and write computer data.

Some issues remain unresolved. But most copy-protection schemes became available with the 1997 introduction of DVD video players and DVD-ROM drives in the United States. While both products involve the playback of DVD-Video movies, the introduction of DVD-ROM drives that allow software distribution renewed interest in copy protection. The final agreement on copy protection for DVD-Video involved extensive interindustry discussion among content owners (such as movie studios), computer manufacturers, and the consumer-electronics industry.

Historical Look at Digital Copyright Protection and DVD

Although copyright protection stands as a longtime issue, the advent of digital content has complicated the interpretation of laws and policies. Unlike analog copies, digital copies provide perfect replicas of the master. In addition, a company or individual could globally distribute digital copies over the Internet with no degradation. As a result, the need for copy-protection policies and methods for digital technologies remains a priority for producers and manufacturers. Hollywood studio executives had this situation in the forefront of their minds when in March 1996 the Motion Picture Association of America and the Consumer Electronics Manufacturers Association invited members of the computer industry's technical working group to a meeting in Los Angeles.

Copy Protection Technical Working Group

The formation of the Copy Protection Technical Working Group (CPTWG) helped to resolve stalemates over what type of copy protection to apply to DVD technologies. As the group reached an agreement, it decided that copy-protection methods should remain transparent for the legitimate viewing and enjoyment of the content, while preventing anyone from making unauthorized copies. Within the agreement, the group also established two key principles, in that the content should include self-protecting and self-describing features.

Encryption

The establishment of self-protecting content led directly to the use of encryption. By definition, encryption preserves the confidentiality of a message passed between persons and emphasizes only the inclusion of authorized recipients. The encryption of copyrighted video or audio information, however, controls access to the content. License agreements maintain the secrecy of the decryption information and allow compliant playback systems to follow specific usage rules designed to protect the content from unauthorized copying after decryption.

Since computer manufacturers insist that copy protection have a basis in voluntary adoption, rather than a mandate through legislation, the use of encryption systems addresses a policy issue for the manufacturers. With encrypted content, a bit-for-bit copy made to a noncompliant system cannot be viewed in the absence of licensed decryption methods. As a result, legitimate but noncompliant systems can exist without creating a loophole in the copy-protection system.

The principle of self-describing content requires the embedding of copy-control information into the content data stream. As a result, the copy-control information can propagate along with the desired video and audio information without any special processing. Application of the self-describing content principle alleviated a controversy surrounding the early Copy Generation Management System method and the two bits that identified the copy-protection level for a given title.

Copy Generation Management System

During the computer industry's technical working group meeting in 1996, the Motion Picture Association of America and the Consumer Electronic Manufacturers Association created the Copy Generation Management System (CGMS) approach to copy protection of motion pictures. Moreover, the two entities explained how CGMS would apply to content released on DVD and computer systems equipped with DVD-ROM drives. Essentially, the plan indicated that all computer systems should preserve, detect, and subsequently operate according to the stipulations of two CGMS bits that associate with all digital copyrighted motion-picture content distributed on a DVD-Video disc.

The computer industry responded immediately and negatively. In its view, the proposed technological approach established ineffective methods for enforcing laws that required the integration of copy-protection technology into products. While willing to study technical methods of imposing copy protection on computer systems, the computer industry preferred voluntary implementation of copy protection. In addition, the computer industry referred to the 1992 Audio Home Recording Act intended for the protection of digital audio content. As the Act below shows, existing provisions applied to consumer-electronics products such as stand-alone compact disc players and exempted computer systems.

Audio Home Recording Act

"An Act that prohibits the importation, manufacture, or distribution of any device, or the offering or performance of any service, the primary purpose of which is to circumvent any program or circuit that implements a serial copy-management system."

• "The Act requires a serial copy-management system in all digital audio recording devices and digital audio interface devices imported, manufactured, or distributed in the United States. Such a system allows unlimited first-generation digital copying of sound recordings, but prevents the making of digital copies from copies."

• "The Act also establishes a royalty system in which importers and manufacturers of digital audio recording devices and digital audio recording media make royalty payments on each device or medium they distribute. Such payments are collected by the Copyright Office and distributed annually to record companies, performers, music publishers, and songwriters."

CGMS/A and CGMS/D

Embedded in line 21 of the outgoing NTSC video signal, CGMS/A information controls the amount of legal copies allowed per disc. As a complement to Macrovision, CGMS/A data has priority over any Macrovision anticopy signals programmed for the same line. Before equipment used for copying DVD discs can utilize CGMS/A, it must recognize the CGMS/A format. The copy-protection system marks contents with standard CGMS flags of "copy never" or "copy once."

When establishing a channel, connected devices such as a DVD player and a digital TV exchange keys and authentication certificates. From that point, the DVD player encrypts the encoded video signal during the sending of the signal to the receiving device. In turn, the receiving device includes decoding hardware used to decrypt the CGMS/A signal. In practice, digital display devices will receive and display all data, while digital recording devices will only receive data not marked "copy never." The recording device must also change the CGMS flags to zero copies for source data marked "copy once." Because of the coding and specific uses of digital technologies, CGMS/D will work for the next generation of digital TVs and digital video recorders and requires new DVD players with digital connectors.

DVD Encryption

The main requirements set for the DVD-Video encryption method reflected the different concerns of movie studios, computer manufacturers, and the electronics industry. All parties agreed that the DVD-Video copy-protection system should prevent the unauthorized "casual consumer copying" of DVD-Video content onto consumer digital recording formats and devices in the home. In addition, the group agreed that the copy-protection schemes would not prevent piracy involving highly sophisticated attacks by individuals who had obtained support from professional-level resources.

Implementation of DVD-Video copy protection involved requirements that:

- the digital content remain unviewable for a scrambled data stream and unchanged from the original when unscrambled;
- the compressibility of the bit stream and picture quality remain unaffected; and that
- the encryption methods meet export standards established by the U.S. government.

The group resolved the first two issues by applying the encryption after the MPEG compression step, rather than before compression. Applying the encryption before compression would eliminate the basis for high-compression factors. With the last issue, the group conceded that copy protection would not reach full effectiveness unless supplemented by more conventional policing methods.

Digital Transmission Content Protection

In draft form, the technical implementation principles for DVD-Video copy protection stipulated that compliant playback systems would have encrypted digital outputs. With the adoption of these principles in 1996, the CPTWG formed the Data Transmission Discussion Group to define the requirements of digital transmission technologies and to solicit technical proposals for those technologies.

After fielding 11 proposals, the group centered on the Digital Transmission Content Protection (DTCP) method developed by Hitachi, Intel, Matsushita, Sony, and Toshiba. Implementation of DTCP involves the authentication and key exchange (AKE) procedure by both the DVD video player and the destination device.

AKE procedure ensures that only compliant destination devices may access the content. After initializing AKE, the source device encrypts and transmits the content and the decryption keys needed by the destination.

The DTCP approach specifies two levels of AKE. Based on the use of digital signatures and a public-key-based cryptographic system, full AKE requires copy-control information such as "do not copy" or "no copies allowed" before the transmission of content. Restricted AKE relies on a shared or common-key cryptography that requires fewer hardware or software resources for implementation. Rather than function with resource-hungry "do not copy" commands, restricted AKE uses the "single copy allowed" or "copy freely" commands.

More recent copy-protection technologies address the need for protecting copyrighted audio and video content for physical distribution on prerecorded media. The copy-protection schemes consider digital transmission and the recording of authorized copies that remain protected from second-generation copying.

Other technologies have emphasized the use of digital watermarking technologies that embed usage conditions transparently in the content and carry the conditions across both digital and analog environments.

Bringing the process full-circle, content providers and manufacturers have opted to integrate copy-protection technologies into a coherent architecture. With this approach, copy-protection technologies protect the content, use system resources efficiently, and do not require additional hardware. The combination of technologies provides copy protection for audio or video content regardless of the delivery method. In addition, the combined technologies can establish a licensed change-of-content protection if the initial source distributes the digital content in an encrypted form.

Copy Protection and DVD

DVD-Video manufacturers apply one of four types of copy protection, and they have begun to study the use of the same type of watermark protection as seen with DVD-Audio discs. Macrovision adds a rapidly modulated color burst signal and pulses in the AGC to the composite and S-video outputs. The serial copy-generation management system (SCMS) included with each DVD-Video disc prevents copies of copies. Another copy-protection standard, called the content-scrambling system (CSS), uses data encryption to prevent the reading of media files directly from a disc.

Decryption circuitry in the DVD video player decodes the data before displaying the programming on the screen. DVD-ROM drives and video-decoder hardware and software exchange encryption keys, allowing the decrypting of the video data before the encoder displays the information. The fourth system, called the Digital Copy Protection System, also exchanges encryption keys and uses authentication certificates to establish a secure playback channel.

With each system, no encryption is required for content that does not have copy protection. The technology relies on flags that mark the content, thus sending "copy-many-times", "copy-once," "don't-copy," and "no-more-copies" signals back to the copy-protection hardware. Given the capabilities of the hardware, players can authenticate the signal to do nothing more than reproduce audio and video and receive all data.

DVD Playback and Copy Protection

In terms of copy protection, every DVD playback system has vulnerabilities. The strategies developed by the movie industry and the consumer-electronics industry consider each of those vulnerabilities. Figure 5-1 uses a block diagram of a DVD video player to show the vulnerable locations.

Within the DVD video player or DVD-ROM drive, raw data travels from the optical pickup unit, the RF signal processor, and a digital signal processor to decoding circuits. In addition, the data signal also travels through an NTSC/PAL decoder that manipulates the digital signal into an analog format. As shown

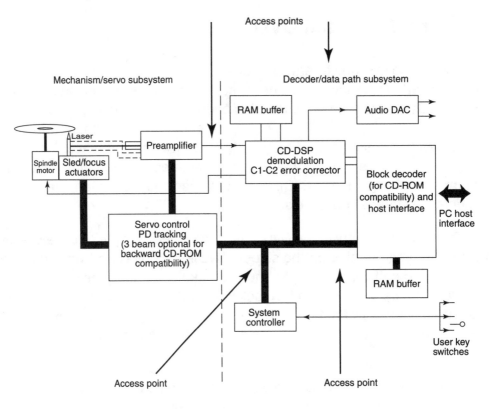

Figure 5-1

in Figure 5-1, scrambled and unscrambled DVD video and audio streams appear in decompressed forms after the decoding process.

Content-Scrambling System (CSS)

The content-scrambling system prevents the unauthorized copying of DVD audio and video information through DVD video decoders and recordable storage devices. During implementation, CSS selectively scrambles each video-title set using unique keys stored and encrypted on the disc. Each disc title uses unique keys encrypted by the CSS Licensing Authority. Scrambling of the video and audio information occurs during the mastering process.

The digital keys allow the playback of copyrighted material on DVD-ROM discs only if the copyright owner grants permission. Coding circuitry individually encrypts three digital keys. As a result, the second key will become available and function only with the first key in place. The third key becomes available and functions only with the second key in place and provides the decrypting mechanism for the compressed audio and video information. A decoder housed in the drive obtains and decrypts the original keys before descrambling the data. In addition, the MPEG-2 decoder ensures the use of only approved hardware or software by challenging the drive for the necessary decryption keys.

CSS relies on bus authentication and encryption to prevent digital-to-digital copying from computer to computer. During the challenging process, a DVD-ROM drive must check the validity of the intended data destination before sending the data. To prevent the playback of illegal copies, the DVD-ROM decoder card checks the validity of the sender. As a result, the implementation of CSS in a computer system requires mutual authentication. The final piece of the CSS solution requires the use of a time-variable key so that illegal mutual authentication cannot occur.

Given the relatively recent breaking of the content-scrambling system, computer security experts have begun to point out the flaws of this security model. Due to the need to comply with federal export regulations, the content-scrambling system relies on a 40-bit encryption key. But the proprietary algorithm used within the keys does not have the robustness of algorithms used with other public keys. The versatility of DVD technologies has also become a factor in breaking CSS. Although each DVD video player or DVD-ROM reader has unique keys that unlock the encryption key in a disc, each disc includes copies of the same decryption key that, in turn, include every unlocking code for each player.

In operation, the content-scrambling system for DVD-Video discs starts at the movie studio. First, the studio transfers the motion picture into the digital domain by applying MPEG-2 compression, assembling soundtracks, menus, subtitles, and special features as specified in the DVD-Video book. Next, CSS data encryption occurs either at the studio or at the disc-production plant. With step three, the compressed, formatted, and encrypted information transfers to the DVD master recording. Another layer of encryption located in the lead-in area of the master protects the content-encryption key. Playback of the replica may occur through a stand-alone DVD video player or a DVD-ROM drive.

Macrovision

In response to the capability to record copyrighted audio and video information from a DVD video player, Macrovision developed an anti-taping process for VHS videotapes and digital video systems. After considering the operating characteristics of VCRs and televisions, Macrovision introduced an encryption scheme that takes advantage of automatic gain control (agc) and Colorstripe. Within VCRs, agc circuits react quickly to any change in signal strength. By comparison, the agc circuits found in televisions react slowly to any change in signal strength.

Macrovision uses this difference when modifying the video signal by placing pulses within the vertical blanking intervals of the video signal. Although a television can display a Macrovision-encrypted picture, a VCR cannot record a viewable scene. Copies of a Macrovision-encrypted tape will display as dim or noisy pictures that have no or little color. In addition, the copy may exhibit a loss of video or a tearing picture. Within Macrovision encryption, Colorstripe uses changes in color-burst information to produce annoying lines across the picture in playback of an illegal copy.

In playback in a DVD-ROM drive, an additional step secures an authenticated communication path across the interface between the host PC and the drive that has the CSS license. Establishment of this secure channel allows the DVD-ROM drive to pass the protected disc key to the host PC for descrambling and playback of the encrypted content. In turn, the content travels from the drive to the host PC during disc playback.

The copy-protection system for DVD-Video also prevents compliant playback systems from reading unauthorized bit-by-bit copies made to recordable DVD media. A bit-by-bit copy process copies every piece of data on the disc in sequence, regardless of the disc content. To accomplish this, disc manufacturers pre-emboss or factory prerecord the sector reserved for the DVD-Video or DVD-Audio disc decryption keys. As a result, the recordable blank cannot record a copy of the disc decryption key associated with the bit-by-bit copy transfer of content. As a result, the copy will not play back.

Watermarking

Supported by Hitachi, IBM, NEC, Pioneer, and Sony—and following an earlier integration of originally separate proposals by IBM and NEC—the Galaxy watermarking system uses Primary Mark and Copy Mark as methods for preventing unauthorized recording and playback of copyrighted video content over consumer devices or personal computers. The system offers playback control, record control, and generational copy control through the application of four copy protection states: "Copy Free," "One Copy," "No More Copy," and "Never Copy." The Primary Mark and Copy Mark standards specify the states in video content.

Primary Mark consists of eight bits of transparent digital watermark data that embeds in the digital video signal. A compliant device detects the Primary Mark data in both the uncompressed and compressed video streams. The first two bits of Primary Mark contain copy-control information (CCI) and represent "Copy Free," "One Copy," and "Never Copy" in data that does not contain Copy Mark information. While the next two bits represent analog protection system (APS) trigger bits, the content owner has control over the remaining four bits.

IBM DataHiding technology allows a content owner to embed a highly transparent, reliable, and secure watermarking message directly into the digital video data. Embedding the watermark into the video stream prevents removal without damaging visual quality. With IBM DataHiding technologies, the embedding process modulates multiple bits of invisible message by quasi-random pattern and then adds the bits to the luminance components of each pixel in the frame or field of digital video data.

A perception model controls the added amount for each pixel by taking a count of the visual effect of embedding additional image characteristics. As a result, the automatic and adaptive IBM DataHiding approach ensures maximum detectability of the embedded data, while preventing any deterioration of the quality of the embedded image. Statistical inference methods extract the embedded message.

Although Copy Mark operates as another transparent digital watermark, it does not interfere with the Primary Mark data. With the Copy Mark approach, a compliant device inserts and detects Copy Mark data in both baseband and MPEG-2 domains. For example, a DVD recorder could insert Copy Mark data into the "One Copy" content to change the status to "No More Copy" for the purpose of generation copy control.

Detecting the Primary Mark involves the use of the adaptive period-detection algorithm with a predetermined false positive error ratio. The algorithm and ratio allow reliable detection of the Primary Mark with even heavily degraded content. In addition, the Primary Mark can survive the successive processes of studio-video processing, MPEG-2 compression, VHS recording, and MPEG-2 recompression.

Several layers of protection prevent the copying of a second-generation copy from an unauthorized copy. If the CCI contained in the watermark calls for either "copy freely" or "single copy allowed," then copying can proceed. If the watermark can update to "no more copies allowed" in the authorized copy, a copy may also occur. But if the CCI shows a "do-not-copy" or "no-more-copies-allowed" command, the compliant recorder shuts down and will not create a copy. The update method may remark the content in the recorder or alter a digital token carried along with the content before the making of the authorized copy.

Content Protection For Recordable Media (CPRM)

Recently introduced for implementation with DVD-RAM recorders, the content protection for recordable media (CPRM) copy-protection scheme senses a signal and encrypts the data if it receives a signal for onetime copying. With CPRM, digital content providers such as broadcasters can specify whether their content can be copied freely or one time only—or whether it cannot be copied at all. CPRM has emerged as a key technology solution for recorders built for export to the United States.

Copy Protection For DVD-Audio

After discussions with major music-label representatives in 1998, IBM, Intel, Matsushita, and Toshiba announced the Framework for Copy Protection of DVD-Audio. Similar to the copy-protection solutions applied to DVD-Video, the framework uses both encryption and watermarking technologies to prevent the playback of music and related content on unlicensed, noncompliant products. Due to widespread customer acceptance of audio compact discs and players, the DVD-Audio framework allows a single unencrypted copy of every DVD-Audio disc for personal use at a sound quality less than or equal to the audio compact disc specification. Existing compact disc readers will ignore the watermark indicating "no more copies allowed." The message remains in place for compliant DVD recorders and should inhibit second-generation copying of those CDs. Within the DVD-Audio framework, the content provider has the capability to set four copy-control information parameters called C, Q, T, and R. Table 5-1 lists these parameters and descriptions of associated functions.

Table 5-1: DVD-Audio Copy Control Parameters

Parameter	Function
C — Copy Permission	Allows more than one copy
Q — Sound Quality	Allows higher levels of sound quality, depending on the discretion of the content owner. The highest level is the full quality of the original DVD-Audio in either multi-channel or super quality stereo.
T — Transaction	Allows properly equipped DVD-Audio players to connect by modem to a location on the Internet. Electronic transactions may override basic copy-control information at the content owner's discretion and allow a transaction for an added fee.
R — Related Content	Determines the authorization status for copies of each element of the related content. The authorization status is "copy allowed" or "not allowed."

In early 1999, the Recording Industry Association of America responded with the Secure Digital Music Initiative, or SDMI. In brief, the SDMI seeks to create specifications that improve copyright protection for music within consumer products. While not wanting to place numerous legal constraints on the interoperability of optical disc products or the use of MPEG-3 files, the SDMI seeks methods for allowing the industry to adhere to the Audio Home Recording Act.

Regional Playback Control (RPC)

Regional codes provide motion picture studios with a method for controlling the home release of movies in different countries. As the potential economic impact of DVD technologies becomes more apparent, controlling the home release of movies in Europe also grows in importance for several reasons. At one level, studios may release screen versions of a movie in Europe well after the video release in the United States. In addition, movie studios have concerns about distribution rights.

As a result, the DVD-Video standard includes regional codes that prevent the playback of discs in other regions of the world. Moreover, each player includes a code for the player-purchase region. The region number for the player and discs appears as a number or numbers superimposed on a world globe. Discs with codes that do not match the player code will not play back in the particular player. With this, a consumer may purchase a disc that has the code for one country and then find that the disc will not play in another country.

As shown in Figure 5-2, the regional codes define six regions for DVD playback. Since regional codes remain an option for disc manufacturers, a disc arriving without codes will play in any player in any country. If the disc includes a region code or a set of regional codes, the codes remain a permanent part of the disc.

With a large number of DVD discs produced in the United States, the selectivity given through regional playback control (RPC) has caused controversy. Videophiles from regions other than the United States cannot play the titles marked with the Region 1 code.

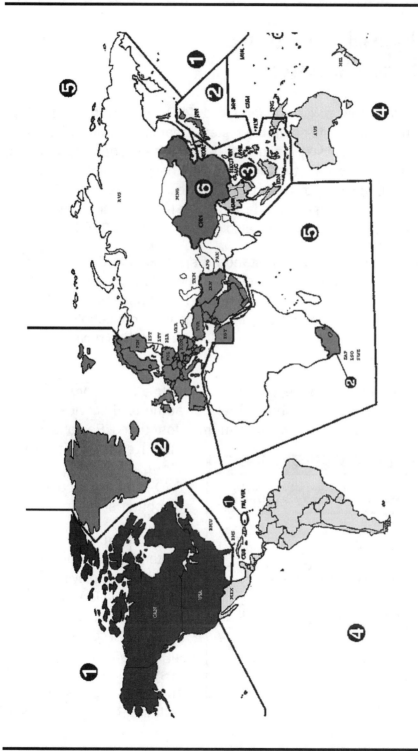

Figure 5-2

Regional Playback Control and Contents-Scramble System

Every DVD-ROM drive sold since January 1, 2000, must support the RPC-II standard set by the contents-scramble system organization. In addition, personal computers manufactured since that date must include hardware and software that meet the RPC-II standard. In a very basic sense, the standard protects against the copying of DVD-based movies. To playback DVD movie software with the specified regional code, either the hardware or software used as applications on a PC system side is also required to meet RPC-II.

The combination of the RPC-II standard specification drive and DVD-Video movies protected with regional codes will not allow reproduction of the disc contents. The CSS prohibits changing the RPC-II specification drive to an RPC-I setting. When implemented at the consumer household, a viewer may change the region recognized by the RPC-II specification drive five times after the initial region set.

After the fifth region change, the drive goes into a Parm—or no change allowed—condition. But drive manufacturers or authorized service centers can reinitialize the Parm condition a maximum of four times. Regional codes operate only with DVD-Video discs and exclude DVD-ROM discs containing computer software.

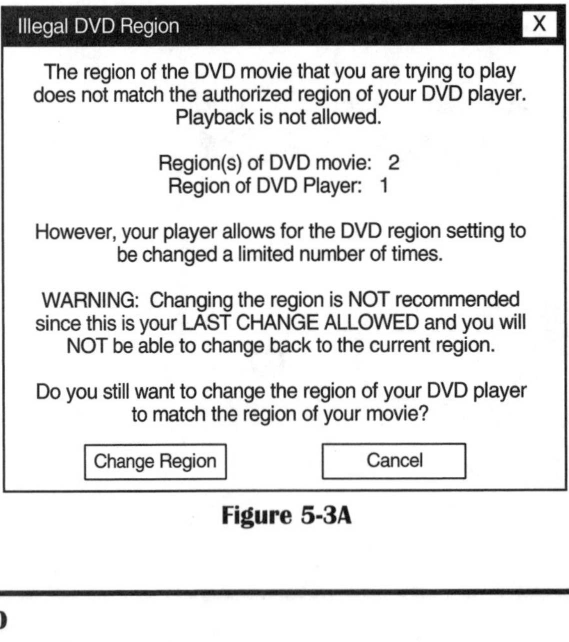

Computer-playback systems check for regional codes before playing movies from a DVD-Video. Drive-utility information usually identifies RPC II compliance during the system boot-up process. Figures 5-3A and 5-3B show messages associated with the RPC-II compliance.

Illegal DVD Region   X

The region of the DVD movie that you are trying to play does not match the authorized region of your DVD player. Playback is not allowed.

Region(s) of DVD movie: 2
Region of DVD Player: 1

However, your player allows for the DVD region setting to be changed a limited number of times.

WARNING: Changing the region is NOT recommended since this is your LAST CHANGE ALLOWED and you will NOT be able to change back to the current region.

Do you still want to change the region of your DVD player to match the region of your movie?

[Change Region]   [Cancel]

Figure 5-3A

```
┌─────────────────────────────────────┐
│                                      │
│  Illegal Region Code !               │
│                                      │
│                                      │
│    Your system is not suitable       │
│      to play this DVD - Disc !       │
│                                      │
└─────────────────────────────────────┘
```

Figure 5-3B

High-Definition DVD Encryption

At the conclusion of Chapter 4, we took a brief look at newer DVD technologies derived from DVD-Video and High-Definition Television. The encryption technology devised for the new HD-DVD players uses a combination of encryption tools and smart-card technologies to produce the extended conditional access (XCA) copy-protection system.

With this approach, the credit card-sized smart card fits into a reader slot located on the chassis front. The smart card includes a processor that contains mathematical algorithms or deciphering keys. Each set of algorithms allows the descrambler to access subscription and pay-per-view programming. Without the smart card in place, a decoder cannot obtain access to the algorithm needed to address the programming.

Authorizing the receiver involves the sending of an encrypted message to the player that initializes playback of the movie. Since the authorization message is a combination of the player serial number and the key card number, the smart card will not interchange between players. Encryption of the data streams occurs at the production site.

When an encrypted packet arrives at the player, it passes through the conditional access module (CAM) before traveling to the demultiplexer. The CAM works as a decryption engine and interfaces with the smart card. During reception of the encrypted signals, the CAM requests the next set of decryption keys from the smart card. At the beginning of each MPEG-2 packet, a two-bit field called the transport scrambling flags (TSF) provides a value that indicates the presence of either an unencrypted or encrypted data stream.

If the TSF indicates the presence of an encrypted data stream, the MPEG-2 packet passes to the decryption engine. At this point, the CAM uses the key obtained from the smart card to change the packet back into an MPEG-2/DVB transport packet. With the digital video broadcasting (DVB) packet conversion in place, the system can process the video and audio information.

Conditional access at the receiver relies on the insertion of a smart card containing the correct deciphering key into the receiver and the authorization of the receiver. Although the conditional access systems have major similarities, differences also exist. Those differences include the size of the key, the mathematical algorithm, and the security of the system. In addition, some services use electronic countermeasures that randomly change the encryption algorithm and change the length of the key.

6

DVD MPEG and Dolby Signal Compression

Introduction

As the capability to store not only audio and video signals but also program information and other computer data with DVD technologies has grown, providers have had to contend with the need for additional bandwidth and storage requirements. Calls for more colors, higher resolution, faster frame rates, and overall higher quality have placed additional pressures on transmission and reception systems. As an example, 24-bit color video at 640 x 480 resolution transmitted at 30 frames per second translates into 26 megabytes of data per second.

Compressing the audio and video information frees space. In addition, the process reduces the amount of power needed to transmit the signal. Additional compression works well for scenes that have less complexity and movement. Decreased compression provides a higher quality picture.

Converting Analog Signals into Digital Signals

With all current systems, the video content originates as an analog signal. As mentioned in Chapter 1, analog-to-digital circuitry converts analog signals to digital data. During the conversion process, the coding and decoding of the signals consider the frame rate, spatial resolution, and color resolution in response to the need for high-quality video images. Three processes—sampling, quantization, and binary notation—occur during the conversion of analog video information into a compressed digital signal, ensuring that the reproduction of high-quality video images exists.

Frame Rates

Every portion of video information breaks down into a series of frames per second. Nonfilm video production has a standard of 30 frames per second, while film video has a standard of 24 frames per second. Each frame splits in half to form a field containing odd lines and a field containing even lines. A standard television displays an analog video signal with the odd field first and the even field second. Sixty interlaced fields show every second. With computer and high-definition television displays, progressive scanning displays each line in sequence and an entire frame 30 times per second.

Color Resolution

Color resolution refers to the number of colors displayed on the screen at one time. Again, the standard television broadcast has a different color resolution than the resolution seen with computer displays. Designated as YUV, the standard analog video display format presents color resolution in terms of the seven-bit, 4:1:1, or 4:2:2 format, which equals 2 million displayable colors. The standard analog-video display format also presents color resolution in terms of the eight-bit, 4:4:4 format, which equals 16 million colors. A 24-bits-per-pixel computer display shows 16.7 million colors.

Spatial Resolution

Spatial resolution measures the size of the picture. As with color resolution, no direct correlation between analog video resolutions and computer display resolutions exists. For example, a standard analog video signal displays a full image without the borders seen with computer displays. The NTSC standard used in North American and Japanese television uses a 768 x 484 display, while the PAL standard for European television has a slightly larger display at 768 x 576. Due to the differences between analog video and computer video, conversion of analog video to a digital format must consider each difference to prevent downsizing of the video image and loss of resolution.

Limitations of Sampling and Quantization

Sampling and quantization produce large amounts of digital information. With video signals, each second of video equals 162 million bits of data. Without using some method for compressing the data, even a small portion of a video signal would become too unwieldy for efficient reproduction. While the uncompressed video-signal data would require huge storage devices, it would also require the use of larger bandwidths to carry even small numbers of channels.

One second of video information contains 30 frames of images, while each frame contains 1.2 million pixels at 3 bytes per pixel, or 3.6 megabytes per frame. As a result, each minute of video information contains 6.4 gigabytes of data. Within this transmission, the 30 frames of video information per second ensure the quality reproduction of motion, and the luminance bandwidth of 5.2 MHz provides the proper reproduction of brightness, contrast, and picture detail. The video signal has 416 horizontal lines of resolution and a signal-to-noise ratio of 55 decibels. With a horizontal scanning rate of 15.734 kHz, the 5.2 MHz luminance bandwidth places 544 pixels on the active portion of each horizontal scanning line.

Another key measure for the transmission of a video signal is the lines of resolution. As opposed to scanning lines, lines of resolution represent the number of transitions that occur in a space equal to the picture height. With the NTSC system, the transmission of 80 lines of resolution requires a bandwidth of 1 MHz. As a result, the NTSC system with a 4.2 MHz bandwidth has a maximum number of 336 lines of resolution.

Compressing Video Signals

During the compression process, different factors affect the amount and quality of the compression. Those factors are:

- Real time vs. non-real time
- Symmetrical vs. asymmetrical
- Compression ratios
- Lossless vs. lossy

- Interframe vs. intraframe
- Bit-rate control

Real-Time vs. Non-Real-Time Compression

During compression, some systems capture, compress to disk, decompress, and play back video at 30 frames per second with no delays, or in real time. Other systems capture some of the 30 frames per second and play back only a portion of the frames. With non-real-time compression, an insufficient frame rate that occurs at less than 24 frames per second causes the reproduced video to have a jerky appearance. Moreover, the missing frames may contain extremely important lip-synchronization data that prevent the correct matching of audio information with video information.

Symmetrical vs. Asymmetrical Compression

Video images compress and decompress either symmetrically or asymmetrically. With symmetrical compression, the compression, storage, and decompression of the video images occur at the same rate. Asymmetrical compression and decompression occur as a ratio of the number of minutes needed to compress one minute of video.

Compression Ratios

Compression ratios refer to a different quantity than asymmetric ratios. In terms of video compression and decompression, the compression ratio corresponds to a numerical representation of the original video in comparison to the compressed video. For example, a 200:1 compression ratio represents the original video as 200 and the compressed video as 1. Compression ratios vary with the compression standard.

For example, the MPEG standard usually has compression ratios of 200:1, while the JPEG standard normally has a maximum compression ratio of 20:1 for high-quality images. With all standards, more compression results in higher compression ratios but lower video quality.

Lossless vs. Lossy Compression

Two types of video compression exist: lossless and lossy. As the name implies, lossless compression doesn't lose any information during the compression process. Decompressing the compressed file produces information identical to the original information. Lossy compression, on the other hand, loses some data while compressing a video data stream and relies on the power of the human eye and brain to fill in the lost information. The human eye and brain can perceive 24 still images shown in rapid sequence as fluid motion.

Interframe vs. Intraframe Compression

The intraframe-compression method compresses and stores each video frame as a discrete picture. By comparison, the interframe-compression method transmits and receives only the differences between frames and creates a reference frame. During compression, each subsequent frame of the video compares to the previous frame and the next frame. With only the difference transmitted and received, interframe compression substantially reduces the amount of data.

Bit-Rate Control

With most forms of digital transmission, the bit rate signifies the speed of transmitted data from transmitter to receiver. Compared to baud rate, the bit rate specifies the number of bits per second carried across a communications channel such as a phone line, serial cable, or satellite transponder. The baud rate describes the transmission rate for data within the channel. The digital transmission of signals relies on symbol rates or the sending of two bits at the same time. With this, the baud rate remains the same, while the bit rate doubles.

In terms of conserving bandwidth, bit-rate control may be the most important compression factor. With the transmission of television signals, quality of the reproduced frames is the highest priority. As an example of bit-rate control, international standard H.320 videoconferencing COder-DECoders (CODECs) can compress the video plus audio into as little as 56 kilobits per second—or about 1.2500th of the original signal—and provides a low-detail image at about one video frame per second. Business-grade videoconferencing typically requires transmission of at least 256 kilobits per second for good quality pictures at about 15 video frames per second. Excellent motion handling near 30 frames per second is possible at transmission rates of 768 kilobits per second and higher.

Adaptive Rate Control

Unlike a single-source MPEG compression, a broadcast service can adapt the rate control for several image and audio sources simultaneously. Adaptive rate control spanning multiple programs can give the highest bandwidth to complex sources while reducing the bandwidth to another source, but requires a more complex uplink-control facility. Yet this type of statistical multiplexing will sometimes lead to blurs or artifacts when the combined ideal bandwidth of the programs on a single transponder is too high. In these cases, one or more programs will have their bit rates dropped to meet the real bandwidth of the transponder. By careful program scheduling, broadcasters can minimize the impact of the fixed transponder bandwidth on the broadcast quality.

As a complicating factor, adaptive rate control of multiple sources requires real-time encoding for some of the programs. Thus, compression and quality will not be as high as possible with non-real-time compression. In addition, broadcasters also encrypt the signal to reduce piracy of programs at the production facility.

MPEG Standard

The Motion Pictures Experts Group (MPEG) mission grew out of earlier standards work for digital compression of still pictures. In terms of optical disc technologies, an international standards committee created in 1988 defined methods to digitally code video and audio on compact discs. MPEG defines the structure of the bit stream. It also defines the decoding process used to reconstruct bit streams into frames of video and audio samples via a predefined rule base, or algorithm. By 1990, the MPEG committee had developed a data-structure syntax for source input format (SIF), in which video and compact disc audio used a combined data rate of 1.5 megabits per second. The MPEG-2 project later expanded to include HDTV- and SDTV-rate programs over many mediums such as disc, broadcast, and tape.

MPEG-1

During operation, the MPEG-1 compression system nearly matched the quality seen with VHS videotape playback systems. Even though MPEG-1 worked for film, it did not yield the same results for interlaced broadcast-video transmissions. The MPEG-1 standard defines the ability to process fields with a resolution up to 4095 x 4095 and bit rates of 100 megabits per second. In addition, MPEG-1 defines a bit-stream syntax for compressed audio and video optimized to not exceed a bandwidth of 1.5 megabits per second. With this, the compression standard has bandwidth restrictions that fit the capabilities of single-speed uncompressed CD-ROM and digital audio tape (DAT) specifications.

MPEG-2

In 1992, more than 200 international companies contributed to the MPEG draft development that demonstrated strong support for a new technology specification. As opposed to MPEG-1, MPEG-2 includes enhancements originally intended for the MPEG-3 standard that cover the compression of broadcast-interlaced television signals. From there, MPEG-2 has become a compression standard for HDTV, DVB, and for high-density compact disc technologies. When considering direct broadcast satellite systems, both MPEG-2 and MPEG-2 "near compliant" stand as standard approaches to video and audio signal compression.

Other MPEG Formats

The new MPEG-4 standard builds from the success of digital television, interactive graphics applications that create synthetic content, and interactive multimedia such as the World Wide Web that allows distribution of and access to content. From this, MPEG-4 provides standardized technological elements that enable the integration of the production, distribution, and content access needs presented through the three areas. The MPEG-7 standard covers multimedia content such as images, graphics, 3D models, audio, speech, and video, and represents a standard for information searching. MP@HL provides a shorthand notation for a specific quality and resolution of MPEG: 4:2:0 quality, high-definition video.

MPEG-2 Operation

Figure 6-1 shows a block diagram of the MPEG-2 encoding sequence. During operation, the MPEG compression process examines each frame and compares the contents of the frame on a pixel-by-pixel basis to the previous frame. If the pixel values in the new frame match those in the original frame, the MPEG-compression processor deletes the new frame. In addition, the MPEG processor also examines a range of pixels for areas of identical color and tone.

When two frames match, the MPEG processor inserts a special small marker that instructs the MPEG decompression processor to restore the pixel. If frames have pixels with identical color and tone areas, the MPEG processor removes the duplicate areas and sends on only one pixel. An instruction accompanies the lone pixel and contains information needed to replicate the color and tone areas a specific number of times.

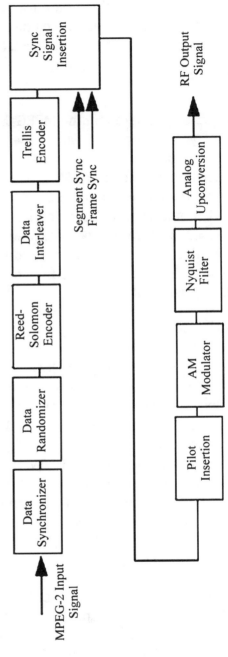

Figure 6-1

Although the MPEG compression scheme cannot condense volumes of data to a low enough level, the lossy characteristics of MPEG take advantage of the ability of the human brain and eyes to fill in any information gaps. As a result, the compression encoder can look for near matches rather than exact matches of data. Adjusting the nearness of the match also controls the amount of compression. Compression of a file at a ratio higher than 3:1, however, will result in the averaging of intermediate tones and allows pixilation—or the placement of visible blocks in an image—to occur.

Statistical Multiplexing

DVD systems not only utilize the MPEG compression scheme, but also include encoder circuitry that limits the amount of data. When a large amount of activity in the reproduced picture causes the number of matches and near matches to decrease, the encoder software responds by lowering the precision of the compression. Statistical multiplexing gathers statistics on the amount of data in each channel and feeds the information back to the MPEG compression system for the purpose of balancing the load.

If one channel has low amounts of activity in the reproduced picture and higher match rates, the system allows more precise matches to occur in the paired channel that has more activity and lower match rates. The opposite occurs for channels that have high amounts of activity in the reproduced picture. As a result, the system parameters, selected compression ratios, and the mix of channels affect the compression scheme. Frame-by-frame analysis, compression, and load balancing occur in real time.

MPEG Encoding

During the first step of the encoding process, the encoder circuitry reduces the active area from the NTSC format of 704 x 480 down to 352 x 240. In addition, the circuitry translates the color information from the NTSC format to the YUV format. While the translation compacts the color signal, the YUV format also separates the color information into independent brightness and hue values. When the human eye views any color, the luminance (or brightness) information exists as the dominant component. Since hue is less significant than brightness in terms of color, the MPEG encoder eliminates 75% of the chrominance values.

During the compression process, any unneeded information is immediately discarded. For example, the NTSC broadcast format uses only 480 out of the possible 525 scan lines to hold image information. The additional 45 scan lines contain information needed for the analog transmission of the signal but unnecessary for the digital transmission of the signal. Discarding the 75% of the chrominance values and the analog-only information allows the MPEG compression scheme to work with only 124 megabits of video data per second, rather than the original 162 megabits of information.

With the data, flag, identifier, and error-correction information in place, a data packet is 147 bytes long. The first two bytes contain the service-channel identification, a 12-bit number that ranges from 0 to 4,095 that identifies the channel for the packet. The third byte contains the four-bit-long flag, an identifier for the encryption code. The next 127 bytes contain the video data. The final 17 bytes are used for forward-error correction.

Discrete Cosine Transformation

The production and playback of a DVD-Video disc requires the encoding and decoding of a signal several times. As a result, signal degradation can occur. To minimize signal degradation, encoding methods employ a 4:2:2 rather than a 4:2:0 chroma-subsampling scheme. With MPEG-2 defining the compressed subsampling methods, a 4:2:2 ratio contains twice as many chroma samples as 4:2:0 subsampling.

The MPEG-compression standard relies on discrete cosine transformation (DCT) for the translation of 8 x 8 blocks of image pixels into sets of numbers. The DCT technique works by removing redundancies from the images. Rather than compress the image, the complex mathematical process of discrete cosine transformation changes the video signal into a form that easily compresses. During the process of compressing the NTSC signal, the video frame divides into 8,100 small individual blocks or boxes. By comparison, the compression of a PAL or HDTV signal results in more blocks. The process also groups the blocks together into five columns called macro blocks and then moves the blocks into an order that increases the efficiency of the compression.

At the beginning of the process, all information about the top left pixel in a given block stores in its complete form. In the second step of the process, only the difference between the next pixel and the base pixel stores. For example, in the transformation of a signal that represents only the blue sky, the difference between the first pixel and the next pixel would equal zero. The zero value for the difference would continue for all the pixels in the block and only the difference values would store. If the televised scene includes white and gray clouds, the difference value would change. With the clouds in the lower half of the block, the bottom pixels might differ from the base pixel by changes equaling a negative one or a positive three. After completion of the process, the values of each pixel in the block are weighted according to the specifications of the system.

Each set of pixels describes one level of detail, with low-detail images represented by many zero values and high-detail images represented by fewer zero values. In essence, each value given through the DCT represents energy at a specific frequency. Rounding off the results of the transformation reduces the number of possible values and produces a better chance for identical values. Although transformation is not the same as compression, frames that feature lower detail compress more than frames with higher levels of detail. Discrete transformation produces a frame called an I-frame, or intraframe.

Spatial and Temporal Compression

MPEG-2 encoding uses spatial compression within each frame. In addition, MPEG-2 encoding uses block-encoding techniques and temporal compression between nearby frames located within the video stream. The application of block-encoding and temporal compression eliminates redundant frame-to-frame information. While not used on all frames set for compression, the encoder uses motion estimation to determine the amount of needed compression. To remove redundancy, the system compares frames that incorporate motion estimation with previous frames (called predicted or

P-frames), or with both previous and future frames (called B-frames or bidirectionally predicted frames). A typical sequence of frames would include one I-frame every 15 frames and a P-frame every third frame, except during the use of an I-frame.

Adaptive Quantization and Variable Length Coding

During the compression process, the system approximates the amount of compression needed for each block. To do this, the compression system looks for long strings of zeros in the data. Rather than storing the entire string such as 000000000000000, the system stores a phrase that means "15 x 0." Consequently, more consecutive zeros contained within the data translates into saved space.

Since long strings of zeroes rarely occur in practice, the compression code tries to round off all values from negative one to positive one down to zero. If the data stream remains too large, the circuit will attempt to round off all values from positive two to negative two down to zero. This process continues until the proper amount of data compression results in the reproduction of only about 25 megabits per second of video information.

At this point, quantization has a major impact on the size of the final encoded video stream. Larger constants offer fewer possible values and increase the compression ratio. The increased density of compression allows the loss of information and the degradation of video signal quality. Quantization ensures that the video stream data rate never exceeds the throughput of the target output device.

During operation, the encoder accesses quantized and transformed values from the lowest to the highest frequencies. As a result, the quantized data becomes strings of identical values that comprise a single token. In turn, each token indicates the value and the number of times that the value repeats.

Encoding the tokens involves the assignment of the most common tokens to symbols that have the shortest possible length. With this process, further compression of the data occurs through the distribution of token frequencies. The MPEG standard further increases the compression by eliminating any redundant data that appears on more than one frame. Throughout the encoding process, the MPEG encoder has the capability to look ahead as many frames as desired to seek repetitive blocks. A pointer that references a single copy of the block replaces identical blocks of pixels common to two or more successive frames.

Variable Bit-Rate (VBR) Encoding

Delivery of a high-quality video within the storage capacity of a DVD requires the application of variable bit-rate (VBR) encoding. With the use of VBR, an MPEG-2 encoder can encode high-activity sequences with higher data rates and simpler sequences with lower data rates. Similar to statistical multiplexing, VBR allows a bit rate to fluctuate constantly around a target rate for the purpose of achieving optimal output image quality.

By comparison, VBR encoding attempts to minimize the storage requirements of a single video stream, while statistical multiplexing minimizes multiple video streams so that the streams will simultaneously fit within a constrained channel.

VBR encoding can occur either in real time or through a two-pass encoding technique. During the first pass, the encoder takes numerous statistical measurements of the incoming video to determine which frames will require more bits to achieve the highest video quality. The stored statistics correspond with each frame in the sequence. After analyzing the sequence, VBR scales the frame-by-frame bit allocations up or down to make the sum of the bits fit the available storage. An encoder uses the allocations in the second pass to encode the incoming video.

Single-pass VBR encoding utilizes an algorithm that can predict the output video quality during encoding and then modify the output bit rate. As a combination, the frame-by-frame bit-rate modification feature used in statistical multiplexing, plus the capability of the architecture to accurately predict the difficulty of encoding the material, yield an efficient yet extremely high-quality encoding solution. Recordable DVD technologies utilize the single-pass encoding method.

Inverse Telecine

The telecine (or 3:2 pull-down) process converts film captured at 24 frames per second into video running at 60 fields per second. During operation, telecine scans frames in an interlaced format and creates fields, because scanning each frame twice generates only two fields per frame and only 48 fields. To increase the number of frames and fields, the telecine system scans alternate frames three times and produces three fields instead of two.

As a result, the system scans incoming frames in a 3:2:3:2 cadence and produces 60 fields from the 24 frames. With only two fields in a single frame, the first and third fields become duplicated during the third scanning of the frame. But the encoder does not see information indicating which fields repeat. Therefore, the encoder must find the duplicated fields and—using inverse telecine—eliminate the duplicates before encoding occurs. High-quality DVD encoders utilize inverse telecine encoders, because of the large amount of original film material set for encoding onto the disc.

Forward-Error Correction

Encoding a digital signal onto an analog carrier frequency involves the breaking up of data into discrete packets, because any transponder frequency will be carrying several different data streams simultaneously. During the encoding process, the multiple streams must interleave in an organized manner so that the receiver can reproduce the data in the same form. Interleaving of data in this fashion is referred to as multiple channel per carrier, or MCPC.

The use of interleaved audio and video data requires the transmission of additional information along with actual information. A packet identifier (PID) fits into the data stream and informs the receiver about the type of data. Synchronization packets keep the audio and video information synchronized, while system-information packets carry other vendor-related information.

Since propagation delays and real-time transmission can cause the dropping out of packets, the compression and decompression of video and audio information relies on error correction. Two modes of error correction exist. While the high mode uses 30 megabits per second for information and 10 megabits per second for error correction, the low mode uses 23 megabits per second for information and 17 megabits per second for error correction. Due to the rate differences, the high error-correction mode requires 3 decibels more of power.

Forward-error correction (FEC) ensures the accurate reproduction of a signal. Without error correction, propagation delays would cause some of the data to drop out. As a result, the reproduced video would resemble a patchwork of colored blocks or a frozen image. The generation of the FEC information-signal takes place during the actual transmission of the television signals. During this process, a complex mathematical process called a syndrome produces and codes the continuously changing details of the television data signal as a separate part of each television signal.

The syndrome contains sufficient information to allow the decompression processor to correct and fully recover its own original information. At the receiver, a set off processes review the syndrome and recreate any information lost due to an error. But an extremely high bit-error rate caused by heavy rains or snow can cause the automatic error correction to fail, resulting in the reproduction of incorrectly placed small picture blocks, blocks of colored snow, or static-like clicking sounds. Generally, a receiver will mute both the sound and video automatically if the error correction fails.

Decoding the Compressed Signal

Decoder circuitry restores the deleted information so that the reproduced picture matches the original scene. A digital-to-analog converter translates the video signals from the digital format to the NTSC-standard analog format. Audio signals travel through MPEG decompression IC and then through another set of digital-to-analog converters for each stereo channel. The decoder must recover and maintain specific timing information and perform complex data processing during the decompression and decrypting of the video and audio information. In addition, the decoder processes the digital-to-analog conversions.

Compressing the Audio

MPEG-2 Audio

The MPEG-2 audio standard for low bit-rate coding of multichannel audio supplies up to full bandwidth left, right, center, and two surround-sound channels, plus an additional low-frequency enhancement channel, and up to seven commentary/multilingual channels. Due to the need for compatibility, the MPEG-2 audio-compression standard also extends the stereo and mono coding of the older MPEG-1 audio standard to half sampling rates of 16 kHz, 22.05 kHz, and 24 kHz for improved quality for bit rates at or below 64 kilobits per second per channel.

Dolby Pro Logic

The Dolby Surround Pro Logic matrix system combines the left, center, right, and a limited bandwidth surround channel into two channels. During playback in a monophonic-only system, the two channels go through a summing process. When used in a stereophonic system, the two channels serve as the right and left input channels. Feeding the two channels into a Dolby Pro Logic Decoder allows the matrixed four channels to unfold and become available for playback.

The design of the Dolby Surround Pro Logic system places the matrixed signal within the stereo signal. As a result, the Pro Logic system functions within stereo television broadcasts, the transmission of audio satellite signals for both C-band and digital satellite systems, stereo cable transmissions, stereo FM radio transmissions, stereo laser disc, stereo videotape, and video games. All Dolby Digital AC-3 decoders include digital Dolby Pro Logic decoder circuitry.

Dolby Digital AC-3

Direct broadcast satellite systems use the Dolby Digital AC-3 format to transmit 120 stereo music channels to business and commercial establishments through a single transponder. In comparison to the Dolby Pro Logic format, the Dolby AC-3 format takes advantage of digital audio coding, a type of perceptual coding. In practice, perceptual coding seeks to eliminate the data that a human ear cannot hear, while maintaining desired data. Digital audio coding allows the use of lower data rates with a minimum of perceived degradation of sound quality. As a result, perceptual audio coding places more information into the available spectrum. In addition, the Dolby digital version of perceptual coding handles multichannel audio.

While Dolby AC-3 works as a compression format, it also applies superior noise-reduction techniques through the lowering of noise when no audio signal is present. With an audio signal, strong audio signals cover the noise at all frequencies through auditory masking. Generally, noise reduction occurs only at nearby frequencies. To accomplish this task, Dolby Digital AC-3 divides the audio spectrum of each channel into narrow frequency bands that correlate closely to the frequency selectivity of human hearing. As a result, coding noise is very sharply filtered and remains close in frequency to the audio signal being coded. The audio signal masks the noise and causes the noise to remain imperceptible to human hearing. With no audio signals present for masking, Dolby Digital AC-3 reduces or eliminates the coding noise.

All this occurs through the use of a "shared bit pool" arrangement, in which bits distribute among different narrow frequency bands. Dolby Digital AC-3 can process at least 20-bit dynamic range digital audio signals over a frequency range from 20 Hz to 20,000 Hz ±0.5 dB. The bass-effects channel covers 20 Hz to 120 Hz ±0.5 dB. In addition, Dolby Digital AC-3 supports sampling rates of 32 kHz, 44.1 kHz, and 48 kHz. To answer the needs of a wide range of applications, data rates range from as low as 32 kilobits per second for a single monophonic channel to as high as 640 kilobits per second.

The distribution of bits differs according to the needs of the frequency spectrum or dynamic nature of the coded program. Auditory masking ensures the use of a sufficient number of bits to describe the audio signal in each band. In addition, bits distribute among the various channels and allow channels with greater frequency content to demand more data than channels with less frequency content. This type of auditory masking allows the encoder to change frequency selectivity and time resolution so that a sufficient number of bits describe the audio signal in each band. Consequently, Dolby Digital AC-3 can use proportionally more of the transmitted data to represent audio.

With the Dolby Digital AC-3 standard, higher sound quality and multichannel surround sound encode at a lower bit rate than required by just one channel on a compact disk.

The use of a sophisticated masking model and shared bit pool arrangement increase the spectrum efficiency of Dolby Digital AC-3. Rather than use data to carry instructions to the decoders, AC-3 can use proportionally more of the transmitted data to represent audio. As a result, AC-3 has higher sound quality delivered over six discrete channels of sound. Compared to Dolby Surround Pro Logic, AC-3 also includes left, center, and right channels across the front of the room, and discrete left surround and right surround channels for the rear of the room. All five main channels have a full frequency range of 3 Hz to 20,000 Hz. A subwoofer could be added to each channel, if desired.

A sixth channel—the low-frequency effects channel—sometimes contains additional bass information used to increase the audio impact of scenes such as explosions and crashes. Since the sixth channel has a limited frequency response of 3 Hz to 120 Hz, it is sometimes referred to as the "0.1" channel. All six channels in a Dolby digital system have a digital format that allows the transfer of data from the producer's mixing console to a home playback system without loss.

7

DVD Recordable Technologies

Introduction

During the development stages of DVD-ROM technologies, the computer industry remained active in the design process and viewed the technology as a fast, large capacity CD-ROM. But the speed and capabilities of DVD-ROM technologies have become a factor in supplanting the use of CD-ROMs with DVD-ROMs. The storage capacity and data-transfer capabilities of DVD-ROM technologies also provide business solutions for operations that require access to large amounts of data. Dual format titles that play on both DVD video players and DVD-ROM readers include movies with an associated game or multimedia content.

DVD-ROM, DVD-RAM, DVD-R, DVD-RW, and DVD+RW

In 1995, a subgroup of the computer industry called the Technical Working Group (TWG) defined the specifications for DVD-ROM. In addition, the TWG recommends current and future forms of computer-based applications for the DVD-ROM and DVD-RAM formats. Since DVD-ROM operates as a super-set of DVD-Video, the players designed for DVD-Video will play DVD-ROM discs or DVD-Video/ROM hybrids. The creation of the DVD-ROM format also led to the development and standardization of recordable formats that include DVD-RAM, DVD-R, and DVD-RW.

The TWG lists the following requirements for the DVD-ROM format.

- Single format for computer and TV-based applications.
- Backward read compatibility with existing CD-ROMs.
- Forward compatibility with future R/W and WORM discs.
- A single file system for all content and disc media types.
- Low-cost drives and discs.
- No mandatory container.
- Reliable data storage and retrieval.
- High on-line capacity.
- High performance for both sequential and nonsequential data types.

DVD-ROM

DVD-ROM discs have many of the characteristics of CD-ROM discs. Because a DVD-ROM disc provides at least seven times the capacity, however, it offers a much more versatile media platform for complex multimedia applications. With many multimedia applications and games utilizing MPEG-2 video, the additional storage capacity offers the capability to give added realism to games and provide richer content for multimedia applications.

Compared to the writing of data to a CD-ROM disc, the writing of data to a DVD-ROM disc relies on shorter manufacturing technology, the production of a DVD-ROM relies on shorter wavelength semiconductor lasers. Because increasing the numerical aperture of the objective lens results in a smaller laser spot on the disc, the DVD disc has a smaller track pitch and smaller pit sizes. In addition, the combination of the Reed-Solomon error-correction algorithm (featuring an enhanced error-correction capability to minimize redundancy), a more efficient data-recording modulation code, and radial increase in the area used for data storage results in 4.7 gigabytes of storage capacity on a DVD-ROM disc.

DVD-ROM Sector Format

Figure 7-1 shows the sector format for a DVD-ROM disc. Each sector begins with a read-only identification field embossed onto the disc surface during the manufacturing process. In the figure, the permanently embossed,

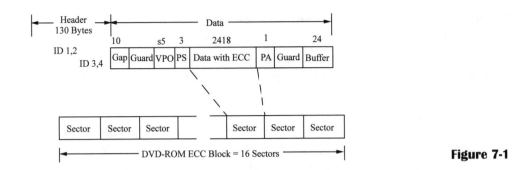

Figure 7-1

read-only header information occupies 130 bytes, while the error-control code (ECC) block takes up 16 sectors. As Figure 7-2 shows, the headers divide between the inner and outer diameters of the disc by one-half track and have sequential sector numbers.

The identification, or ID, fields within the header identify the physical location of the sector and remain separate from the user recordable data field. As a result, the 2,567-byte-long data field remains permanently readable. While

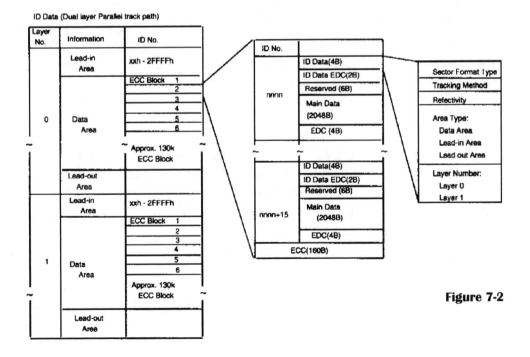

Figure 7-2

ID1 and ID2 contain the sector numbers for the following land sector, ID3 and ID4 contain the sector number for the following groove sector. Combined with the polarity information of the header readout signal, the information found in this control area establishes accurate ID information for any sector at the innermost part of the disc.

Guard fields at each end of the data field prevent degradation from occurring during repeated rewrites of data. In addition, the lead-in areas of all DVD discs contain information that identifies disc format structure as DVD-ROM, DVD-RAM, DVD-R, DVD-RW, or DVD+RW. The data structure of the lead-in area remains consistent across all DVD formats.

Compared to a CD-ROM with a minimum pit length of 0.83 micrometers, a single-layer DVD-ROM disc has a minimum pit length of 0.4 micrometers. In addition, the DVD-ROM disc has a track pitch of 0.74 micrometers that compares favorably with the 1.6-micrometer track pitch seen with a CD-ROM. The number of pits corresponds with the capacity of the disc. Reducing the pit size and track pitch provides increased capacity. Land sectors beginning with ID1 and ID2 offset toward the inner disc diameter, while land sectors beginning with ID3 and ID4 offset toward the outer disc diameter. Groove sectors beginning with ID1 and ID2 offset toward the outer disc diameter, while groove sectors beginning with ID3 and ID4 offset toward the inner disc diameter. By changing the offset sequence between land and groove tracks, the design of the DVD-ROM allows the drive to reliably switch its tracking servo between land and groove tracking.

DVD-ROM Disc Layout

Figure 7-3 shows the DVD-ROM disc layout. The disc manufacturing and optical recording methods used for DVD-ROM make it possible for a single drive to read the four types of DVD-ROM media. With this, future DVD-ROM drives will continue to play back DVD-RAM discs. Table 7-1 lists the storage capacities of different DVD-ROM types.

DVD-RAM

Recordable versions called DVD-RAM, DVD-R, DVD-RW, and DVD+RW build on the potential of the DVD-ROM technology. DVD-RAM discs have all

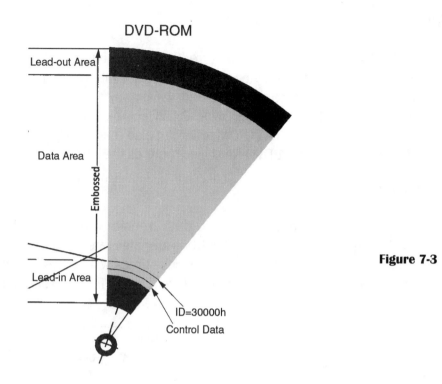

DVD-ROM

Figure 7-3

Table 7-1: DVD-ROM Disc Storage Capacities

DVD-ROM Type	Storage Capacity
DVD-5 Single-layer, single-side DVD-ROM disc	4.7 gigabytes
DVD-9 Dual-layer, single-side DVD-ROM disc	8.5 gigabytes
DVD-10 Single-layer, dual-side DVD-ROM disc	9.4 gigabytes
DVD-18 Dual-layer, dual-side DVD-ROM disc	17 gigabytes

the benefits of DVD-ROM, as well as the added advantage of rewritability. As a result, a DVD-RAM user can record and rerecord from 2.6 to 5.2 gigabytes of information onto one disc. Because of this, DVD-RAM works well as an option for backing up data, creating document archives, and generating multimedia titles and presentations.

DVD-RAM *Discs*

Single-sided DVD-RAM discs manufactured before the latter part of 1999 have a storage capacity of 2.6 gigabytes. Decreasing track pitch and pit lengths allowed manufacturers to produce a single-sided, 4.7-gigabyte DVD-RAM for distribution in the year 2000. Single-sided, type 2 DVD-RAM discs come with or without a cartridge. As a result, a DVD-ROM drive can also read a DVD-RAM disc. As shown in Figure 7-4, the type 1 DVD-RAM disc requires the use of a cartridge.

DVD-RAM *Data Transfer Rates*

The media specification determines the data transfer rate for DVD-RAM drives. The 2.6-gigabyte disc has a 1,385-Kbps transfer rate, while the 4.7-gigabyte disc has a 2,770-Kbps transfer rate. Access times will also evolve with an increase in disc rotational speed, reducing drive latency. Further reductions

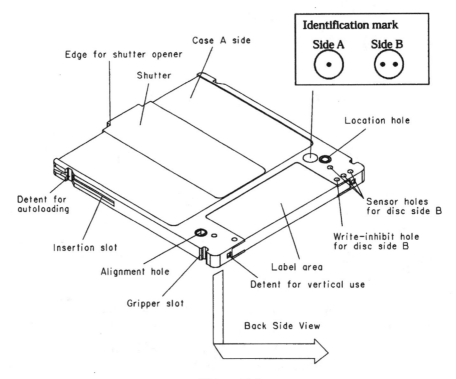

Figure 7-4

in access time will come from mechanical improvements, a more robust servo technology, and mass reductions in the optical pickup.

Zoned Constant Linear Velocity

DVD-RAM discs and drives rely on a phase-change recording technology that uses a laser to heat the inner surface of the disc and create a magnetic polarity change. In addition to this phase-change technology, DVD-RAM discs also rely on the zoned constant linear velocity (ZCLV) method, rather than the traditional constant linear velocity (CLV) method. ZCLV writes and reads data using the constant angular velocity method to specific zones on the disc and provides higher capacity and faster access speeds. Compared to the CLV method, in which the angular velocity continuously changes, ZCLV changes the angular velocity from zone to zone and maintains a constant average linear velocity, constant data rates throughout the disc surface, and constant data recording rates. The technique writes data on both the land and groove of the disc, while molding the address information in the form of pits.

Defect Management

As shown in Figure 7-5, the DVD-RAM disc rewritable data area divides into 24 zones matched with an associated spare area that replaces any defective sector in the user area. Comparing the DVD-RAM disc layout to the DVD-ROM disc layout seen in Figure 7-3, it becomes evident that the DVD-RAM disc has rewritable data areas and read-only embossed data areas. The DVD-ROM disc, however, has only embossed data areas.

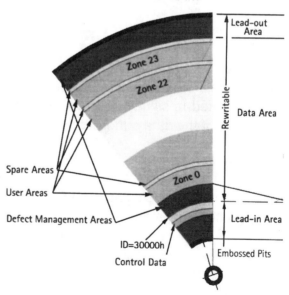

DVD-RAM

Figure 7-5

117

Four defect-management areas handle defective sector addressing. Two defect-management areas reside in the lead-in area, while the other two reside in the lead-out area. Since the four areas contain the same information, each provides an additional level of redundancy for improved reliability. As shown in Figure 7-6, each defect-management area includes lists of defective sectors and replacement sectors.

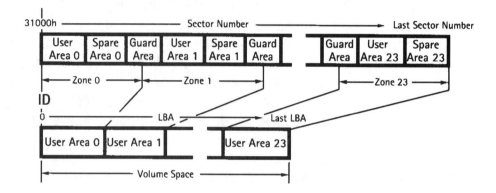

Figure 7-6

Wobbled Land-and-Groove

When first introduced, DVD technology featured a spiral on the disc and placed data around the spiral. Unfortunately, the placement of the data sometimes resulted in signal crosstalk between adjacent tracks. In addition, the readability of the data suffered.

As shown in Figure 7-7, the high-frequency wobbled groove eliminates the use of linking sectors in the format and increases reliability. Moving to the wobbled groove signals shown in Figure 7-8, the data tracks have a wobbled appearance, a constant pitch, and reflected light interference. Data records alternately on land and groove. In addition, the land/groove combination forms a continuous spiral track that has a logical track pitch of 0.74 µm. With this approach, a 1.48 µm distance remains in place for the physical track pitch, or the distance from a land track to the next land track.

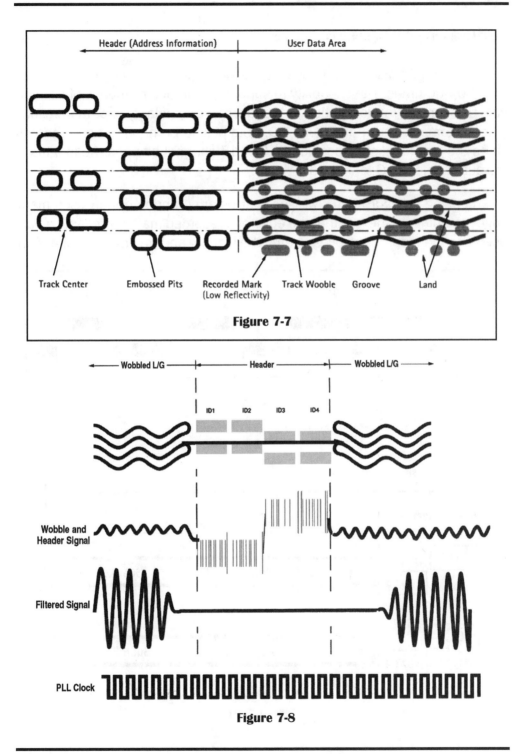

Header (Address Information)   User Data Area

Track Center   Embossed Pits   Recorded Mark (Low Reflectivity)   Track Wooble   Groove   Land

Figure 7-7

Wobbled L/G   Header   Wobbled L/G

ID1   ID2   ID3   ID4

Wobble and Header Signal

Filtered Signal

PLL Clock

Figure 7-8

Data Position and Polarity Randomization

A DVD-RAM disc accommodates the writing and rewriting of data more than 10,000 times. The capability to support numerous rewritings of data occurs through the randomization of the location and polarity of data in recordable sectors. As shown in Figure 7-9, data-position randomization randomly shifts the recording start position by 0 to 15 channel bits and the lengths of the guard fields by 0 to 7 bytes.

Looking at Figure 7-10, we see that polarity randomization uses mark-edge recording, or the fact that the edge of a recorded mark represents a data bit. Since the recording process treats the leading and trailing edge of a mark

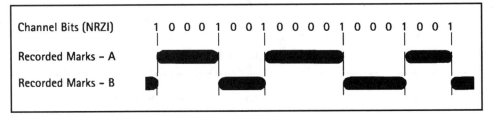

Figure 7-9

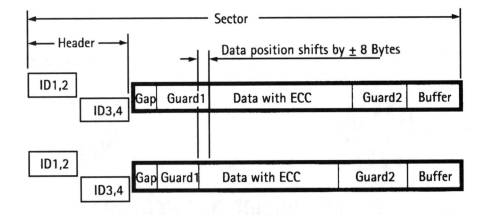

Figure 7-10

equally, the polarity of a recorded mark has no importance and does not affect the ability to retrieve data. The application of random-polarity inversion causes the location of marks and spaces to become uniform when averaged throughout the overwrite cycles. As a result, the overwrite cyclability improves, and the disc achieves greater capabilities to accept new data.

Given the storage capacity seen with a DVD-RAM disc, the capability for rewriting information to the disc, and the compatibility with other DVD formats, DVD-RAM technology very well may become the top storage medium option of the future. Yet the use of a cartridge, rather than a disc, may slow consumer acceptance of the technology. Cartridges with single-sided discs allow removal of the disc and allow operation as a bare disc.

DVD-R

DVD-R offers full compatibility with DVD-ROM, DVD-Video, and DVD-Audio discs. As a result, DVD-ROM drives and DVD video players can play back information recorded onto a DVD-R disc. DVD-R discs use the equivalent of the CD-R multisession writing with two types of incremental writing.

Dye Recording

Along with the CD-R and other Write-Once, Read-Many (WORM) disc formats, the DVD-R employs dye recording. In this process, the disc consists of a dye layer sandwiched between a polycarbonate substrate and a gold reflective layer. The use of the dye layer requires that the reflective layer have the reflectivity needed for successful playback, while remaining chemically inert. DVD-RAM disc recording layers may use a metal-stabilized cyanine green dye, a phthalocyanine golden brown dye, or an azo blue dye.

When the laser heats the disc during the recording of data, the dye layer absorbs heat and causes a physical change in the polycarbonate and reflective layers. In addition, the optical properties of the dye change. The combination of these three factors causes an optical contrast between recorded and nonrecorded areas to occur.

Incremental Writing

With DVD-R type 1, the ISO-9660 system using the UDF Bridge file system can read the DVD-R disc. DVD-R type 2 enables a drag-and-drop file transfer and uses the UDF Bridge file system without relying on ISO-9660. Table 7-2 compares the DVD-R types.

Table 7-2: Comparison of DVD-R Types

	TYPE 1	TYPE 2
Single Layer	Yes	Yes
Dual Layer	Yes	Yes
Storage Capacity	3.95 Gigabytes per Side	4.7 Gigabytes per Side
Recording Method	Organic dye layer, 635nm laser	Organic dye layer, 635nm laser
Minimum Pit Length	0.44 microns	0.40 microns
Track Pitch	0.80 microns	0.74 microns
Track Format	Wobble pre-groove	Wobble pre-groove
Modulation	EFT+	EFT+
Error Correction	RSPC	RSPC

Both types of incremental writing place each section of data within a bordered area by a border-out marker. A border-in marker precedes the next bordered area. In addition, each bordered area begins with the UDF file system and ends with a virtual allocation table (VAT). The DVD-R format uses the following data areas of the disc.

- Power calibration area
- Recording management area
- Lead-in area
- Data recordable area
- Lead-out area

DVD-RW and DVD+RW

Developed by Pioneer and based on the DVD-R standard through the use of a similar track pitch, mark length, and rotation control, DVD-RW discs will remain compatible with most DVD drives and players. Also marketed as DVD

Rewritable discs, a DVD-RW disc is a rewritable version of a DVD-R disc that offers 1,000 rewrites. A DVD-RW disc has a 4.7-gigabyte capacity.

Like DVD-RAM, the DVD-RW and DVD+RW technologies build around the phase-change erasable formatting technique and offer compatibility with most DVD drives and players. A DVD-RW formatted disc differs from a DVD-RAM formatted disc, however, in that the former sequentially records data. In contrast, a DVD-RAM formatted disc provides random access to recorded data. Figure 7-11 shows the DVD-RW groove recording.

Proposed and developed by Hewlett-Packard, Philips, and Sony with the support of Verbatim, Ricoh, and Yamaha, the DVD+RW standard offers discs that have a three-gigabyte-per-side capacity and do not require the use of a cartridge. DVD+RW discs can record using either the CLV format for sequential video access or the CAV format for random access. DVD-RW and DVD+RW discs function as an excellent platform for authoring tools or archived data.

As with DVD-RAM discs, both the DVD-RW and DVD+RW formats use the wobbled-groove recording technique, which places address information on land areas for synchronization when data writes to the disc. As a combination, the use of a wobbled groove, the CLV format for sequential video access, and the CAV format for random access ensures compatibility between

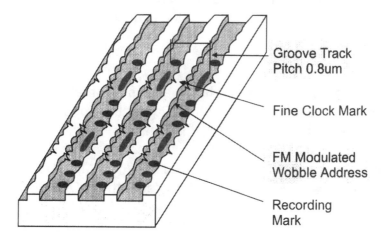

Groove Track
Pitch 0.8um

Fine Clock Mark

FM Modulated
Wobble Address

Recording
Mark

Figure 7-11

the DVD-RW and DVD+RW discs and existing technologies. According to manufacturers, DVD-RW and DVD+RW discs will accept 1,000 erasures and rewrites. Table 7-3 summarizes the recordable disc types, associated formats, and compatibility with readers.

Table 7-3: Recordable DVD Computer Discs and Capabilities

DVD Type	Format	Capacity	Number of Rewrites
DVD-R	Write-once. Provides sequential write, similar to CD-R. No overwrite capability.	4.7 Gb	0
DVD-RAM	Random access storage, similar to floppy disk or CD+RW.	4.7 Gb	10,000+
DVD+RW	Limited sequential rewritability.	3.95 Gb per side	1,000
DVD-RW	Limited sequential rewritability.	3.95 Gb per side	1,000

Future DVD Applications in Computing

Members of the DVD Forum have begun work on the next generation of optical disc format called high-density DVD, which may store approximately 20 gigabytes of data per layer. The improved storage capacity comes from the use of new laser technologies and mastering techniques.

DVD Multi

In an attempt to ensure compatibility across recordable DVD standards, the DVD Forum introduced the DVD Multi. Rather than operate as a new format, DVD Multi uses a set of specifications that define which DVD drives will read and write for designated categories of discs. DVD drives branded with the DVD Multi logo will read DVD-Video, DVD-Audio, DVD-ROM, DVD-RAM, DVD-RW, and DVD-R discs. In addition, recorders branded with the DVD Multi logo must have the capability to write to DVD-RAM, DVD-RW, and DVD-R discs. DVD compliant video players will read DVD-Video and DVD-Audio discs, as well as DVD-RAM, DVD-RW, and DVD-R discs. In much the same way, DVD-Audio players will read all DVD-Audio and all DVD recordable disc formats.

8

DVD Video Player Circuits: Power Supply

Introduction

Whether operating in a computer system, video system, or audio system, video players consist of electronic and mechanical systems. Starting with an overview of power supplies, Chapter 8 begins a four-chapter focus on the electronic systems used within a DVD player. While this chapter defines the purpose of electronic systems and provides an overview of common power-supply designs used within DVD players, Chapter 9 continues the discussion with a look at the optical pickup unit, motor controls, signal processors, and microcontrollers.

Electronic Systems

An electronic system is made up of a group of electronic components interconnected to perform a function or group of related functions. Those components are the source, circuit, and load, as shown in Figure 8-1A (on Page 126). The source is a device—such as a power supply in a DVD player—that develops a voltage or a combination of voltages. Figures 8-1B (on Page 127) and 8-1C (on Page 126) compare a block diagram and an exploded diagram of DVD video players with the block diagram shown in Figure 8-1A.

In order to take advantage of the force associated with an electric charge, and in order to use that force to produce work, we must control the flow of electrons. A load is a device that performs a specific function when current flows through it. Because a load opposes current in an electric circuit, it has

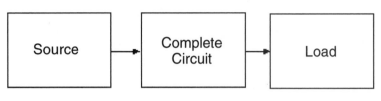

Figure 8-1A

resistance. We can define resistance as the property of a device that opposes current in an electric circuit.

Electron flow can only occur if a complete path exists from the source to the load and then back to the source. Therefore, a complete circuit must exist for electron flow. The insertion of a switch—one of the simplest control devices—allows the control of the electron flow. A switch is a device that opens and closes the path for electrons.

Electronic systems divide into analog and digital circuits. An analog circuit has an output that varies smoothly over a given range and has an infinite number of voltage and values. Each of those values corresponds with some

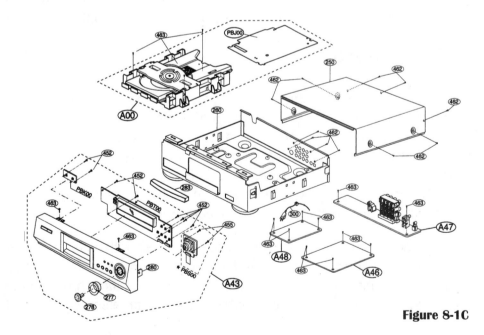

Figure 8-1C

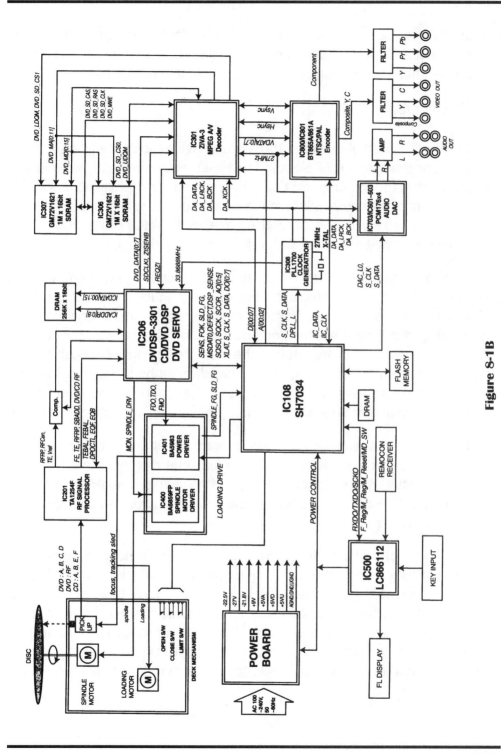

Figure 8-1B

portion of the input. Digital circuits have either an "on" or an "off" output state. Application of an input signal to a digital circuit produces either of the output states but—unlike the analog circuit—no intermediate output conditions.

Source Voltages

In electricity and electronics, the term voltage describes a "difference in potential," or the amount of electric force that exists between two charged bodies. A volt is the standard unit of measurement for expressing this difference in potential. Because this force in volts causes the movement of electrons, it is defined as the electromotive force (emf). Voltage is defined as either a positive or negative force with reference to another point.

If we have two bodies that have an opposite charge, or a difference in potential, and then connect those bodies with a conductor, the charged body with a more positive potential will attract free electrons from the conductor. As the free electrons move from the conductor to the charged body, the conductor assumes a positive charge due to the loss of electrons. Because of this, excess electrons in the other, more negative-charged body begin to flow into the conductor. This flow of electrons is called current and continues as long as the difference in potential exists. The basic measure of current is the ampere.

Polarity of the source voltage used in a dc circuit doesn't change. In direct current (dc) circuits, electrons flow in only one direction. In alternating current (ac) circuits, the direction of electron flow changes periodically. Due to the changes in direction, the polarity of the source voltage also changes from positive to negative.

The ability of a circuit or device to pass current is defined as conductance. Depending on its size and type of material, a conductor carries electricity in varying quantities and over varying distances. A large diameter wire provides a greater surface area, has less resistance to current, and can carry more current. A material such as copper has better conductance characteristics than a material such as platinum. An inverse relationship exists between conductance and resistance. Conductance is measured in siemens or mhos.

Passive Components

Devices with different values of resistance are connected into circuits to control the amount of current. Since resistance opposes current, the current in a circuit is always inversely proportional to the resistance in a circuit. If the resistance increases, then the amount of current decreases; if the resistance decreases, then the amount of current increases. Resistance is measured in ohms, milliohms (.001), kilohms (1000), and megohms (1,000,000). A resistor is a device that offers a certain amount of opposition to the flow of current.

Capacitors store an electrical charge, acting as buffers in power supplies or as filters that prevent voltage spikes from reaching sensitive, solid-state electronic devices. A capacitor exists whenever two conductors are separated by a dielectric. Capacitance occurs with the separation of two or more conducting materials by an insulating material. We measure capacitance with basic units called the farad (1), the millifarad (.001 farad), the microfarad (.000001 farad), and the picofarad (0.0000000000001 farad, or pF).

The capacitance value depends on the amount of total surface area taken by the conducting materials, the amount of spacing between the conducting materials, and the thickness and type of insulating material. The different types of capacitors range from Mylar to electrolytic.

An inductor is a conductor surrounded by a magnetic field. Inductance is a value associated with coils and is measured in basic units called the henry (1H), the millihenry (.001 henry or mH), and the microhenry (.0000001 or µH). The inductance value of a coil depends on size, number of windings, and type of core material. Small coils have lesser values than large coils, while coils with a higher number of windings have larger values. When considering core materials, powered iron cores yield a higher inductance than brass or copper cores.

Inductance also has reactance and impedance values. The impedance value of an inductance varies with the value of the ac frequency and the value of the inductance. Any increase in the frequency or the inductance values also increases the inductive reactance.

Characteristic Impedance

Impedance is a measure of resistance to current flow and, as mentioned, varies with the value of the ac frequency and the value of the inductance. Any type of conductor—gold, copper, aluminum, etc.—has a resistance to current flow that results in a loss of power. Moreover, the movement of electrical charges on the outer skin of a conductor will combine with the movement of electrical charges within the conductor to produce additional delays and losses. When we view the opposition of conductor to current flow as a combination, we can measure the characteristic impedance of the conductor as a resistance in ohms. Manufacturers rate the cables used for video, audio, and data transmissions according to characteristics impedance.

In any electronics system, the characteristic impedance of the transmission cables and the devices that make up the system becomes extremely important. Since every electronic component has characteristic impedance, we must ensure that the characteristic impedance of the cable matches the characteristic impedance of the component. Mismatches of characteristic impedance can occur through inadequate system designs, crimped transmission cables, or poorly constructed cables. Any mismatch in characteristic impedance will cause a signal loss to occur.

Resonance

Resonance occurs when a specific frequency causes the inductances and capacitances in either a series or parallel ac circuit to exactly oppose one another. With resonance, a single particular frequency emerges as the resonant frequency and three basic rules follow.

- Capacitors and inductors with larger values have lower resonant frequencies.
- Capacitors and inductors in series have low impedance at the resonant frequency.
- Capacitors and inductors in a parallel circuit have high impedance at the resonant frequency.

Active components

While passive components provide resistance, inductance, and capacitance, active components such as diodes, transistors, and integrated circuits manipulate voltage and current through switching and amplification. Active components are semiconductors, or devices consisting of materials that neither fully conduct nor fully resist electricity. A diode is a two-terminal semiconductor device that conducts under specific operating conditions. As shown in Figure 8-2, pn-junction diodes are constructed of a more negative n-type material at the cathode and of a more positive p-type material at the anode.

An ideal diode acts as an open switch when reverse-biased and as a closed switch when forward-biased. The term bias refers to the no-signal dc operating voltage or current between two of the elements of a semiconductor device. When forward-biased, a more positive voltage applies to the positive p-type material than to the negative n-type material. Reverse biasing applies a more negative voltage to the positive p-type material than to the negative n-type material.

A zener diode is a special type of diode that operates when reverse-biased. Because of this, a zener diode maintains a relatively constant voltage despite any variations in the diode current. Zener diodes work well as voltage regulators. Figure 8-3 shows the schematic symbol for a zener diode.

Transistors can amplify small ac signals or switch a device from its on state to an off state and back. Any electronic system will have at least one transistor performing a task. To name a few of those tasks, modern electronic equipment uses transistors for signal transmission, video and audio signal amplification, and voltage regulation.

Anode ▷| Cathode

Figure 8-2

Figure 8-3

Like diodes, transistors will not function without a source of energy. In most cases, this energy takes the form of an applied dc voltage. Depending on the task given the transistor, various methods of applying the dc voltages exist. In a normally biased transistor, the emitter junction is always forward-biased, while the collector junction is always reverse-biased.

A bipolar-junction transistor can operate as a switch by driving the device back and forth between saturation to cutoff. Switching transistors have a delay between each input transition and the time when the output transition begins. The output transition for a switching transistor takes a given amount of time to occur. Because transistor switches have internal resistance and leakage resistance, the device never completely restricts the flow of current or allows all current to pass. Capacitance found within transistors prevents the device from switching instantaneously.

By careful chemical composition and arrangement, it's possible to create a very small transistor directly on a layer of silicon, using various technologies to manipulate the material into the correct form. These transistors are small, fast, and reliable and use relatively little power. In its very basic form, an integrated circuit such as the one shown in Figure 8-4 is a group of transistors manufactured from a single piece of material and connected together internally, without extra wiring. Integrated circuits are also called ICs or chips and contain passive and active elements while performing a complete circuit function or a combination of complete circuit functions.

After the invention of the integrated circuit, it took very little time to realize the tremendous benefits of miniaturizing and integrating larger numbers of transistors into the same IC. The use of additional transistor switching allowed the implementation of more complicated functions. To accomplish this, manufacturers miniaturized components to a much greater extent and integrated large numbers of transistors, while increasing hardware speed and managing power consumption and space requirements. Large-scale integration (LSI) refers to the creation of integrated circuits that contain hundreds of transistors.

IC packages may house anywhere from a dozen to millions of individual components. Since computers and microprocessor control systems require

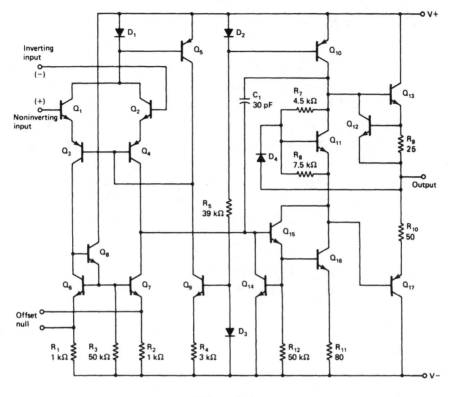

Figure 8-4

hundreds of thousands of those functions, cost and size savings are critical. Integrated circuits provide the most efficient method of packaging those functions within a small area. Standard digital ICs are available for every conceivable logic application. Along with those benefits, ICs also offer increased reliability and higher operating speeds.

After the invention of LSI integrated circuits, integration and miniaturization technologies continually improved and allowed the manufacture of smaller, faster, and cheaper chips. Very large-scale-integration (VLSI) builds millions of transistors onto one IC and, as a result, packs more logic into a single device. With VLSI technology, the functions once performed by several different logic ICs became enclosed within one package.

Voltage Supplies

Every stage in an electronic device requires some type of voltage supply, because of the signal amplification required to allow the system functions to occur. Amplification is an increase in the voltage, current, or power gain of an output signal. Although systems may use an ac power line input, the components within the system rely on dc voltages. We can categorize dc voltages into the low (12V dc - 35V dc), medium (150V dc - 400V dc), and high (15 kV-25 kV dc) ranges. Using a television receiver as an example, the low-voltage supply provides the necessary voltages for semiconductor operation, while the mid-range and high voltages are required for the deflection, focus, and cathode-ray tube circuits.

Every electronic voltage supply has four distinct parts that involve rectification, regulation, and filtering of the source voltages. Transformers either step up or step down the voltages to the levels required by circuits. Rectification involves the conversion of the required ac voltage value to a pulsating dc voltage. Regulation is defined as the maintenance of a consistent output at the power supply source. With a regulated power supply, changes in the input voltage do not affect the operation of some stages in the system. Filtering smooths the pulsating dc voltage into a usable, constant dc supply voltage.

Rectifying the AC Line Voltage

Rectification involves the conversion of the required ac voltage value to a pulsating dc voltage that may have either a positive or negative polarity. Depending on the application, linear power supplies may use one of four ac-to-dc voltage diode rectifier circuits to deliver either a half-wave or a full-wave output. The full-wave bridge features four diodes that rectify the full secondary voltage on each alternation of the ac wave. Full-wave bridge rectifiers are used in cold and hot grounding systems and are generally applied to large-screen televisions.

Integrated Rectifiers

Advances in the production of integrated circuits have allowed manufacturers to place all the active components of a full-wave or bridge rectifier into one semiconductor package. For example, a single one-inch square package can contain a bridge rectifier capable of handling an average forward current of 25 mA and surges as high as 400A. The performance of an integrated rectifier package is equivalent or superior to that provided by conventional diode-rectifier circuits.

Filtering

Every type of rectifier circuit uses some type of filter circuit to smooth the pulsating dc output voltage given through rectification and to remove as much rectifier output variation as possible. The most basic type of filter consists of an electrolytic capacitor connected across the output of a half-wave rectifier. Other filter types take advantage of the reactance properties of inductors or utilize a combination of a power transistor and a capacitor. We define the varying voltage across the filter capacitor as the ripple voltage.

Active Filters

Many power-supply circuit designs will supplement a filter capacitor with an active power filter circuit. Usually consisting of either a single power transistor or a combination of a filter driver transistor and a power transistor, the active filter circuit eliminates 60 Hz and 120 Hz ripple voltages and any residual audio frequency or horizontal frequency voltages. With the active filter shown in Figure 8-5, a power transistor connects in series with the rectifier output. Any ripple voltages cause increases in the current flowing through the transistor.

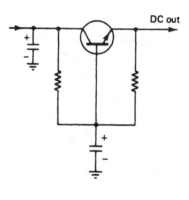

Figure 8-5

In turn, the increased current causes an increase in the reverse bias of the transistor and decreases the amount of conductance. As a result, the voltage at the output of the transistor also decreases.

Regulation

Regulation is the maximum change in a regulator output voltage that can occur when the input voltage and load current vary over rated ranges. We can also define regulation in terms of line regulation and load regulation. While line regulation of a voltage regulator shows the amount of change in output voltage that can occur per unit change in input voltage, the load regulation rating of a regulator indicates the amount of change in output voltage that can occur per unit change in load current. An ideal voltage regulator will maintain a constant dc output voltage, despite any changes that occur in either the input voltage or the load current.

Regulation is required because every device in the circuits that feeds off the low voltage supply has an internal resistance and draws some amount of current. Without some type of voltage regulation, the combination of internal resistance and current flow creates a voltage drop across the resistance and a resulting decrease in the output voltage. Regulator circuits stabilize the rectified and filtered power supply voltages, so that the dc level of the voltage does not vary with changes in the line or load.

The basic types of regulators are the shunt regulator and the series regulator. A shunt regulator is in parallel with the load, while a series regulator is in series with the load. Zener diode regulators are a form of shunt regulator. Transistor regulators are a form of the series regulator. Both types of particular applications have advantages and disadvantages. Regulator circuits for linear power supplies range from a zener diode, transistor circuits working as series-pass regulators, silicon controlled rectifier (SCR) circuits working as phase-control regulators, and integrated three-terminal regulators.

Zener Diode Regulators

The most basic type of voltage regulation occurs through the use of a zener diode and takes advantage of the reverse breakdown characteristic of the diode. That is, when a zener diode operates in the reverse breakdown region, the diode will have a constant voltage across it, as long as the zener current remains between the knee current and the maximum current rating.

As shown in Figure 8-6, a zener diode regulator circuit places the load resistance in parallel with the diode. Therefore, the load voltage will remain constant, as long as the zener voltage remains constant. If the zener current increases or decreases from the allowable range, then the zener and load voltages change.

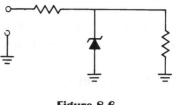

Figure 8-6

Consequently, the success of a zener diode regulator in maintaining the load voltage depends on keeping the zener current within its specified range.

Integrated Circuit (IC) Regulators

Many modern power supplies rely on an IC voltage regulator, because of the characteristics provided by the IC technology. IC voltage regulators hold the output voltage from a dc power supply constant over a wide range of line and load variations. Fixed voltage IC regulators provide specific positive or negative output voltages. While an adjustable IC regulator allows either a positive or negative output voltage to adjust within specific limits, a dual-tracking IC regulator establishes equal positive and negative output voltages.

Voltage Dividers

A voltage divider establishes a method for providing more than one dc output voltage from the same power supply. The most basic voltage divider places a number of resistors across the power supply terminals. For example, a three-resistor voltage divider can provide three different output voltages. With this, terminal A might supply +300V dc, while terminals B and C could supply +250V dc and +100V dc. The values of the resistors are chosen to accommodate the amount of current required by the load connected to the particular terminal.

Switch-Mode Power Supplies

With switch-mode power supplies, the block diagram changes slightly. Rather than begin with a transformer, the SMPS begins with a full-wave rectifier circuit connected directly to the line and then progresses to a high-frequency transformer, a power transistor, and a pulse generator. Figure 8-7 shows a block diagram for a typical switch-mode power supply.

SMPS Components

Like the linear power supplies discussed in Chapter 2, switch-mode power supplies contain a mix of passive and active components. These components include bipolar-junction transistors, rectifiers, silicon control rectifiers, shunt regulator ICs, optoisolators, filter and bypass capacitors, resistors, metal-oxide resistors, and thermistors. Each component type affects the performance of the switching power supply and involves tasks such as feedback, control, rectification, overvoltage and overcurrent protection, regulation, isolation, filtering, and voltage division.

When considering the operation of an SMPS, it's easier to consider the components by function. For example, filter capacitors either filter the rectified—and sometimes doubled—ac line input voltage or filter the output voltages from the SMPS. Other types of capacitors in the circuit provide bypass

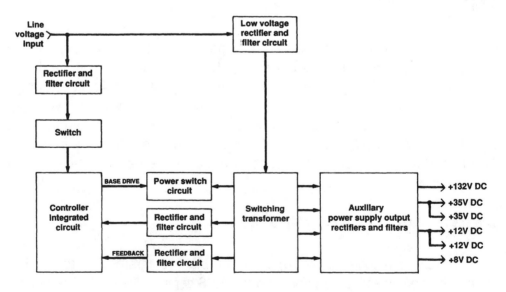

Figure 8-7

paths. SMPS power supplies also contain a combination of general type resistors and flameproof resistors, metal-oxide varistors, and thermistors. While the general type resistors are often found in voltage divider circuits, the flameproof resistors are found in the return circuit for the switching regulator or in the ac line circuit. Metal-oxide varistors (MOVs) and thermistors protect against severe surges and appear in the ac line circuits, while optoisolators or optocouplers establish isolation.

Active components such as bipolar transistors, metal-oxide-semiconductor field-effect transistors (MOSFETs), and SCRs may operate as part of a feedback circuit, as regulators, or in overvoltage and overcurrent protection circuits. Bipolar-junction transistors function in a feedback circuit or may function as the SMPS switching device. The type of transistor used in the particular circuit varies with the function. For example, a power transistor capable of handling high voltages will work as a switching device.

In addition to transistors, MOSFETs and SCRs may appear in the switching role. SCRs are also found in overvoltage and overcurrent protection circuits. Rectification occurs through the use of either discrete or packaged diodes. Most SMPS units use diodes for ac line rectification or in voltage doubler circuits. The switched power supplies usually rely on some type of three-pin IC regulator for regulation of the output voltages.

SMPS Operation

All switch-mode power supplies use a high-frequency switching device such as a transistor, MOSFET, insulated gate bipolar transistor, SCR, or triac to convert the directly rectified line voltage into a pulsed waveform. An SMPS that has a lower power requirement will feature a conventional transistor or MOSFET as a switcher, while high-power SMPS units will rely on an IGBT, SCR, or triac. Each of the last three components offers latching in the on state and high-power capability. This type of capability, however, also requires more complex circuitry to ensure that the semiconductors turn off at the correct time.

The switching on and off of the transistor closes and opens a path for dc current to flow into the transformer. With the flow of current producing a changing magnetic field in the transformer primary, a changing magnetic field also develops in the transformer secondary winding. As a result, voltage is induced in the secondary winding. Rectifiers and filters in the secondary circuit rectify and filter into stable supply voltages.

SMPS Input

After rectification of the line voltage, the SMPS may have two possible dc inputs. With the first, 150V dc - 160V dc arrives at the SMPS after the direct rectification of 115V ac -130V ac line voltage. Some SMPS units, however, require a higher input voltage. In this case, a voltage doubler supplies 300V dc - 320V dc to the SMPS input. Other designs rectify a 220V ac - 240V ac line voltage and also supply the 300V dc - 320V dc to the SMPS input.

While rectification of the line voltage occurs through the use of a full-wave bridge rectifier or a voltage doubler, the input to the SMPS also includes inductors and capacitors for the purpose of filtering line noise and any voltage spikes. Those components also eliminate the transmission of any radio frequency interference generated by the power supply back into the ac line. As mentioned, most designs feature metal-oxide varistors across the input lines for additional surge protection.

Switch-Mode Regulators

Switch-mode regulator circuits provide the advantage of having a control device that has minimal power dissipation for the entire duty cycle. In particular, switch-mode regulator circuits provide:

- the capability to produce an output voltage higher than the input voltage;
- the capability to produce either a positive or negative output voltage from a positive input voltage;
- the capability to produce an output voltage from a dc input voltage.

A switch-mode regulator circuit uses a control device—such as a bipolar transistor, a field-effect transistor, or a silicon controlled rectifier—to switch the supply power in and out of the circuit and regulate the voltage. Switching occurs because of the ability to send the device into either saturation (the completely on state) or into cutoff (the completely off state).

The duty cycle of the device, or the ratio of "on" time to "off" time, establishes the regulation of the output voltage level. Therefore, regulation in a switch-mode power supply occurs through the pulse-width modulation or the pulse-rate modulation of the dc voltage. Pulse-width modulation varies the duty cycle of the dc voltage, while pulse-rate modulation varies the frequency of the dc pulses.

Figure 8-8 is an illustration of pulse-width modulation. In the figure, the on-cycles of the pulse train energy double as the time periods for storing energy in a magnetic field. During the off-cycles of the pulse train, the stored energy provides output power and compensates for any changes in the line voltage or the load. The pulse-width modulation of the switching transistor changes the conduction time of the device by varying the pulse frequency.

With a low load resistance and the line voltage within tolerance, the switch-mode power supply switches the power into the power supply for only a short period of time. Either a high load resistance, a low line voltage, or a combination of both conditions will cause the switch-mode power supply to transfer more energy over a longer period of time into the power supply. As a result, the switching frequency varies from a higher frequency for lower loads to a lower frequency for higher loads.

SMPS Transformer Operation

Switch-mode power supplies do not include any type of conventional power transformer and, as a result, do not have line isolation. At the input of the power supply, a small, high-frequency transformer converts the pulsed waveform taken from the switching device into one or more output voltages. Other components following the high frequency rectify and filter the voltages for use by signal circuits.

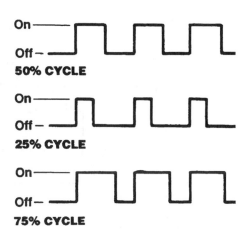

Figure 8-8

Isolation in the SMPS system

Although the SMPS doesn't provide line isolation, use of the high-frequency transformer establishes an isolation barrier and the type of characteristics needed to operate in the flyback mode. Depending on the circuit configuration, a small pulse transformer or an optoisolator sets up feedback across the isolation barrier. The feedback controls the pulse width of the switching device and maintains regulation for the primary output of the SMPS.

Most small switch-mode power supplies, such as those used for DVDs, use optoisolators for feedback. An optoisolator is a combination of an LED and a photodiode in one package and establishes an isolation barrier between low-voltage secondary outputs and the ac line. Whenever a primary output voltage reaches a specified value, a reference circuit in the output turns on the LED. In turn, the photodiode detects the light from the LED and reduces the pulse width of the switching waveform. This establishes the correct amount of output power and maintains a constant output voltage.

Iso-Hot Grounding System

As shown in Figure 8-9, an iso-hot chassis utilizes a combination of the cold and hot grounding systems through the connection of one portion of the

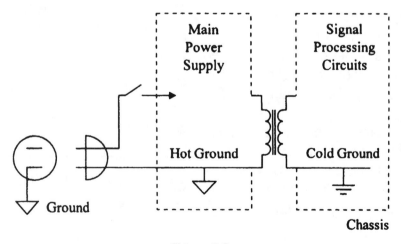

Figure 8-9

receiver to earth ground and the other portion to the ac line ground. Due to the existence of three different grounding systems, technicians must take special care when using test equipment and when moving from one system to the other. An iso-hot chassis combines the better points of the cold and hot chassis into a different power supply approach and allows the isolated connection of video accessories—such as DVD players and VCRs—to the standard television receiver. Because of this, the iso-hot design continues to use an isolated transformerless system, but also includes a separate cold chassis ground. Any direct connection between the two types of grounding systems will damage the receiver, as well as any attached test equipment.

DVD Video Player Power Supply

Conversion of signals within the DVD player can only occur through the application of dc voltages throughout the receiver. Each of the dc voltages works as a source voltage for a particular circuit. Power supplies convert the pulsating ac voltages found at electrical outlets into the regulated dc voltages required by the individual circuits. The power supply used in a DVD video player also provides a range of voltages needed for the audio and video processing circuits, digital circuits, and the displays.

While Figure 8-10 (on Page 144) shows a block diagram for the power supply found in a Zenith model DVC2200 video player, Figure 8-11 (on Page 145) shows a schematic diagram of the power supply circuit. Moving from left to right, the player utilizes a free-running, pulse-width modulated supply. At the bottom center of Figure 8-11, the primary of the transformer references to hot ground rather than cold ground.

At the top left of Figure 8-11, voltage from the ac line applies to BD101, a bridge rectifier that produces approximately 160V dc. Again moving from left to right, the voltage feeds to two circuits after leaving the rectifier and filter capacitor C905. From there, the 160V dc applies to pins 1 and 3 of the PT901 transformer primary and pins 3 and 5 of the switching circuit labeled IC901.

Applying the voltage to transformer and switching transistor generates a start-up voltage for the integrated circuit and causes a current to pulse through

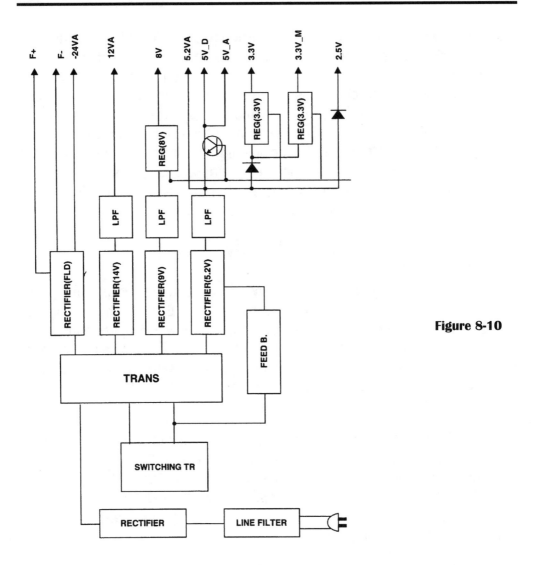

Figure 8-10

the primary of the transformer. As the current reaches maximum potential and the transformer saturates, a magnetic field induced in the transformer collapses and reverses polarity. Once the current reverses polarity, the voltage at pin 2 of the transformer becomes negative.

From there, the negative voltage applies to C111 and switches transistor Q101 off. C903 controls the operating frequency for the power supply; the frequency varies with changes in the load. With the DVD player in standby

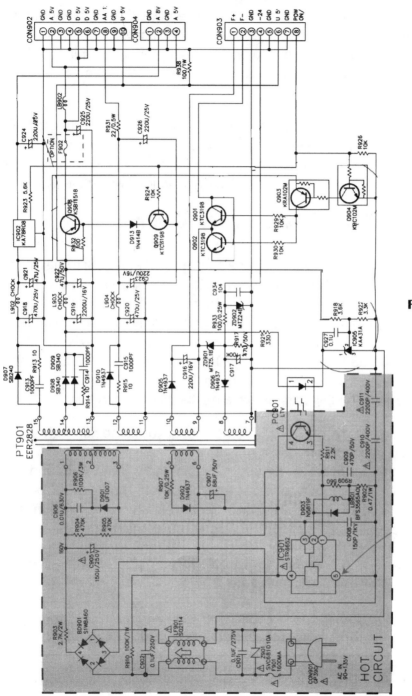

Figure 8-11

mode, the power supply oscillates at approximately 125 kHz. When the DVD player operates, the frequency decreases to approximately 55 kHz. When the magnetic field has completely collapsed, the voltage found at pin 2 becomes positive, forward biases D903, and causes the transistor found within IC901 to switch on.

Current flowing through the transformer primary creates a magnetic field that magnetically couples energy from the primary to the transformer secondary. As a result, the secondary produces dc supply voltages for the main circuit board, the display, and the mechanical subassemblies contained within the player.

DVD Video Player Power-Supply Regulation

Regulation measures changes in load current. Moving back to Figure 8-11, we see that IC902 establishes a +8V dc line that remains loaded regardless of whether the player operates or remains in standby mode. When the DVD player goes into standby mode, Q909 doesn't conduct, and the switched voltages remain at a low level. The bias voltage developed through the +8V dc line and R924, D913, and R932 forward biases Q908 into conduction. When this occurs, the circuit establishes a ground path through R933 for the +9V dc line and provides the necessary loading to maintain a regulated power supply.

Functioning as part of IC901, another transistor combines with an error amplifier found in IC905 and the optocoupler found within PC901 to control the switching time of the first transistor functioning within the IC and maintains the +8V dc supply. As a result, regulation occurs through the controlled switching of the on/off time of the two transistors. The error amplifier constantly samples the output of the +8V dc line and feeds the results to the optocoupler. If the voltage on that line exceeds 8V, the error amplifier begins to conduct harder. In turn, PC901 applies a feedback voltage from pin 3 to pin 2 of transformer PT901.

All this creates a feedback circuit that switches the transistors on and off. A higher-than-normal voltage on the +8V dc line indicates that the output voltages have begun to increase. Switching the two transistors on and off causes the output voltages to decrease. A lower-than-normal voltage on the

+8V dc line causes a third transistor to switch off for a longer time period and allows the first to conduct longer. With this, the output voltages increase back to the operating level.

DVD Player Operating Voltages

With the DVD player turning on normally, the power-on command received from either the front panel control or remote control causes the main circuit board to apply +5V dc through pin 3 of CN801, the power supply connector, and to Q903, the on-off control transistor. As Q909 becomes forward-biased, the voltage produced at the output of the transistor represents a digital low value.

Placing the low signal at four locations on the power supply board causes the circuit to generate the dc voltages needed for operation. At Q908, the application of the low signal causes the transistor to switch on, saturate, and produce the +5V dc supplies. Applying the signal to the base of Q909 causes the transistor to switch off. Given that action, the 5V regulator operating within Q901 initializes Q902 and establishes the positive and negative filament supply voltages. Coupling the low signal to Q909 not only switches the transistor on, but also sets the load needed for the +12V dc line.

Overvoltage and Overcurrent Protection

When considering regulator circuits such as the series-pass transistor, we should remember that a short across the load would destroy the pass transistor because of the excessive load current. Most devices that rely on a series-pass regulator also include a current-limiting circuit. The use of an overcurrent protection circuit adds a transistor and a series resistor to the series-pass regulator circuit.

With the resistor connected to the base and emitter terminals, the current-limiting transistor can only conduct if the voltage across the resistor reaches approximately 0.7V dc. If the resistor has a value of 1 ohm, conduction only occurs if the load current (IL) equals:

$$0.7V \text{ dc} / 1 \text{ ohm} = 700 \text{ mA}$$

Any load current less than 700 milliamps allows the current-limiting transistor to remain in cutoff. Any increase of the load current above the 700-ma level, however, causes the transistor to conduct. As a result of the conduction by the current limiter, the voltage at the base of the series-pass regulator transistor decreases. With a decrease in the base voltage, the transistor has a reduced conduction, and the load current begins to decrease to less than 700 milliamps.

Overvoltage Protection Circuits

As opposed to series-pass regulators, shunt regulators require protection against overvoltage conditions at the input. If the dc input voltage to the regulator rises above a specified level, the shunt regulator transistor conducts harder so that the output voltage remains constant. With this, the transistor also dissipates more heat.

Overcurrent Protection in the DVD Power Supply

Again looking at Q903 (in Figure 8-11), resistor R910 connects from pin 4 of IC901 to ground. As a result, the resistor functions as the emitter resistor for transistor T1. If operation of the DVD player generates enough current to apply 0.6V dc across the resistor, transistor T2 switches on and shunts the drive voltage for transistor T1 to ground. With this, the power supply shuts down.

An overvoltage condition causes a zener diode found within IC905 to conduct and pull the base voltage of Q903 low. With Q903 operating as a power supply control, pulling the base voltage down to a low level causes the power supply to shut down. The zener diode connects to Q904, the shutdown switch.

DVD Video Player Circuits: Optical Pickup Unit

Introduction

While it may seem reasonable to compare the optical pickup unit (OPU) used in DVD players and readers to a phonograph needle, the precision required for the tracking of the disc by the OPU has little in common with the old phonograph technology. The servo systems within a CD or DVD player maintain the focus and tracking of the OPU within micrometers. All this occurs because of the minute differences in depth between pits and lands and the extremely short wavelength of the laser light emitted by the laser diode.

Basic Operation of DVD Video Player Optical Electronics

As seen on the left side of the DVD video player block diagram shown in Figure 9-1 (on Page 150), an optical pickup unit reads and retrieves data from the disc. Modern OPUs include a laser diode, optics, focus and tracking actuators, and a photodiode array. Figure 9-2 (on Page 151) shows the basic elements of an OPU. Looking at the enlarged diagram at the left, we see that the semiconductor laser diode emits a low-energy beam of light toward a reflecting mirror. A servomotor positions the beam onto the correct track of the disc by moving the reflecting mirror. When the laser light reflects from the disc, servos react to the information by controlling the focus and tracking. The servo maintains the tracking of the OPU by keeping the amplitude of the reflected beams equal.

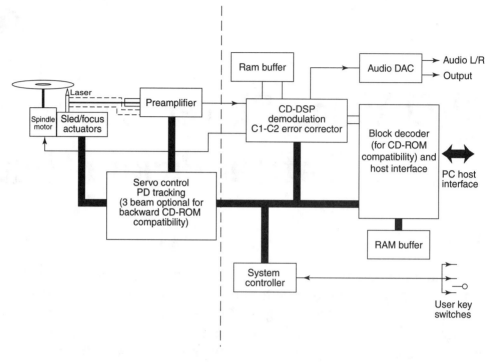

Figure 9-1

From there, a well-corrected lens found beneath the platter gathers and directs the beam toward an objective lens. An objective lens focuses the beam onto the disc and collects the reflected light. The last lens directs the beam toward the photodetector. Viewed as a mechanical system consisting of a spindle or turntable, clamper, and the servo assembly, the tracking assembly controls the focus, tracking, and retrieval rate of the optical pickup unit. The mechanical system also includes the OPU sled and sled motor as well as the loading drawer.

In turn, the photodetector produces an electrical signal. Light reflected from the pits found on the disc has an out-of-phase relationship with light reflected from the lands. The photodiode measures the 180° differences in intensity and converts the differences into electrical pulses. A digital-to-analog converter interprets the pulses and converts the signals into series of corresponding 0s and 1s.

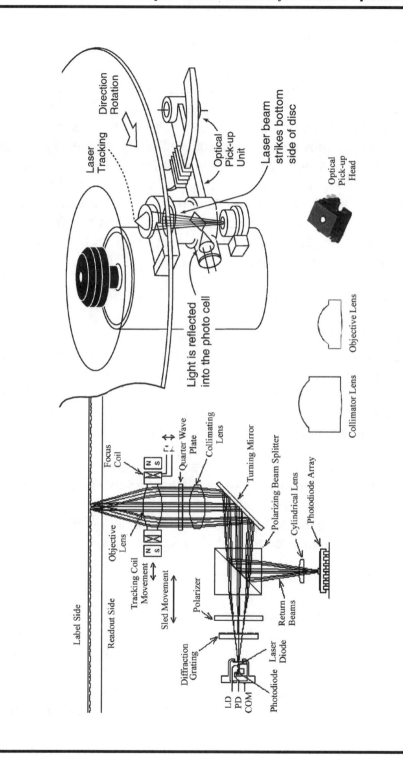

Figure 9-2

Optical Pickup Unit

An optical pickup unit contains the laser, lenses, mirror, and photodiode needed to translate the information stored on a DVD disc into electrical signals. Once the circuitry attached to the OPU converts the electrical signals into data, other circuits provide error correction. Shining a laser on the disc and then measuring the strength of the reflection from the pits and lands allows the reading of information from the disc. For example, the pit depth of a CD-ROM disc equals one-fourth the wavelength of the laser beam in the transparent substrate on the CD-ROM disc. The substrate has a refractive index of $n=1.5$. As a result, the light reflected from a pit has a 180° out-of-phase relationship with the light reflected from the adjacent land.

Semiconductor Laser Diodes

All optical recording technologies rely on lasers as the source of light. DVD players rely on red light lasers, rather than the infrared lasers seen with compact disc audio players. In addition, modern OPUs combine the laser diode and photodiode array into one device. Semiconductor laser diodes used in DVD video players and readers have moderate power at approximately 50 milliwatts and a short wavelength at 680 nanometers.

Shorter wavelengths can focus on smaller spots at the diffraction limit. Since the diameter of a focused spot has a direct relationship with wavelength, reducing the wavelength by a factor of two also decreases the focused spot diameter by the same factor. As a result, the combination of short wavelength and small pit size quadruples the data storage density.

Construction of Semiconductor Laser Diodes

Semiconductor laser diodes continue to gain new product applications, because of decreases in the laser wavelength. With the latest generation of visible laser diodes (VLDs) operating at or near a wavelength of 635 nanometers, semiconductor laser diodes have wavelengths similar to those seen with a helium neon (HeNe) gas laser. Given the lower cost, compact size, and reliability seen with semiconductor laser diodes, the devices have replaced HeNe lasers for many applications. The semiconductor laser diodes have become especially well suited for applications that require battery or low-voltage operation.

Any type of semiconductor has electrical conductivity characteristics that fit between the high conductivity of metals and the low conductivity of insulators. Most semiconductor laser diodes consist of a chemical combination of gallium and arsenic called gallium arsenide, or GaAs. The manufacture of GaAs lasers begins with ingots of gallium arsenide crystals mounted on glass plates with wax and cut into 0.5 mm slices.

After the forming of the slice, the diffusion of impurities in from the surface produces the semiconductor junction. Cutting the blocks into one- or two-millimeter sizes and then sandwiching the blocks between two gold-clad metal discs forms the individual semiconductor laser diode. With the light-emitting region, or the junction from which the radiation originates—remaining as a few micron thick layer—the completed laser diodes attach to a copper heat sink on one side and a small electrical contact on the other.

Figure 9-3 is a diagram of a simple gallium arsenide laser, while Figure 9-4 (on Page 154) is a photograph of the semiconductor laser diode. The cleaved ends of the laser diode form the mirrors that provide feedback and output

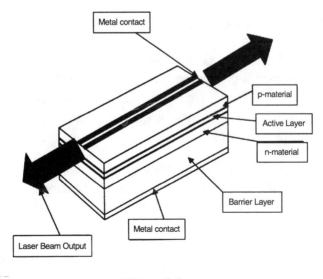

Figure 9-3

coupling. In addition, the manufacturing process roughens the two sides, reduces reflection, and prevents lasing the diode cavity. Available loop gain within the laser cavity limits the output of the laser, while amplifier gain of the active medium remains dependent on the current density through the junction.

As shown in Figure 9-5, semiconductor laser diodes emit coherent light through stimulated emission. Current flow provides the excitation needed to produce light. The energy of the photon resulting from this recombination equals the energy associated with the energy gap and takes the form of electromagnetic radiation.

Output Characteristics of GaAs Lasers

Gallium arsenide lasers have very few of the characteristics typically associated with lasers. Within the GaAs laser, the small dimension of the junction that produces light provides a beamwidth of several degrees that compares with the narrower beamwidths seen with typical gas lasers or crystal lasers. A gallium arsenide laser has a 2- or 3-nanometer spectral beamwidth.

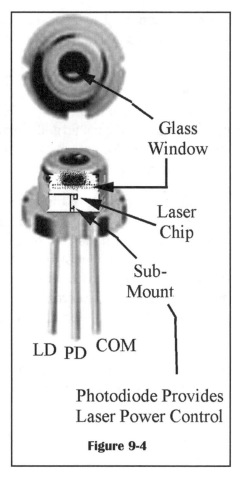

Glass Window

Laser Chip

Sub-Mount

LD PD COM

Photodiode Provides Laser Power Control

Figure 9-4

As a result, a gallium arsenide laser appears as a small bright area source of radiation. Although gallium arsenide lasers do not possess the directionality and monochromaticity characteristics found with other lasers, GaAs lasers have other characteristics that match favorably with communications applications. With this, a GaAs laser modulates easily at high frequencies through the modulation of the current through the junction. In addition, a GaAs laser provides efficient and rugged operation within a small, inexpensive package.

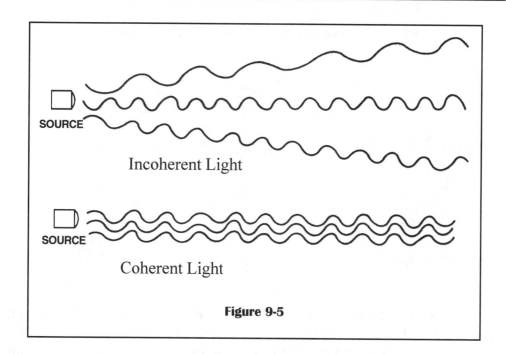

SOURCE

Incoherent Light

SOURCE

Coherent Light

Figure 9-5

Dual Lasers Used for DVD Readers and Players

As mentioned, the semiconductor laser diode and optical pickup unit must have the capability to precisely illuminate the data-readout area of the optical disc. For a DVD disc of any type, the optical focused spot size must have a focus size no larger than 0.6 μm. Going back to Chapters 2 and 3, DVD discs and optical pickup units require a much smaller focus size than compact discs and optical pickup units. In addition, the difference in numbers of layers and substrate thickness between compact discs and DVD discs also requires more powerful lasers for the DVD application. Table 9-1 (on Page 156) compares the compact disc and DVD laser diode specifications.

To ensure that DVD readers and players can read and play both compact discs and DVD discs, several manufacturers have introduced laser diodes that have two output wavelengths. Until these designs reached the marketplace, some readers and players employed dual pickup heads that rotated the separate lasers into place for either a compact disc or a DVD.

Table 9-1: Comparison of Laser Diode Optical Specifications

	Compact Disc	DVD
Objective Lens Focal Length	2.3 mm	3.37 mm
Working Distance	1.3 mm	1.5 mm
Numerical Aperture	0.45	0.60
Laser Diode Wavelength	780 nanometers	650 nanometers
Servo Error Detect Method	Knife-edge	Astigmatism
Tracking Error Method	3-beam	3-beam or DPD
Track Sensitivity	1.10 mm/V	1.35 mm/V
Track Signal Level	0.21V dc	1.4V dc
RF Signal Level	1V dc	1V dc
Focus Signal Level	0.54V dc	0.8V dc
Focus Range	0.8 mm	0.8 mm

Optimization of the reflection film allows operation at both 650 nanometers for DVD discs and 780 nanometers for compact discs. Although the new laser package fits within a standard package, the two lasers require separate drivers. In addition to offering compatibility, the new laser package also provides a more precise focus spot, an advanced digital learning servo, and a more reliable traverse mechanism. The servo control varies the speed of the spin motor for either a compact disc or a DVD disc.

Next-Generation Semiconductor Laser Diode Technologies

Given the impact of DVD technologies on the marketplace, manufacturers have also responded with more powerful, 426-nanometer blue output lasers intended for next-generation DVD readers and players. With the more powerful gallium nitrade laser, new DVD technologies gain the potential for higher storage capacities. Next-generation DVDs with 400-nanometer lasers and high-density signal processing technology will have a capacity of 15 gigabytes per side.

Other technologies promise to improve the capacity to as much as 27 gigabytes per side. In late-1999, Pioneer Electronics demonstrated a 27.4-gigabyte optical disc system that can store four hours of 1,080i high-definition video at an average variable bit rate of 13.4 megabits per second. The system relies on a 405-nanometer violet laser that reads out signals from each layer of a two-layer disc. Since prototype discs designed for the system have a narrow track pitch of approximately 0.37 microns, Pioneer Electronics also relies on three-beam crosstalk cancellation.

Spindle, Spindle Table, and Spindle Motor

Manufacturers refer to the platform that holds the disc as the spindle, spindle table, or spindle platter. The spindle automatically centers the disc and spins at a constant rate because of the spindle motor. The purpose of this system is to spin the CD at the correct speed. Unlike records that spin at a constant rate, DVD discs spin at different rates depending on where the laser beam is located. Depending on the cost of the player, a spindle motor may be either a brush-type or brushless dc motor. Most manufacturers rely on direct-drive spindle/spindle motor combinations. The clamper—a magnet found on the opposite side of the disc—maintains the position of the disc on the spindle.

Sled and Sled Motor

As mentioned, the optical pickup unit mounts onto a sled that allows the OPU to move across the disc. Supported on guide rails, the sled moves according to commands from the microcontroller and may either allow the OPU to track completely across the disc for normal play or may move the OPU to a specific position over the disc when in the search mode. Most manufacturers rely on conventional direct-drive dc motors to push the sled. Figure 9-6 is a photograph of the sled and sled motor.

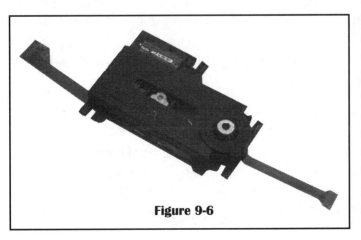

Figure 9-6

Sled Movement

Given the need for movement across the disc, the OPU mounts on a sled. The adjusting speed of the disc motor results in the reading of the data at a constant rate. Because the disc contains spiral tracks, the motor speed decreases as the scanning moves from the beginning near the center of the disc to the end at the edge of the disc.

Automatic Focusing

Several factors affect the focusing of the optical electronics. At one level, a typical optical disc does not have a perfectly flat plastic substrate. Instead, the plastic substrate will show slight warping. At another level, small tilts of the axis could cause vertical motions of the disc surface during operation. Typically, vertical movements as much as ± 100 μm occur during the operation of an optical disc. Because an objective lens has a numerical aperture of 0.5 or higher, the focused beam has a depth of focus of a fraction of λ/NA or a fraction of a micron. Moreover, the focused spot must remain within the depth of focus while the disc rotates at speeds of several thousand rpm and wobbles in and out of focus by as much as ± 100 μm in each revolution. As a result, every player or reader requires the use of an autofocus mechanism to keep the disc continually in focus.

When the disc becomes out of focus, the astigmatic lens creates an elongated spot on the detector. Depending on the amount of blurriness, the elongated spot may illuminate quadrants one and three or quadrants two and four of the detector. As a result, the combination signal $(S_1 + S_3) - (S_2 + S_4)$ provides a bipolar focus-error signal that feeds back to the voice coil for maintaining focus automatically.

Automatic Tracking Control

Information on an optical disc records around a series of concentric circular tracks or as a continuous spiral. Manufacturing errors and disc eccentricities caused by mounting errors or thermal expansion of the substrate may cause a given track to wobble in and out of position as the disc spins. As an example, a given track might be as much as ±100 μm away from its intended position at any given time. Because a focused spot has a width of less than 1 μm, the spot may not strike the correct location at all times and requires an automatic tracking scheme. Given the mechanical rotation rates of the disc, the frequency response of the track following actuator does not cover more then a few kHz. The return beam provides the feedback signal for controlling the position of the objective lens within the tracking coil.

Three-beam Tracking

Most DVD video players use a radial tracking system based on the three-beam approach. With this, the laser beam emitted from a semiconductor laser unit passes through a diffraction grating to produce two extra light sources that appear to each side of the main beam. The collimator lens takes the three beams and produces a completely collimated, or parallel, beam.

Twenty microns separate each spot from the other. Two additional photo-detectors operate alongside the main quadrant detector and pick up these subsidiary beams. Error control circuitry measures the two side beams measured for intensity. If the three beams remain on track, two subsidiary photo-detectors have equal amounts of light and have more brightness because of tracking only lands. Any sideways movement of the disc causes unequal measurements of intensity to occur. In turn, a track following servomotor repositions the objective lens. The central beam has reduced brightness given through the tracking of both land and pits.

As Figure 9-7 (on Page 160) shows, the receptor diode splits into quadrants and locates between the horizontal and vertical focal points of the beam. Any vertical deviation of the disc causes the spot to become elliptical and causes a current imbalance to appear between each opposing pair of quadrants. As a result, a servomotor moves the objective lens up or down to ensure that the spot remains circular.

Lenses

Collimating and focusing a laser diode is perhaps the most critical prerequisite in any laser diode application. While the characteristics of a laser

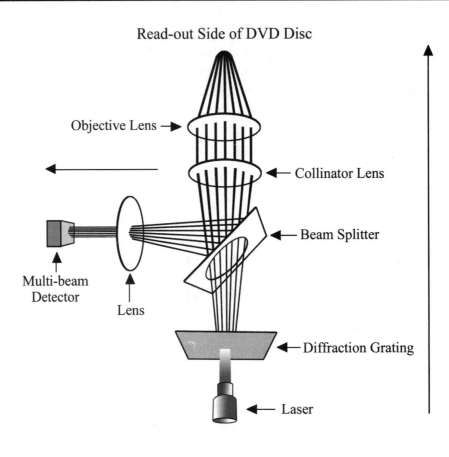

Read-out Side of DVD Disc

Objective Lens →

Collinator Lens

Beam Splitter

Multi-beam
Detector

Lens

Diffraction Grating

Laser

Figure 9-7

diode may seem appropriate for an application, the laser diode must match with the appropriate optics to create a usable beam. Most optical pickup units utilize one collimating lens and a second focus lens.

But some DVD video players use a single lens for collimating and focusing the beam. The manufacturers rely on an astigmatic objective lens rather than the series of lenses seen in older optical pickup units. With the exception of the diffraction grating and turning mirror, most manufacturers of DVD optical assemblies eliminate all other optical components such as the beam splitter.

As shown in Figure 9-7, the diffraction grating converts the emitted light into a signal that takes the form of a central peak accompanied side peaks. Splitting and polarizing the beams transmits polarizations parallel to the page. From there, the emerging and polarized light travels through a collimating lens.

In either application, semiconductor laser diodes require a collimating lens that has a large numerical aperture. With this, the lens can efficiently capture the widely divergent perpendicular axis. The lens consists of two aspheric surfaces on a single piece of glass and have numerical apertures that range from 0.4 to 0.6. In addition, the lenses have few aberrations. Astigmatic objective lenses use molded glass for focusing the laser beam to a diffraction-limited spot.

As the collimated light travels through a 1/4-wave plate, it converts into circularly polarized light that focuses down onto the disc. If the light strikes a land, the light reflects back into the objective lens. By comparison, if the light strikes the pit, it does not reflect. The reflected light again passes through the 1/4 wave plate in the reverse direction. Because of this, the reflected light becomes polarized perpendicular to the original beam or vertical with respect to this page. When the vertically polarized light strikes the polarizing beam splitter, it will reflect though the focusing lens and the cylindrical lens before imaging on the photodetector array.

Figure 9-8 (on page 162) shows a diagram of the astigmatic focus error detection system used in many practical devices these days. As the returned beam goes through an astigmatic lens, the lens focuses the incident beam to a symmetric spot halfway between its focal planes. While the objective lens mounts within a voice coil actuator, a quad detector placed at this plane then receives equal amounts of light on its four quadrants. Using reflected light from the disc, a feedback mechanism drives the lens toward and away from the disc in such a way as to maintain focus at all times. As shown in Figure 9-9 (on page 163), the objective lens collects either convergent or divergent light depending on the placement of the disc with regard to the lens. With the disc further away from best focus, the lens collects convergent light. Placing the disc closer to the lens allows the lens to collect divergent light.

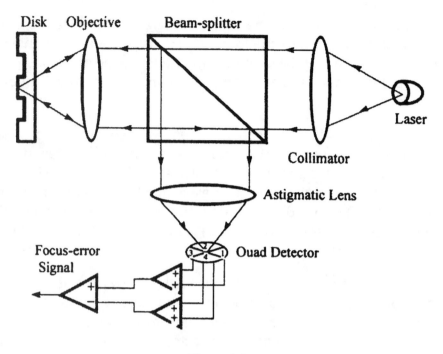

Figure 9-8

Numerical Aperture

The numerical aperture of a lens is NA = sin Φ, where Φ is the half-angle subtended by the focused cone of light at its apex. For example, the 0.5 NA lens used in a DVD video player will have a focused 60° full-angle cone. The diameter of the focused spot equals λ/NA, where λ equals the vacuum wavelength of the laser beam. Higher numerical apertures allow the use of smaller pits and greater storage densities.

Read-Only Optical System Data Amplifier and Laser Supply Circuit

Figure 9-10 shows a schematic diagram for a data amplifier and laser supply circuit for three-beam pickup detectors found in read-only optical

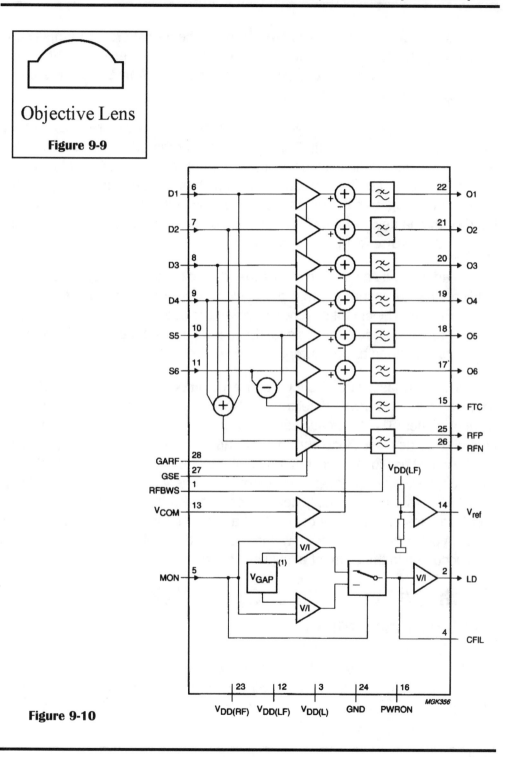

Objective Lens

Figure 9-9

Figure 9-10

systems. The device contains six transimpedance amplifiers that amplify and filter the focus and radial photodiode voltage input signals. In brief, the preamplifier forms a versatile, programmable interface from the voltage output disc mechanism to a digital signal processor.

With the capability to program the interface, manufacturers can set the dynamic range of the preamplifier/processor combination to match low-frequency servo and radio frequency signal data paths. While the analog-to-digital conversion range of the processor establishes the servo channel gain, the preamplifier programs the RF data channel. Given the wide programmable RF bandwidth, the device works for audio/video applications, disc read/write applications, and disc ROM applications.

In addition, a gain switch allows the RF and LF gain to adapt to particular applications. To ensure optimal playback, the system also applies programmable RF gain. The circuit ensures minimal disc access time for the system by generating a Fast Track Count signal that allows the decoder to count the number of tracks during a track jump.

While the laser supply circuit can accommodate astigmatic, single Foucault and double Foucault detectors, it also works with all laser and N- or P-sub monitor diodes. The Automatic Laser Power Control, or ALPC, circuit maintains control over the laser diode current. With an on-chip reference voltage generator, the circuit provides a constant and stabilized output power supply that has a wide voltage supply range, good temperature range, and lower power consumption. A separate power supply connection reduces internal power dissipation and increases efficiency by connecting an external low voltage supply to the circuit. A protection circuit found within the device prevents damage to the laser from occurring in the event of a sagging voltage supply.

Zenith DVD Video Player Optical Pickup and Servo Electronics

Figure 9-11 (on Pages 166-167) shows the block diagram of the optical electronics for the DVC2200 video player. As the diagram shows, the optical electronics features the optical unit, the servo motor assemblies, and a five-channel motor drive IC. As shown in Figure 9-12, the KA3032 motor drive IC uses a transformerless BTL driver to drive the tracking actuator, focus actuator, sled motor, spindle motor, and tray motor. The device features built-in thermal shutdown, voltage lockout, overvoltage protection, and mute circuits. A fully integrated digital servo controls the spindle motor speed and responds to the disc rotational speed.

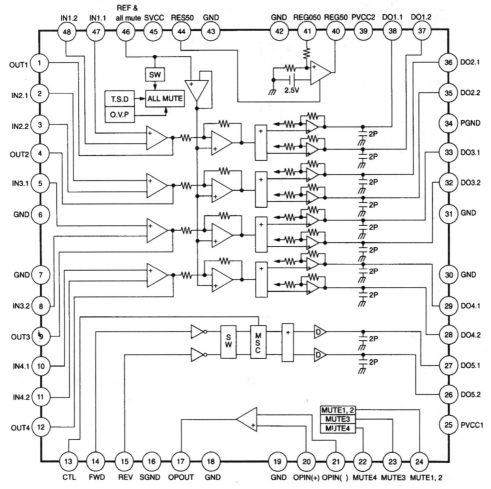

Figure 9-12

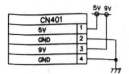

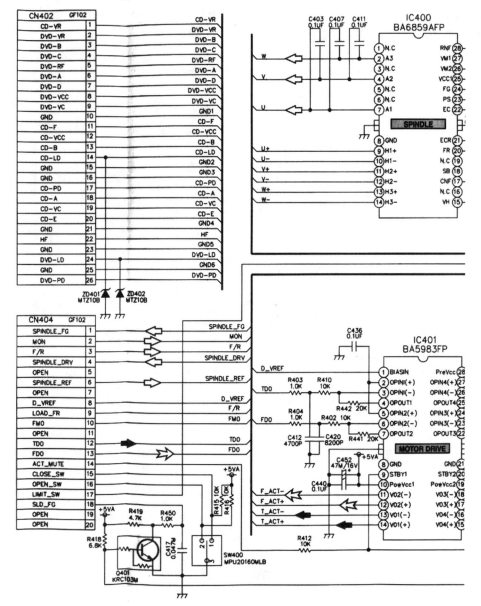

Figure 9-11a *(see next page)*

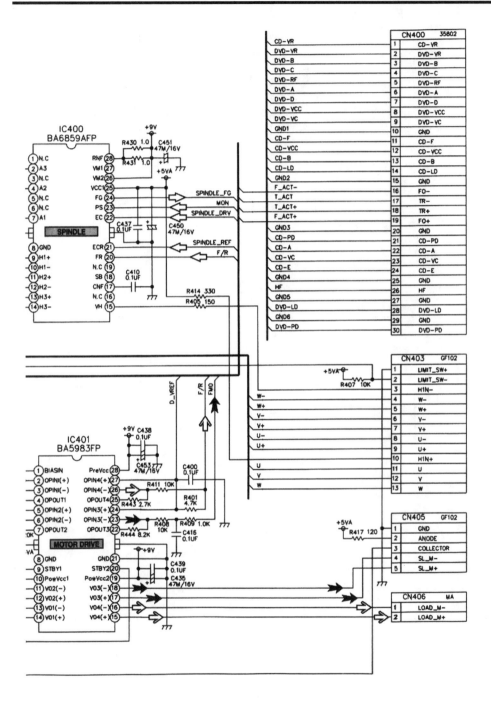

Figure 9-11b *(continued from previous page)*

DVD Video Player Signal Circuits

Introduction

Chapter 9 explained how the optical pickup and semiconductor laser work together in reading the encoded data from the spinning optical disc. As the signal progresses from the OPU, it travels through several different processing circuits. Chapter 10 begins with an overview of frequency and signal characteristics, as well as the factors such as gain and amplification that affect those characteristics. This chapter also looks at basic circuits that process radio frequency (rf), intermediate frequency (if), and automatic gain control (agc) signals, then moving on to an overview of digital signal processors. From there, Chapter 10 takes a detailed look at the signal-processing circuits used within the Zenith DVC2200 DVD video player.

Frequency Characteristics

Electromagnetic wave frequencies cover a wide range that extends from the longest radio waves to the very short waves called cosmic waves. In terms of frequency, this range extends from 10 kHz at the low end to 10^{20} kHz at the high end. Of this range, or spectrum, radio frequencies cover a range from 10 kHz to 3×10^8 kHz.

Along with having frequency ranges, electromagnetic waves also have polarization. As with electrical wiring, electromagnetic wave polarization exists through the direction of electrical and magnetic fields. Two types of polarization occur. When the electrical and magnetic fields of a received signal remain within the same plane of the electrical and magnetic fields of the transmitted signal, linear polarization occurs. Horizontally polarized waves travel along the horizontal plane, while vertically polarized waves travel along the vertical plane. Figure 10-1 depicts linear polarization.

Circular polarized electromagnetic waves have electrical and magnetic fields that rotate in a circular motion. In this case, electrical and magnetic fields that rotate in a right-hand spiral have right-hand circular polarization (RHCP). Electrical and magnetic fields rotating in a left-hand spiral have a left-hand circular polarization. Figure 10-2 depicts circular polarization.

Signals

In terms of electronics, we can define a signal as a voltage or current that has deliberately induced, time-varying characteristics. A signal voltage or current is different than a source voltage or current for several reasons. Every electrical signal has a distinctive shape described in terms of time domain (the amplitude of the signal as a function of time) and in terms of frequency domain (the magnitude and relative phase of the energy).

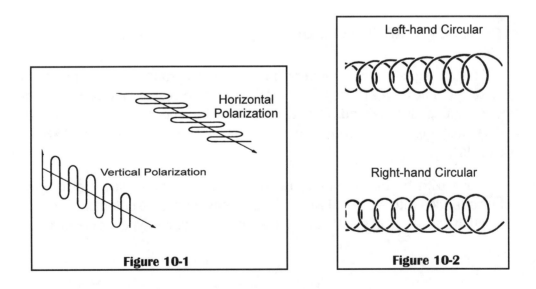

Figure 10-1

Figure 10-2

Phase

In addition, we describe signals that have the same frequency and shape in terms of phase, or when the repetitions of the signals occur in time. In-phase signals have repetitions occurring at the same time, while out-of-phase signals are displaced along a time axis. In an amplifier, the input and output have phase relationships that vary with the configuration of the amplifier circuit. In some amplifier circuits, the output voltage becomes more negative as the input voltage becomes more negative, and then becomes more positive when the input voltage becomes more positive. With the output and input voltages in step with one another, no phase shift occurs. Figure 10-3 shows an example of in-phase signals.

In other amplifier circuits, the output voltage becomes more negative as the input voltage becomes less negative, and less negative as the input voltage becomes more negative. With this, the output voltage signals are out-of-phase with the input voltage signals. Figure 10-4 shows an example of two out-of-phase signals.

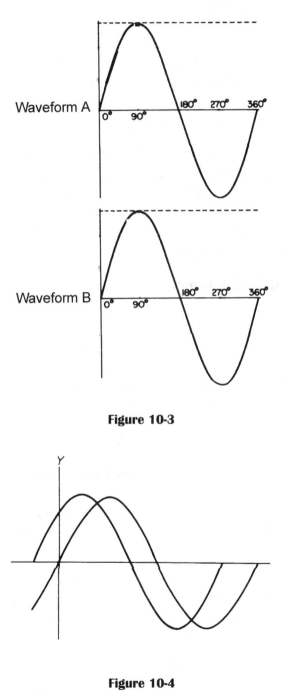

Figure 10-3

Figure 10-4

Signal Band

Radio frequency (rf) signals occupy the frequency range between 10^4 Hz and 10^{11} Hz in the frequency spectrum. As with the low-frequency energy and dc energy seen with supply voltages, we can transmit radio frequency energy over wires. Unlike low-frequency energy, however, we can also transmit radio-frequency energy through space in the form of electromagnetic waves.

Conventional rf transmissions break down into three fundamental categories. While we can define any portion of a radio wave that travels along the surface of the Earth as a ground wave, we call the portion of the wave radiated at an angle greater than horizontal the sky wave. Radio waves that travel from one antenna to another without the affect of the ground or the upper atmosphere are called direct waves.

Radio Frequency Spectrum

As shown in Table 10-1, the rf spectrum divides into eight categories. When considering the uses of each band, it's important how the frequencies differ in wavelength. For example, we could transmit frequencies within the EHF band across very long distances because of the extremely long wavelength seen with those frequencies. In practice, the Earth would absorb much of the power from the frequency waves. Even with those power losses, EHF transmitters still have a great range.

Table 10-1: Radio Frequency Bands

Designation	Abbreviation	Frequency Range (kHz)
Extremely High Frequency	EHF	30,000,000 to 300,000,000
Super High Frequency	SHF	3,000,000 to 30,000,000
Very High Frequency	UHF	300,000 to 3,000,000
High Frequency	HF	3000 to 300,000
Medium Frequency	MF	300 to 30,000
Low Frequency	LF	30 to 300
Very Low Frequency	VLF	10 to 30

Frequencies in the LF band are even more prone to losses due to Earth absorption. Yet the shorter wavelengths seen with those frequencies allow the use of highly efficient antennas. When considering the MF band, note that the commercial AM broadcast band—533 kHz to 1605 kHz—lies with those frequencies. Because of the wavelength of those frequencies, most AM radio transmissions take the form of ground waves.

The HF band covers frequencies used by foreign broadcast stations and amateur radio stations. Given the frequency band, ground wave transmissions have a limited range of 10 to 20 miles. Sky wave transmissions between 30 MHz and 60 MHz, however, have a much greater range.

Frequencies found in the VHF band cover the VHF television bands, or 54 MHz to 72 MHz, 76 MHz to 88 MHz, and 174 MHz to 216 MHz. In addition, the VHF band includes frequencies used for commercial FM broadcast transmissions. Most conventional VHF transmissions involve direct wave transmissions. The UHF band covers UHF television band frequencies, or 470 MHz to 890 MHz. Conventional UHF transmissions also involve direct wave transmissions. The last band of frequencies, the SHF band, has extremely short wavelengths and is recognized as microwave frequencies.

Noise

When we consider the use of signals to communicate, we can define any type of disturbance other than the desired signal as interference, or noise. These extraneous signals may take a variety of forms and can affect both the transmission and reception of broadcast signals. The ability of a system to reject noise is defined in terms of signal-to-noise ratio. A system with a high signal-to-noise ratio has a greater ability to reject noise. Table 10-2 defines common types of noise.

Circuit Functions

Analog and digital circuits perform the basic tasks of amplification, oscillation, and switching and contain combinations of passive and active elements. Passive elements—resistors, capacitors, and inductors—route

Table 10-2: Types of Noise

Atmospheric Noise: Radio-wave disturbances, such as lightning, that originate in the atmosphere.

Common-mode Interference: Noise caused by the voltage drops across wiring.

Conducted Interference: Interference caused by the direct coupling of noise through wiring or components.

Cosmic Noise: Radio waves generated by extraterrestrial sources.

Crosstalk: Electrical disturbances in one circuit caused by the coupling of that circuit with another circuit.

Electromagnetic Interference (emi): Noise ranging between the subaudio and microwave frequencies.

Electrostatic Induction: Noise signals coupled to a circuit through stray capacitance.

Hum: Electrical disturbance caused by a power supply frequency or harmonics of a power supply frequency.

Impulse Noise: Noise generated by a dc motor or generator. Impulse noise takes the form of a discrete, constant energy burst.

Magnetic Induction: Noise caused by magnetic fields.

Radiated Interference: Noise transmitted from one device to another with no connection between the two devices.

Radio-frequency Interference (rfi): Occurs in the frequency band reserved for communications.

Random Noise: Irregular noise signal that has instantaneous amplitude occurring randomly in time.

Static: Radio interference detected as noise in the audio frequency (af) stage of a receiver.

Terrestrial Interference: Unwanted Earth-based communication signals.

Thermal Noise: Random noise generated through the thermal agitation of electrons in a resistor or semiconductor device.

White Noise: Electrical noise signal that has continuous and uniform power.

voltages, provide feedback, and perform a variety of functions, but do not amplify or oscillate. Active elements—transistors and integrated circuits—perform amplification and oscillation. For the most part, however, amplification and oscillation cannot occur without interconnections between passive and active elements.

In electronic systems, each active element and its associated passive elements make up a stage. The three functions of amplification, oscillation, and switching performed by electronic stages and circuits lead to other processes such as modulation, demodulation, heterodyning, frequency multiplication, and frequency synthesis. To varying degrees, all those functions involve basic concepts such as gain, feedback, attenuation, and phase reversal.

Gain

The term "gain" expresses the ratio of input signal voltage, current, or power to the output signal voltage, current, or power of an amplifier. Mathematically, voltage gain appears as:

$$A_V = E_O / E_{IN}$$

where A_V represents the voltage gain, E_O represents the output signal voltage across the load, and E_{IN} equals the input signal voltage. To show the current and power gain, we substitute the output and input current or power values into the equation for:

$$A_I = I_{OUT} / I_{IN} \quad \text{and} \quad A_P = P_{OUT}/P_{IN}$$

The use of more than one stage for amplification produces total amplifier gain, or the product of the voltage gains of the individual stages.

Attenuation

Attenuation is the opposite of gain and is shown as loss. With attenuation, the output signal from an electronic circuit has a lower amplitude or signal level than the input signal. Attenuation is specified as loss through either a linear ratio or in decibels.

Bandwidth

Every amplifier has bandwidth, or a frequency range over which the amplifier has relatively constant gain. For example, typical voltage amplifiers have a bandwidth defined as the range of frequencies over which the output voltage is at least 70% of maximum when a constant amplitude input signal is applied. In this type of amplifier, the output voltage decreases rapidly at frequencies higher than that range and at frequencies lower than that range.

Coupling

Although a single transistor amplifier can provide a large gain, most electronic devices require more gain than one transistor amplifier can develop. Coupling involves the connecting of one or more amplifier stages together through various circuit configurations. The output of one stage is applied to the input of a second stage through resistance-capacitance coupling, impedance coupling, or direct coupling.

Phase

The input and output voltages of an amplifier have phase relationships that vary with the configuration of the amplifier circuit. In some amplifier circuits, the output voltage becomes more negative as the input voltage becomes more negative and then becomes more positive when the input voltage becomes more positive. With the output and input voltages in step with one another, no phase shift occurs.

In other amplifier circuits, the output voltage becomes more negative as the input voltage becomes less negative and less negative as the input voltage becomes more negative. With this, the output voltage signals are out-of-phase with the input voltage signals. In addition to in-phase and out-of-phase relationships, some applications require that signals follow, or lag, a reference signal.

Feedback

Almost every type of signal-generation technique uses feedback to control the frequency (or period) and the amplitude (or level) of an output signal. A feedback signal travels from the output signal to the input of the amplifier. At the input, the feedback modifies the control voltage that determines the size and shape of the output signal. When the feedback voltage has the same polarity or phase as the input signal, we define the feedback signal as positive feedback. Oscillators rely on positive feedback to sustain the oscillations of the amplifier.

The result of positive feedback is the increase of an input signal. A device conducting current and utilizing positive feedback will conduct more current. As the device continues to conduct, the feedback line allows a greater level of feedback signal to travel back to the input until the device saturates. When saturation occurs, the device stops conducting, and the positive feedback re-inforces the action and shuts the device off.

Other circuits rely on negative feedback or the feeding back of part of an output signal to reduce the size and shape of the output signal. In this case, the negative feedback signal has an opposite phase or polarity as seen with the input signal. Many circuit designs use negative feedback to control the gain of an output signal from an amplifier.

Amplification

Amplifiers increase either the voltage, current, or power gain of an output signal. When a signal passes through two or more stages in sequence, we define the circuits as cascade stages. The efficiency of an amplifier is the ratio of signal power output to the dc power supplied to the stage by the power supply. We can classify amplifiers by whether the device amplifies voltage or power. The term "amplifier" may describe a single stage or a transmitter or receiver section consisting of two or more stages of amplification. In a multiple-stage voltage amplifier, all stages contain voltage amplifiers. But a multiple-stage amplifier designed to provide a power output will include a power amplifier in the last stage. The other stages in the amplifier will consist of voltage amplifiers.

Voltage Amplifiers

A voltage amplifier builds a weak input voltage to a higher value, but supplies only small values of current. Thus, a voltage amplifier always operates with a load that requires a large signal voltage and a small operating current. A cathode-ray tube is an example of this type of load. Every voltage amplifier stage has voltage gain shown as the ratio of the output voltage to the input voltage.

Power Amplifiers

Even though voltage amplifiers increase the output voltage, the actual power output may remain at a low value. If the signal must operate some type of current-operated load, such as a speaker, then the low power output will not drive the load. Power amplifiers increase the power gain of the circuit by supplying a large signal current. As the following equation shows, power gain is a product of voltage and current.

$$A_P = P_{OUT}/P_{IN} = A_V \times A_I$$

A_P represents the power gain, P_{OUT} equals the output power, and P_{IN} equals the input power.

Rf Amplifier Stage Operation

The rf amplifier provides both selectivity and amplification, while increasing the voltage level of an if signal applied to its input. Given its flat bandpass, the stage should equally amplify all passing frequencies and reject any signals that lie outside the bandpass. Also, rf amplifiers should have a good signal-to-noise ratio. With these two characteristics in mind, the rf amplifier stage design strengthens desired signals, while canceling internally generated or externally generated noise. Internal noise may arise from the mixer or from the conduction of some semiconductor components. External noise is a product of electromagnetic fields generated by appliances, power lines, and unfiltered automobile ignition systems.

Furthermore, the rf stage should isolate both the oscillator and the mixer from the antenna. Isolating the mixer protects the tuner from any unwanted frequency responses or interference. Isolating the oscillator nearly eliminates any signal radiation or other interference by preventing the oscillator from sending unwanted signals back through the transmission cables. The high-level sine-wave signal generated by the oscillator can combine with the cable capacitance to become a receivable signal.

Rf amplifiers used in receivers usually operate in the class A mode to provide minimum distortion. In addition, an rf amplifier works as a tuned amplifier. At the high frequencies of the signals amplified by rf amplifiers, the internal capacitance of the device produces a low enough reactance that some signal energy feeds back from the output circuit to the input of the amplifier. Depending on the phase relationship between the feedback signal and the input signal, a high-amplitude feedback signal will cause either oscillation or degeneration at the amplifier.

Because of this, rf amplifier circuits usually employ neutralization. A neutralization circuit consists of an adjustable capacitor or neutralizing capacitor that connects from the output circuit to the input circuit. The circuit feeds back a small amount of 180° out-of-phase energy. This small amount of feedback energy cancels the original feedback signal that travels through the amplifier.

Automatic Gain Control

Automatic gain control (agc) circuits take advantage of the forward-bias characteristics of the amplifiers and either change or maintain amplifier gain by adjusting the operating conditions of the amplifier. Because of this, the dc control voltage produced by the agc circuit may push the amplifier toward either saturation or cutoff.

The agc circuit works as part of a closed feedback loop that includes a detector, a filter circuit, a feedback path to the amplifier, and the amplifier stage. When the input signal varies in amplitude, a dc correction voltage feeds from the agc circuit to the amplifier and maintains a constant amplifier gain by controlling the amplifier forward bias. Figure 10-5 (on page 180) shows a block diagram of the agc operation.

If the input signal amplitude increases, the agc circuit prevents the output of the amplifier from increasing by producing a higher dc bias control voltage. The increased bias at the amplifier reduces the gain of the amplifier stage. A

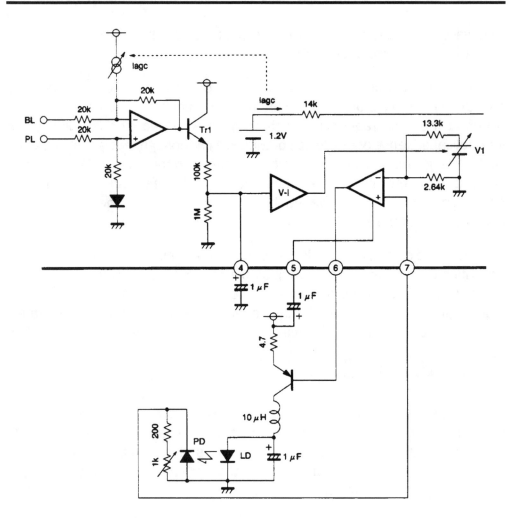

Figure 10-5

decrease in the input signal amplitude causes the agc circuit to produce a lower dc bias control voltage. Here, the decreased bias at the amplifier causes the amplifier stage gain to increase.

As mentioned, agc circuits use the operating characteristics of an amplifier to control amplifier gain. With forward agc, the automatic gain control circuit begins with a no-signal bias that produces the maximum gain of the amplifier. Increasing the bias in a forward direction causes an increased amplifier current, an increased voltage drop across a series load, and a decreased gain value at the amplifier output. In this case, the forward agc circuit pushes the amplifier toward saturation with a control voltage that has the same polarity as the bias voltage and controls gain.

Again starting with a no-signal bias that produces maximum amplifier gain, an agc circuit using reverse agc decreases the forward bias of the amplifier circuit. With a decrease in forward bias, a decrease in current through the amplifier also decreases the gain at the amplifier output. With reverse agc, the automatic gain control circuit uses a control voltage that has a different polarity from the bias voltage and pushes the amplifier toward cutoff to decrease gain.

Rf Automatic Gain Control

To provide the best signal-to-noise ratio, the rf amplifier stage of the DVD video player operates at the maximum gain for rf signal levels that have a minimum threshold level. To provide incremental control over a wide range of signal levels, an rf agc circuit connects to the rf stage and compares the signal level with a fixed dc reference value. Any signal increase above the reference level causes the agc circuit to apply a dc correction voltage to the amplifier stage.

Digital Signal Processing

A digital signal processor (DSP) translates the laser pulses back into an electrical signal. A DSP application converts analog signals to the digital domain for processing and then back for playback or display. With the DVD digital signal processor, all input signals arrive from the real world. Due to this direct connection to real-world signals, the DSP must react in real time and must measure and convert signals, such as analog voice, to digital numbers.

Zenith DVD Video Player Signal Processing

As we begin analyzing signal processing within the Zenith DVC2200 DVD video player, we should take another look at the optical and servo circuits discussed in Chapter 9. As the block diagram in Figure 10-6 (on page 182) shows, the video signal begins with information accumulated by the pickup assembly from the disc. From there, the signal progresses through the rf signal processor and to the DVD digital signal processor (DVD DSP). Output signals from the DVD digital signal processor travel to the system microcontroller and the MPEG decoder.

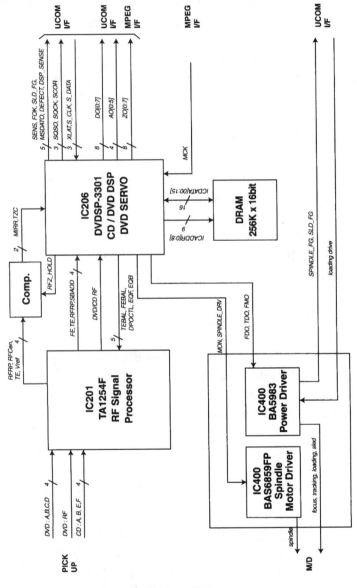

Figure 10-6

Rf Signal Processor

Referring to the diagrams shown in Figures 10-6 and 10-7 (on Pages 184-185), information embedded in an rf signal transfers from the OPU to the main circuit board through a ribbon cable to IC 2A1, the rf signal processor. IC 2A1 amplifies and equalizes the rf signal before the signal exits to IC201, the DVD digital signal processor. In addition, the circuit includes internal rf agc circuits, an internal automatic phase-control (APC) circuit, an internal auto asymmetry circuit, an internal disc-defect detector, and internal focus protect function against disc defects. (An APC circuit synchronizes the horizontal scan by using an automatic phase-control loop and input signals from the sync separator and horizontal output of the television or computer.) Figure 10-8 (on Page 186) shows a schematic diagram of the rf signal processor.

DVD Digital Signal Processor

As the schematic diagram in Figure 10-9 (on Page 187) shows, IC201 provides a number of functions for the DVD video player. The analog front end converts the high-frequency input signal to the digital domain through the use of an eight-bit analog-to-digital converter. An agc circuit, operating before the analog-to-digital converter circuit, establishes the gain control needed for obtaining optimum performance from the converter. An analog-to-digital converter clock circuit (ADCCLC) provides the clocking synchronization for the operation.

Phase-Locked Loops

A phase-locked loop (PLL) contains a voltage-controlled oscillator, prescaler and divider circuits, a comparator, and a quartz crystal, while providing a low-cost alternative to frequency synthesis. The design of the pll provides the most stable operating conditions. During operation, the pll receives an input signal and then compares that signal with the feedback of an internal clock signal generated by the voltage-controlled oscillator (vco). Given the tuning provided by the pll, the vco oscillates at a frequency where the two divided signals are equal and adjusts the feedback signal so that it matches the reference signal applied to the phase detector in both frequency and phase. As a result, the internal and external clock signals synchronize.

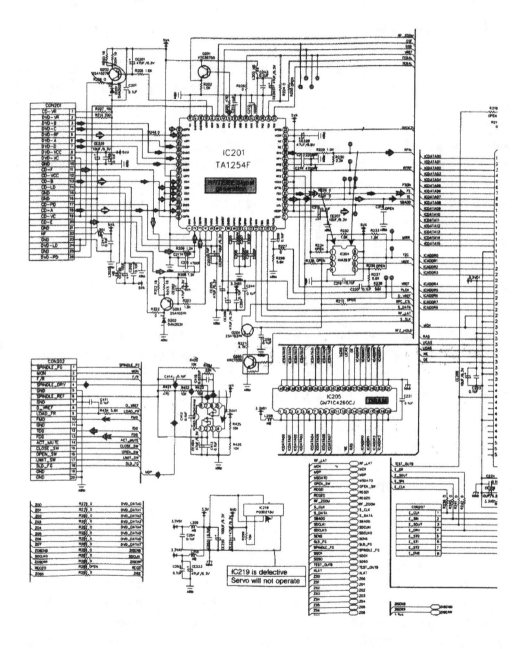

Figure 10-7a *(see next page)*

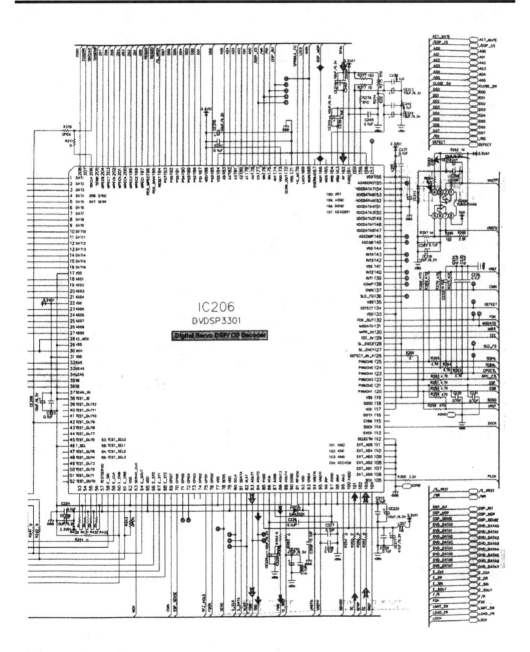

Figure 10-7b *(continued from previous page)*

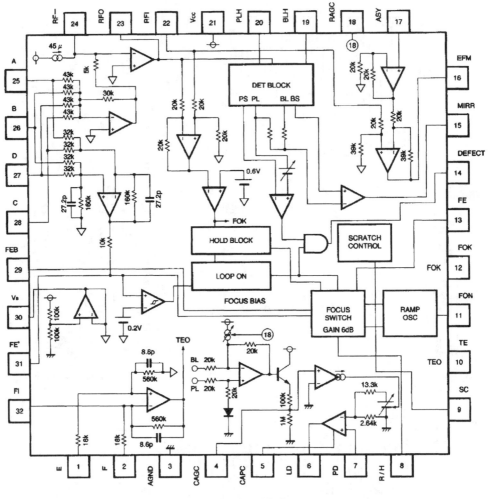

Figure 10-8

Adaptive Slicing

When the amplified and equalized rf signal enters the DVD DSP circuit, a portion of the digital signal processor serves as a data slicer, functions as a 16-to-8-bit decoder, and establishes error correction. With the playback information still embedded in the rf signal, the data slicer retrieves the embedded data and temporarily stores the data in the memory found at IC205. From that point, the data travels to the 16-to-8-bit demodulator located within IC201.

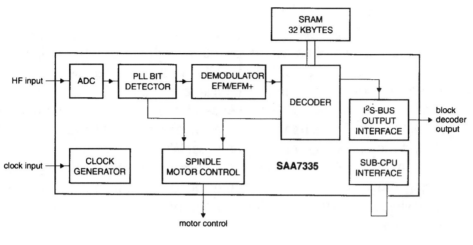

Figure 10-9

A phase-locked loop and bit detector form a subsystem that recovers data from the channel stream. The block corrects asymmetry, performs noise filtering and equalization, and finally recovers the bit clock and data from the channel through the pll. The advanced bit detector offers improved data recovery for multilayer discs and contains two extra detection circuits to increase the margins in the bit-recovery block.

Sixteen-to-8-Bit Demodulator

Two synchronization counters work within the DSP to detect the frame synchronization signals. A coincidence counter detects the coincidence of successive sync frames and generates a sync coincidence signal when two syncs occur 1488 +-EFM+ clocks apart. The main counter partitions the EFM+ signal into 16-bit words and resets after the generation of a sync coincidence and after finding a sync within +-10 EFM+ clocks of the expected sync position.

As a whole, the demodulator decodes the 16-bit EFM+ data and subcode words into eight-bit symbols. The DVD header processor accumulates a selection of bytes from the beginning of the DVD sector. In addition, the DVD header processor defines two header modes for reading the normal sector headers and for filtering the disc physical format information from the control data block in the lead-in area.

Error Correction

Once the decoding has occurred, the signal progresses through error correction for the restoration of any lost bits of data. The double-pass C1-C2 error correction corrects as many as 5 C1 frame errors and 16 C2 frame errors. At the first stage, a cross-interleave Reed-Solomon error-correction decoder uses four of the error-correction bytes to check for correctable errors that could occur during the encoding/decoding process. With interleaving, the 24 data bytes and remaining error-correction bytes pass through a set of delay circuits before going through another Reed-Solomon decoder. Each delay circuit causes the interleaving of the data so that long bursts spread through multiple passes of the second decoder.

The second decoder relies on the remaining error-correction bytes to correct any other errors that may occur in the data bytes. Within the second decoder, interpolation reconstructs bad data that's surrounded by good data. If large amounts of data test as bad, the second decoder signals the microcontroller, and the audio mutes for a fraction of a second. After the data bytes exit from the second error-correction stage, de-interleaving restores the data bytes to the correct order.

Full depth PI and PO error correction allows five corrections per PI row and full depth (2t + e) lesser than or equal to the 16 corrections performed per PO column. (PI and PO designate columns and rows within the error-correction matrix.) The error corrector also contains a flag controller and assigns flags to symbols when the error corrector can't determine the validity of the symbols. C1 generates output flags that C2 reads after de-interleaving for the purpose of generating C2 output flags. An interpolator uses the output flags to conceal uncorrectable errors.

DVD Header Processing

The DVD header processor accumulates a selection of bytes from the beginning of the DVD sector. From there, the processor defines two header modes. One header mode allows the reading of the normal sector headers, while the other enables the filtering of the disk physical format information obtained from the control data block in the lead-in area.

11

DVD Video Player Encoding and Decoding

Introduction

Earlier in this text, we found that much of the DVD technology focuses on the capability to encode and decode video and audio signals. Chapter 11 explains the characteristics of the video and audio signals through block diagrams and waveforms. After providing that basis, the chapter defines typical circuits that process video and audio circuits, as well as circuits used in the Zenith DVC2200 DVD video player. Along with video and audio signal processing, the chapter also covers the circuits that provide the MPEG, NTSC, and PAL encoding and decoding.

Video Signals

Figure 11-1 uses labels to point out the different types of signals associated with the complete composite video signal. While the sync pulses have a consistent amplitude and spacing, the changing amplitude and spacing of the luminance and chrominance signals represent the changes occurring in a transmitted picture. By definition, luminance signals represent the amount of light intensity given by a televised object, cover the full video-frequency bandwidth of 4 MHz, and provide the maximum horizontal detail.

When we look at a picture reproduced on a television screen, we see an orderly arrangement of light and dark areas. As the electron beam deflects across the inside face of the cathode-ray tube, the beam action produces a

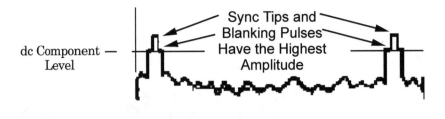

Figure 11-1

tiny spot of light where it strikes the surface. If the beam stayed at one point, then it would burn a permanent spot into the crt. Instead, the beam moves from side to side and from top to bottom as it traces successive, closely spaced horizontal lines. The pattern created by these lines is the raster.

The waveform shown in Figure 11-1 corresponds with the period where the electron beam traces the last four lines at the bottom of the reproduced picture, quickly returns to the top of the screen, and then traces the first lines of the next field. When we break the waveform down into its component parts, the eight lines of picture information are represented at each side of the diagram. At the middle of the waveform, the video waveform is shown as the electron beam returns from the bottom to the top of the picture.

All the information found within the composite video signal fits within a bandwidth of 4 MHz. This wide band of frequencies is necessary because of the different elements that make up a televised scene. In a color television receiver, the different components of the composite video signal contain the information needed to reproduce both a monochrome picture and a color picture.

The signal splits into the luminance, chrominance, and sync components. The changing amplitude and spacing of the luminance and chrominance signals represent the changes occurring in the transmitted picture. Luminance signals consist of proportional units of the red, green, and blue voltages and contain the brightness information for the picture. In addition, luminance signals cover the full video-frequency bandwidth of over 4 MHz and provide the maximum horizontal detail.

In any video picture, motion causes a succession of continuously changing voltages to occur. Also, every scene contains different amounts of light and shade that are distributed unevenly across the picture. Each light and shade element corresponds with horizontal lines and vertical fields that, in turn, match with amplitude variations. Since the amplitude variations correspond with the horizontal and vertical scan rates, a horizontal scan contains rapid amplitude changes, while vertical scans contain lower frequency variations.

Large areas of a constant white, gray, or black produce signal variations that occur at low frequencies. With no rapid changes in intensity or shade, the amplitude has fewer variations. If we take the same area and break it down into small areas of light and shade, the amplitude changes occur at a higher frequency. Video signals can include frequencies ranging from 20 Hz to over 4 MHz. Within that range, high frequencies carry the fine detail of the reproduced picture, and low frequencies cover the detail of large areas. Slow changes in background brightness occur along with changes in fine picture details. Because of this, a video amplifier stage must provide uniform or near-uniform amplification across the frequency band.

The transmitted video signal contains a brightness reference level that provides a basis for adjusting the brightness controls. This level may range from the signal level that corresponds with a maximum white raster, the signal level that produces a black raster, or a level that corresponds with a definite shade of gray. But almost all transmission standards use the level that produces a black raster as the brightness-reference level. The black level remains fixed so that—as the camera moves across a scene—the background brightness varies with respect to black. Every change in the brightness level corresponds with the intensities of the elements that make up the picture.

The luminance signal consists of an ac voltage component that corresponds with the detail in the reproduced picture and a dc voltage component that corresponds with the average background brightness. Maintaining a picture background that has proper brightness level with respect to black requires that the luminance signal retain the dc component. Using the black level as a standard allows any receiver circuit or crt type to match the varying degrees of brilliance seen with the original picture.

The composite video signal also includes vertical and horizontal blanking pulses, or retrace blanking pulses, that have amplitude greater than the black level. Because of this, a blanking pulse always reduces the scanning spot intensity to zero. Retrace blanking pulses blank the electron beam during the horizontal and vertical retrace.

Television broadcast stations use a negative transmission system based on the reduction of power. To make this easier to understand, Figure 11-2 again enlarges the composite video signal seen at the beginning of the chapter and places the waveform against the horizontal and vertical retrace periods. At the transmission point, the tips of the sync pulses cause the maximum radiated power, blanking pulses cause a 25% reduction in the radiated power, black causes another 5% reduction of radiated power, and white causes the radiated power to decrease to approximately 15% of maximum.

Hue, Saturation, and Chrominance

Primary colors are colors that do not result from the mixing of other colors. Video systems use red, green, and blue as primary colors, because the addition of these colors can produce a large number of color mixtures. The complete transmission/reception system begins with red, green, and blue signals at the camera and finishes with red, green, and blue signals at the receiver. Most systems use mixtures of the primary colors during encoding and decoding, because two color-mixed signals can contain all the color information found in the three primary colors.

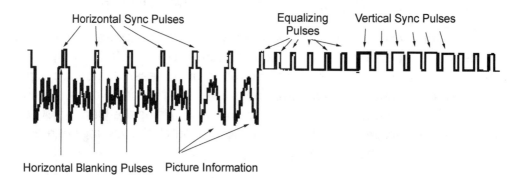

Figure 11-2

As the following equations show, the I- and Q-signals contain proportional amounts of the red, green, and blue signals.

$$I = -0.60\ R + 0.28\ G + 0.32\ B$$
$$Q = 0.21\ R + 0.31\ B - 0.52\ G$$

Combined, the I- and Q-signals must contain all the red, blue, and green color information. Thus, the two signals consist of mixtures of the colors so that the combination provides the correct information.

Although the equations show I- and Q-signals with positive polarities, both signals may also have negative polarities. As such, the polarities of the voltages that correspond with the primary colors will have the opposite polarities from those seen in the equations. Given opposite polarities, the new colors have a hue that is the direct opposite of the primary colors. Therefore, with the positive polarity I- and Q-signals representing mixtures of the primary colors, the negative polarity I- and Q-signals represent mixtures of complementary colors. A complementary color is a color that produces white light when added to a primary color.

With a positive polarity, the I-signal appears as orange, while the negative polarity I-signal shows as cyan. As a result, the I-signal contains all color mixtures between orange and cyan. Every color within these mixtures is a derivative of the red, green, and blue primary colors. Given these colors, the I-signal shows small details of color. A positive polarity Q-signal appears as purple, while a negative polarity Q-signal appears as yellow-green. Consequently, the Q-signal contains mixtures of every color between purple and yellow-green or a set of red, blue, and green mixtures.

In the previous paragraph, we found that the I- and Q-signals correspond to colors ranging between orange and cyan to purple and yellow-green. Applying in-phase and quadrature-phase modulation to the chrominance signal concentrates almost all the color information into one of the chrominance signals. Thus, the color corresponding to a complete chrominance signal resulting from the mixing of a strong I-signal and a weak Q-signal will have an orangish tint. With the opposite conditions, a weak I-signal and strong Q-signal will produce a purplish tint. Equal applications of the I- and Q-signals will yield a color some-where between orange and purple.

Every color signal represents hue, saturation, and luminance. Essentially, the hue, or tint, is the color and is represented as an angular measurement. For example, a blue sweater has a blue hue. When the human eye senses different wavelengths of light for an object, it sees different tints. Saturation represents the degree of white in a color and is represented through ampli-tude measurements. A highly saturated color is intense and vivid, while a weak color has little saturation. For example, a red signal that has low amplitude will have less saturation and will appear as pink.

Within the chrominance circuitry, separate red, blue, and green video channel voltages equal proportionate combinations of the luminance signal and the two subcarrier frequency signals, as shown in the following equations.

$$R = Y + 0.96 (I) + 0.62 (Q)$$
$$G = Y - 0.28 (I) + 0.65 (Q)$$
$$B = Y - 1.10 (I) + 1.70 (Q)$$

Amplitude variations of the complete chrominance signal indicate the amount of saturation within the color information. Therefore, when we mea-sure the amplitude of the chrominance signal, we're measuring the saturation of the signal. If we subtract luminance from hue and saturation, we have chromi-nance. In terms of signals, the chrominance signal is the 3.58 MHz modulated subcarrier signal contained within the composite video signal. Since the hu-man eye can't detect small color details, the full bandwidth of the chromi-nance signal ranges from 0 MHz to 1.5 MHz, and the used bandwidth ranges from 0 MHz to only 0.5 MHz. At the transmission point, color information modu-lates the subcarrier and produces sidebands that extend from 0.5 MHz and 1.5 MHz away from the subcarrier frequency.

Frequency Interleaving

Video signals may range anywhere between 0 MHz and 4.2 MHz during transmission. To provide a transmitted signal with color information, transmission circuitry inserts a chroma subcarrier at 3.58 MHz. In review, color information modulates the suppressed subcarrier and creates sidebands that extend 0.5 MHz above and 1.5 MHz below the subcarrier frequency.

Limiting the bandwidth of the luminance signal to approximately 3 MHz prevents the subcarrier sideband information from mixing with the 4.5 MHz sound carrier and appearing as interference in the luminance portion of the video signal. This would show as patterns in the reproduced picture. Bandwidth limiting prevents interference from occurring between the low-frequency sidebands and the high-frequency luminance signals. Unfortunately, bandwidth limiting also results in some loss of picture detail.

Frequency interleaving—or the interlacing of odd and even harmonic components of two different signals to minimize interference between the signals—allows the transmission of the chrominance signal within the same 6 MHz channel as the luminance and sound signals. Interleaving of the signals occurs because the relationship between transmitted video information and the scanning rate causes video information to appear as an energy burst between every horizontal sync pulse. Chrominance information also appears as an energy burst at the horizontal rate but—because of the introduction of a 3.58 MHz chroma subcarrier—is offset by one-half the horizontal rate. With this offset, the chroma information interleaves with the luminance information.

In Figure 11-3, the frequency components of the luminance signal cluster around the horizontal and vertical scanning frequencies and illustrate the

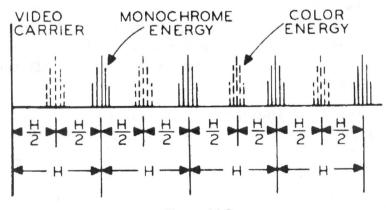

Figure 11-3

process of frequency interleaving. The horizontal scanning frequency (f_H) for a television is 15,734 Hz, and the vertical scanning frequency (f_V) is 60 Hz. As shown in Figure 11-3, luminance frequency pairs fit above and below the horizontal scanning frequency and are separated by 60 Hz gaps.

As a result, a reproduced scene that has 40 pairs of luminance frequencies requires a bandwidth of +-40 x 60 Hz or 2,400 Hz. Due to the 60 Hz separation, open spaces exist between each luminance signal cluster. Each of those spaces occurs at an odd multiple of one-half of the horizontal line-scanning frequency. Due to the relationship between the chrominance signal and the horizontal scan frequency, the chrominance signal frequencies fit, or interleave, between the clusters of luminance signal frequencies.

DVD-Video, NTSC, and PAL

One of the dilemmas faced by DVD manufacturers is achieving compatibility with different video broadcast standards. While the NTSC format has 525 scanning lines at 60 Hz and 29.97 interlaced frames per second, the PAL standard has 625 scanning lines at 50 Hz and 25 interlaced frames per second. All this translates into a difference in picture size and pixel aspect ratio (720x480 vs. 720x576), as well as display rate. To further complicate the dilemma, film has a coded frame rate of 24 progressive frames per second.

DVD technologies rely on MPEG-2 encoding and decoding to ensure the high-quality reproduction of movies and other video programming. Each disc contains one track of MPEG-2 compressed digital video either in the constant bit rate or variable bit rate format. Since the encoding process relies on a 24-frames-per-second progressive source from the original film, the MPEG-2 encoder embeds flags into the video stream to ensure compatibility with either 60 Hz or 50 Hz video standards.

DVD manufacturers have the capability to include additional video and audio so that the disc will play in either an NTSC or PAL standard player. As we saw with the interactive features, however, including additional video or audio information decreases the amount of available space for the playback of desired programming. In almost all cases, the MPEG-2 video is stored in either the NTSC or PAL format.

Players using the PAL/SECAM standard can play NTSC-formatted discs as well as PAL-formatted discs. To accomplish this, the player partially converts the NTSC signal to a 60 Hz PAL signal. The player uses the PAL 4.43 color-encoding format at a 60 Hz scanning rate with 525 lines. Modern PAL standard televisions can reproduce a picture given through this type of signal. With all this, an NTSC-formatted disc will play in a PAL standard player, while a PAL-formatted disc will not play in an NTSC standard player.

Zenith DVD Video Player Encoding and Decoding

As shown in the block diagram in Figure 11-4, the video encoding and decoding portion of the Zenith model DVC2200 DVD video player consists of the ZiVA-3 MPEG A/V Decoder IC, the Philips SAA7126 NTSC/PAL Encoder, two ROHM BA7660FS 6dB Amplifier ICs, a clock generator, and two sets of Synchronous Dynamic RAM (SDRAM). Data travels to the circuits from the Hitachi RISC-based microcontroller. Outputs for the circuits include the audio intermediate frequency (if) signals, the audio/video if connectors, and the servo if signals.

Referring to the block diagram featured in Figure 11-5, the audio decoding portion of the DVD video player includes the Burr-Brown PCM1716 and PCM1600 audio digital-to-analog converters and four operational amplifiers. Input signals travel from the system microcontroller and the MPEG A/V decoder. Dolby Digital AC-3, linear pcm, or MPEG-2 audio output signals travel to the audio/video connectors and support the attachment of home theater systems.

MPEG Audio/Video Decoding

Figure 11-6 (on Page 200) shows the functional block diagram for the ZiVA-3 decoder manufactured by C-Cube. As Table 11-1 indicates, the ZiVA-3 decoder implements 3D audio, karaoke functions, and DVD-Audio in the Zenith DVD video player series. In addition, the ZiVA-3 decoder provides full NTSC and PAL decoding in a 16-megabit SDRAM environment. The ZiVA-3 decoder supports full disc-playback compatibility with DVD, VCD, and CD-DA formats.

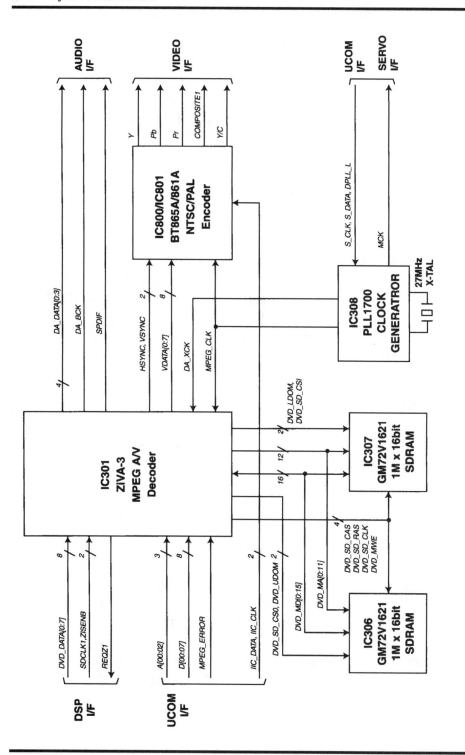

Figure 11-4

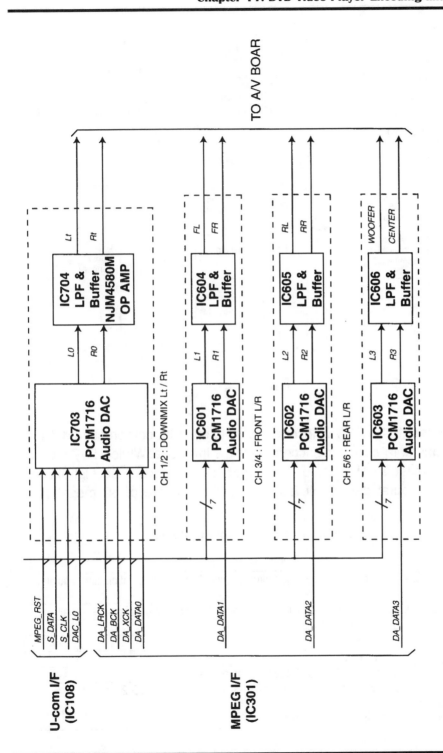

Figure 11-5

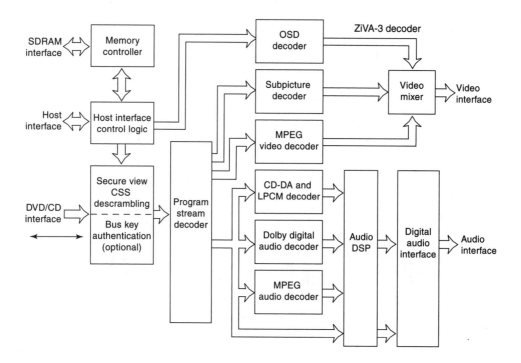

Figure 11-6

At the input, the ZiVA-3 decoder accepts eight-bit compressed data with the data transfer rates varying according to the interface. While a DVD interface has a compressed data rate of 16 megabits per second, an eight-bit host interface with burst data achieves a data transfer rate of 80 megabits per

Table 11-1: Ziva-3 Decoder Features

Karaoke functions, including vocal harmony, chorus, scoring, flange, reverberation, and simulated stereo
Home theater effects, including concert hall, dynamic range compression, and graphic equalizer
Dedicated Dolby Digital 5.1-channel decoder
Digital Theater Sound output
2/4/8-bits per pixel On-screen Display
Zoom and fade-in/fade-out functions for still and motion pictures
MPEG-2, DVD-Audio, and CD-DA Output Channels -- Dolby Digital or MPEG-2 2-channel -- 6 channel Linear PCM
Sample Rates 44.1, 48, 88.2, 96, 176.4, 192 kHz

second. Burst data at the DVD interface increases the data rate to over 100 megabits per second.

NTSC/PAL Video Encoding

Figure 11-7 shows a schematic diagram of the Philips SAA7126 NTSC/ PAL Digital Video Encoder used with the Zenith DVD video player. Basic encoding functions involve subcarrier generation, color modulation, and the insertion of synchronization signals. The SAA7126 encodes digital luminance and color difference signals into analog CVBS, Super-Video (S-video), and simultaneous Red, Green, and Blue (RGB) signals or Cr-Y-Cb signals, while supporting NTSC and PAL standards. As a result, the encoder also supports interlaced and noninterlaced scanning formats.

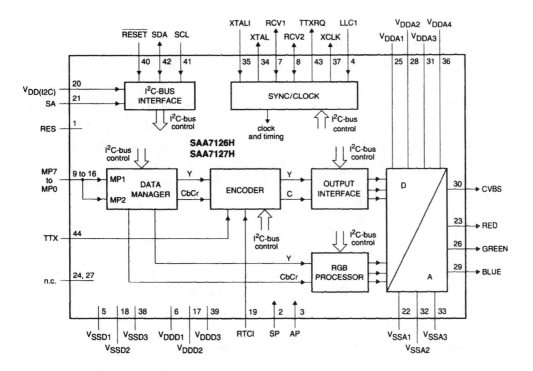

Figure 11-7

Input Signals

The video decoder expects digital Cr-Y-Cb data with digital codes that meet the CCIR 601 standard. Signals travel to and from the encoder through the I 2 C-bus interface. Operating as a standard slave transceiver, the bus supports seven-bit slave addresses and a guaranteed 400-kilobit per second transfer rate. The bus relies on eight-bit subaddressing and includes write and readable registers.

For the chrominance and composite video baseband signal (CVBS) outputs, deviating amplitudes of the color difference signals can be compensated by independent gain control setting, while gain for luminance is set to predefined values. The respectively Cr-Y-Cb path features a gain setting individually for luminance and color difference signals.

Encoder Video Path

The SAA7126 Digital Video Encoder uses the Y, U, and V baseband signals to generate luminance and color subcarrier output signals suitable for use as CVBS or separate luminance and chrominance signals. Utilizing gain levels achieved through the programmable setting of different black signal levels, the encoder modifies the luminance signal. After inserting a fixed synchronization pulse tip level, the circuit sets the blanking level. To enable easy analog post filtering, the encoder interpolates the luminance signal from a 13.5 MHz data rate to a 27 MHz data rate and provides a 10-bit resolution luminance output signal.

Circuitry within the encoder again uses different gain levels to modify the chrominance signal. To accomplish this, the encoder inserts a standard dependent burst signal before the interpolation of baseband color signals occurs. Given programmable amplitude for the purpose of providing either standard signals or special effects, the baseband color signals interpolate from a 6.75 MHz data rate to a 27 MHz data rate. Bypassing one of the interpolation stages makes a higher color bandwidth available for the luminance/chrominance output.

RGB Processing

The RGB processing block dematrixes the digital red and blue color difference signals and the luminance signal to produce red, green, and blue signals. Before the dematrix operation occurs, the circuit applies individual gain adjustments for the signals along. In addition, the block provides two times oversampling for the luminance signal and four times oversampling for the color difference signals.

At the output of the processing block, software controls or minimum output voltages control the output signal given by digital-to-analog converters. Along with converting the encoded luminance and chrominance signals from the digital format to an analog form with 10-bit resolution, the converters also convert the red, green, and blue signals from digital-to-analog at a nine-bit resolution. The processor combines the luminance and chrominance signals to produce a 10-bit CVBS signal.

Synchronization

The synchronization circuit operates in either slave mode or master mode. When operating in the master mode, the circuit generates all necessary timing signals. As a result, the video signal can provide timing signals at the RCV1 and RCV2 ports. In slave mode, the circuit accepts timing information either from the RCV pins or from the embedded timing data found within the video data stream. The slave mode operation also allows the interface circuit to set a vertical sync, odd/even, or field sequence signal at the RCV1 pin.

Filtering Luminance and Chrominance Signals

Luminance and chrominance signals are filtered in accordance with the standard requirements of "RS-170-A" and "ITU-R BT.470-3." For ease of analog post filtering, the signals are twice oversampled with respect to the pixel clock before digital-to-analog conversion. The digital-to-analog converters (dacs) for Y, C, and CVBS are realized with full 10-bit resolution—and nine-bit resolution for RGB output. The Cr-Y-Cb to RGB dematrix can be bypassed optionally in order to provide the upsampled Cr-Y-Cb input signals. While the eight-bit multiplexed Cb-Y-Cr formats are CCIR 656 compatible, operation in the slave mode allows the optional decoding of the SAV (start-of-active-video) and EAV (end-of-active-video) codes.

At input port LLC1, the encoder accepts signals either from the phase-locked loop (PLL) clock generator through the MPEG decoder or from the buffered on-chip clock designated as XCLK. As the encoder processes two independent data streams, the rising edge of LLC1 latches one data stream and the falling edge of LLC1 latches the other. As a result, the encoder can forward one of the data streams containing both video and on-screen display (OSD) information to the RGB outputs.

Closed Caption Encoder

Using this circuit, data for closed caption or extended data services encodes on line 21 and delivers through the control interface. With each pair preceded by run-in clocks, two dedicated pairs of bytes per field become possible and allow the modification of the encoded data line number. The data clock frequency is defined by the NTSC-M standard 32 times horizontal line frequency. Data LOW at the output of the dacs corresponds to 0 IRE, while data HIGH at the output of the dacs corresponds to approximately 50 IRE. The closed caption data can encode for 50Hz field frequencies at 32 times the horizontal line frequency.

Copy Protection

While the encoder provides closed caption and extended data services encoding, it also supports the Macrovision anti-taping signal generation. In addition, the encoder can load data for the copy-generation management system into line 20 of every NTSC field. The data contains information that affects the black and blanking level control, color subcarrier frequency, and the variable burst amplitude.

PAL Video Encoding

The other stream contains only video and travels to the encoded CVBS and S-video outputs. Providing an early composite sync pulse for three clock

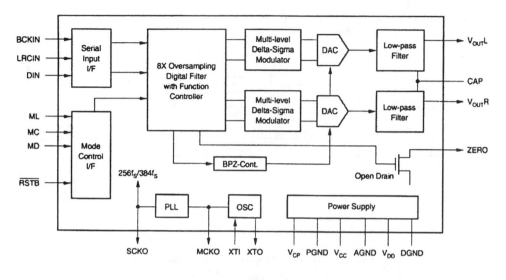

Figure 11-8

periods at the CVBS output establishes the optimum display of RGB signals through a Euro-connector television. Information concerning the actual subcarrier, PAL-ID, and definite subcarrier phase inserts at the RTCI pin and connects to the RTCO pin of a decoder.

The encoder IC synthesizes the color subcarrier frequency and synchronization signals using the signals found at the RTCI and RTCO pins. Wide-screen signaling data loads through the bus and inserts into line 23 for standards using a 50 Hz field rate. Video program system (VPS) data for program-dependent automatic start and stop of compatible VCRs also loads through the bus. During reset and after the releasing of reset, the encoder sets all digital input/output stages to the input mode. With that action, the encoder sets to PAL mode and outputs a "black burst" signal on the CVBS and S-video outputs. In addition, the encoder sets the RGB outputs to the lowest possible output voltages.

Audio Decoding

As shown in Figure 11-8, the Burr-Brown PCM1716 stereo audio digital-to-analog converter includes a phase-locked loop circuit that derives the system clock from an external 27 MHz reference frequency. The converter

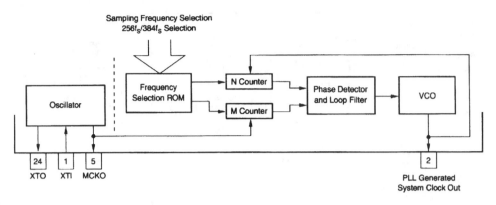

Figure 11-9

works well for applications that combine compressed audio and video data such as DVD, DVD-ROM, set-top boxes, and MPEG sound cards. In brief, the PCM1716 contains a third-order Delta-Sigma modulator, a digital interpolation filter, and an analog output amplifier. While the modulator can accept 16-, 20-, or 24-bit input data, the digital filter performs an 8X interpolation function and includes selectable features such as soft mute, digital attenuation, and digital de-emphasis. The phase-locked loop accepts programming for sampling at standard digital audio frequencies, as well as one-half and double sampling frequencies. Figure 11-9 shows a block diagram of the phase-locked loop function.

Amplifying the Video Signal

As shown in Figure 11-10, the Rohm BA7660FS amplifier operates as a 75-ohm driver that includes a 6 dB amplifier and three internal circuits. The circuit drives the composite luminance and chrominance signals, as well as RGB signals. Each load can drive two circuits, while using a sag correction function to reduce the capacitance of the output coupling capacitor.

Since the amplifier operates from an input voltage ranging from 0V dc to 1.5V dc, it can connect directly to the output of a digital-to-analog converter. An internal power-saving circuit provides simultaneous muting on all three channels, as well as output pin-shorting protection. In addition, the circuit features an internal output protection circuit.

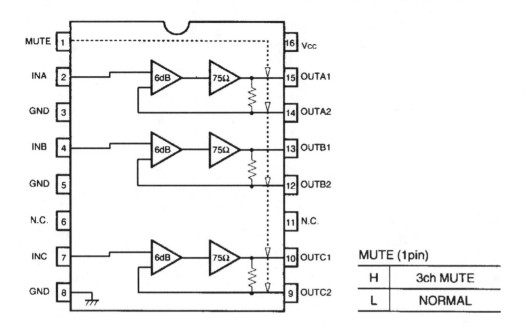

MUTE (1pin)	
H	3ch MUTE
L	NORMAL

Figure 11-10

DVD Video Player Microcontroller and Customer Display Circuits

Introduction

Chapter 12 continues with the analysis of DVD player circuits by examining the operation of the system microcontroller, as well as the customer control, customer display, and remote-control circuits. With the overview of system microcontroller operation, the chapter introduces the operation of RISC-based microcontrollers. In addition, Chapter 12 shows the integration involved with typical DVD video player operations. By closing with a look at customer controls and displays, the chapter shows how circuit functions interface with the needs of the customer.

Microcontrollers

Microcontrollers provide the basic control functions seen in industrial equipment and in consumer electronics products. As a result, the devices have widespread use. But changing consumer industry demands for more processing power have softened the lines between embedded microprocessors, embedded controllers, and digital signal processors. Several manufacturers have introduced devices that combine the functionality of all three devices within one package. Microprocessors differ in the amount of instructions executed, the number of bits processed within a single instruction, and the number of instructions that the processor can execute per second. Microcontrollers employ either the complex instruction-set computing (CISC) architecture or the reduced instruction-set computing (RISC) architecture.

RISC-based microcontrollers provide superscalar architectures that have multiple-execution units capable of executing two or more instructions simultaneously. Superior pipelining schemes add pipeline stages to the processor and allow the placement of multiple instructions in the CPU execution queue. As a result, new instructions in the pipeline begin with each clock cycle.

Each of these architectural improvements has led to the addition of more complex instruction sets to superscalar processors. Due to the increase to 128-bit-wide buses in microprocessors such as the Alpha, CPU word lengths have grown from 16 to 64 bits. With this, 64-bit data words can be divided into two, four, and eight subwords. As a result, a processor involved with digital signal processing, image processing, or multimedia applications can perform as many as eight parallel computations on the data words.

The improved computational power also results from minimum clock speeds of 200 MHz to maximum clock speeds of 600 MHz and higher, along with exceptional integer and floating-point performance. At the high end, data throughput may reach 2 billion instructions per second. Each of the improvements in computational power and throughput also requires the addition of large caches, the use of dynamic execution control, the implementation of multiple execution units, and advances in register logic and branch prediction.

Embedded Microcontrollers

An embedded microcontroller is a highly integrated chip that contains a central processing unit, random-access memory, some form of read-only memory, input/output ports, and timers. Unlike a microprocessor, which also includes all of these components, a microcontroller is designed for a very specific task—that is, a microcontroller controls a particular system. An embedded microcontroller functions as one part of a larger device or system.

Almost every consumer electronics device or home appliance incorporates some type of microcontroller. Typically including a central processing unit, random-access memory, erasable programmable read-only memory, serial and parallel I/O ports, timers, and an interrupt controller, a microcontroller controls some type of process or some aspect of the environment. Embedded microcontrollers work on the same principle as microcontrollers, but usually require the connection to external components before operations can begin. For example, many embedded microcontrollers require a connection to external system memory, because of the processes needed to complete a task. Yet, more sophisticated market applications and declining memory prices have allowed the integration of microcontroller cores with different types and higher densities of memory.

Zenith DVD Video Player Control Circuits

The block diagram shown in Figure 12-1 (on Page 212) depicts the operation of a Hitachi SH6417034 Super H RISC-based microcontroller that provides all control functions for the Zenith DVC2200 DVD video player. Working from left to right, the microcontroller accepts input signals from IC506, which is an interface IC connected to the front panel controls and the remote-control circuits. As the microcontroller accepts user commands through the interface IC, it sends clock and data signals along the main bus to the servo control and signal processing circuits found within the DVD digital signal processor (dsp).

In addition, the microcontroller also sends clock, data, and reset signals to the ZiVA-3 MPEG Decoder. Flash ROM, EEPROM, and DRAM found at IC502, IC503, and IC504 store static and dynamic commands for the microcontroller.

Main Microcontroller

As shown in Figure 12-1, the SH6417034 microcontroller utilizes a RISC-type instruction set and integrates the functions required for system configuration onto a single integrated circuit. The microcontroller executes most instructions in one system clock cycle and features a 32-bit internal architecture for enhanced data-processing capabilities. With the device controlling all system configuration functions, it also includes peripheral functions such as large-capacity read-only and random-access memories, a direct memory access controller, timers, a serial communication interface, an analog-to-

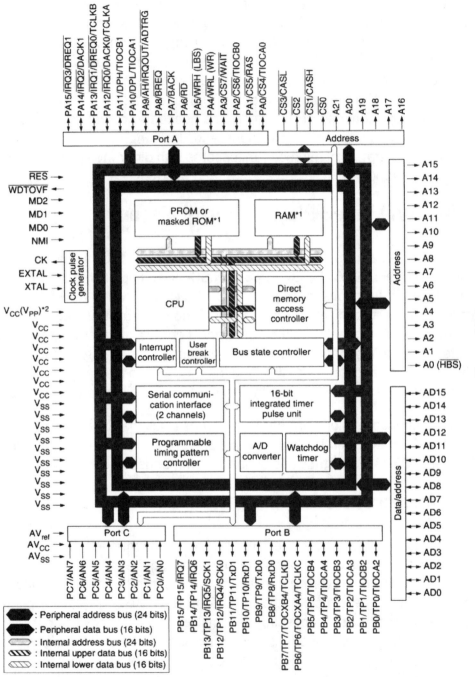

Figure 12-1

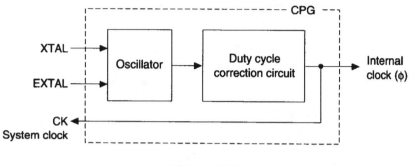

Figure 12-2

digital converter, an interrupt controller, and input/output ports. External memory access support functions allow direct connection to SRAM and DRAM devices. In addition, the microcontroller accepts data from EEPROM devices programmed by users.

As shown in the schematic diagram in Figure 12-2, the SH6417034 includes a built-in clock pulse generator that supplies the microcontroller and any connected external devices with clock pulses. As the schematic shows, the clock pulse generator consists of an oscillator and a duty cycle correction circuit. Through the use of the oscillator, the microcontroller synchronizes to the oscillation frequency of the crystal resonator.

An integrated bus state controller (BSC) divides address space and provides control signals for memory and peripheral circuits. The functions found within the bus state controller allow the connection of the microcontroller directly to DRAM, SRAM, ROM, or peripheral devices. (DRAM, or Dynamic Random Access Memory, provides a temporary storage space for data, while SRAM, or Static Random Access Memory, operates as a temporary form of memory and offers faster access times than DRAM.) The elimination of external interface circuits through the use of the BSC decreases the operating cost of the microcontroller and facilitates high-speed data transfers.

Setting the DRAM enable bit to digital 1 generates the DRAM interface function and allows the direction connection between the microcontroller and the memory devices. The additional setting of the multiplex enable bit in the DRAM control register to a digital one directly connects the SH6417034 to

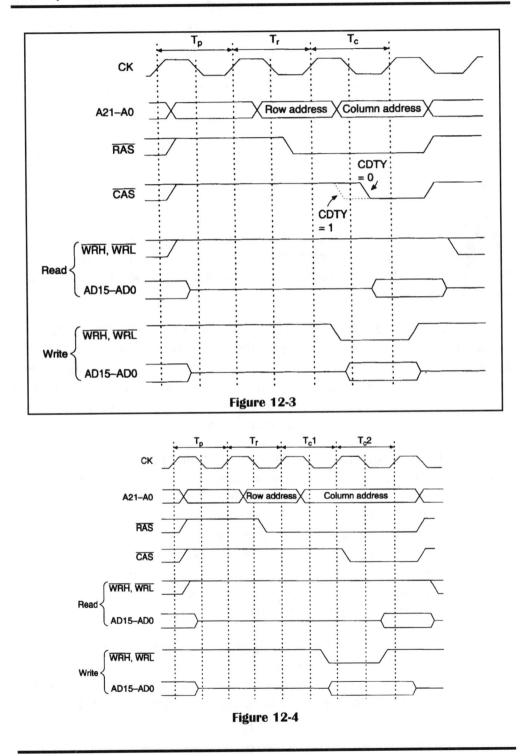

Figure 12-3

Figure 12-4

DRAM devices that require the multiplexing of address and column addresses. As shown in Figures 12-3 and 12-4, the microcontroller relies on short pitch and long pitch DRAM access.

Using the RW1 and WW1 bits in WCR1 and the DRW1 and DWW1 bits in WCR2, the microcontroller can select either type of timing. With the bits set to a digital zero, the microcontroller relies on short pitch timing and the DRAM pitch and column addressing occurs in one state. Setting the bits to a digital one establishes long pitch timing and causes the DRAM pitch and column addressing to occur in two states.

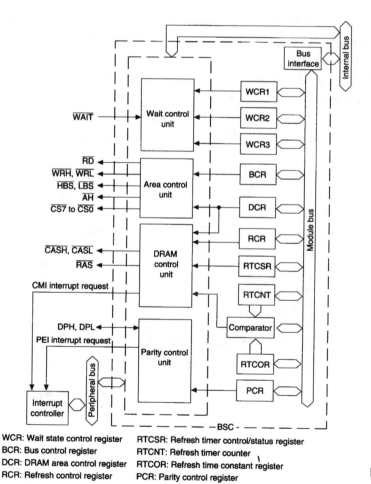

WCR: Wait state control register
BCR: Bus control register
DCR: DRAM area control register
RCR: Refresh control register

RTCSR: Refresh timer control/status register
RTCNT: Refresh timer counter
RTCOR: Refresh time constant register
PCR: Parity control register

Figure 12-5

As mentioned, the bus state controller also allows the direct connection between the microcontroller and peripheral circuits that require address or data multiplexing. The multiplexing occurs on pins AD15 through AD0 in area six of the microcontroller. With the multiplexed input/output enable bit in the bus-control register (BCR) set to one, the area six space changes into an address/data multiplexed input/output space that multiplexes addresses and data. As Figure 12-5 (on Page 215) shows, accesses in the address/data multiplexed I/O space happen in four states. With the A14 address bit set to zero, address output and data input/output occur on the eight-bit wide AD7 to AD0 bus. Setting the A14 address bit to one enables the addressing operation on the 16-bit wide AD15 to AD0 bus.

Given the bus arbitration characteristics of the microcontroller, the device can release the bus to external devices as requested. The SH6417034 utilizes two internal bus masters, with priority given to the bus master residing within the main processor. A second bus master resides within the direct memory access controller. An external device has priority when generating a BREQ bus request (a bus request by an external device that requires ownership of the bus for a given process). Figure 12-6 shows the bus release procedure.

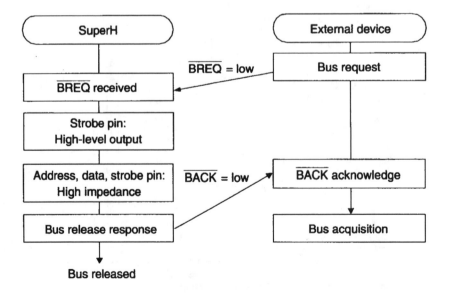

Figure 12-6

The four-channel, direct-memory access controller operates in place of the processor and performs high-speed burst transfers between external devices. The devices must use a data acknowledgment (DACK) transfer-request signal and have access to external memory, include on-chip memory, and use on-chip supporting modules. Using the DMAC reduces the burden on the CPU and increases overall operating efficiency.

In addition to communicating through the main bus, the microcontroller also relies on a serial communication interface (SCI). Given two independent but identical channels, the serial communication interface supports asynchronous and synchronous serial communication. Moreover, the SCI has a multiprocessor communication function that establishes serial communication between the microcontroller and the DVD digital signal processor.

An analog-to-digital converter module located within the SH6417034 accepts analog signals over a maximum of eight channels. Operating by successive approximation with a 10-bit resolution, the A/D converter has a single mode and a scan mode. In the single mode, the module performs analog-to-digital conversion on a single channel. In the scan mode, the module monitors analog inputs on one or more channels. Analog-to-digital conversion begins with the first channel in the group and—once the first channel conversion has completed—continues cyclically with the next selected channels.

Customer Preference Controls

Control of any DVD video player begins with the customer interface. With electronic tuners, the customer interface and the control system begins with some type of keypad or remote-control device. In addition, the customer interface includes either a channel display based on light-emitting diodes (LEDs) or an on-screen display (OSD).

Selection and tuning begin when the customer uses either a pushbutton, keypad, or remote-control device to start instruction sets into motion. In addition to working with receiver controls, the customer also needs some method for finding which channel is selected. Along with providing some type of customer control, the DVD player must also have either a display that uses LEDs or an on-screen display.

The user interface to the DVD player is a remote control. All DVD player manufacturers are required to have similar buttons and functionality on their remotes, including play, stop, pause, next program, previous program, title menu, root menu, up, down, left, right, enter, and return. Additionally, remote controls must include a numeric keypad, although this may be hidden in an access panel within the remote.

Frequency Synthesis Section

In addition to microprocessors and memory devices, electronically controlled tuners rely on frequency synthesis for maintaining the exact selected frequency.

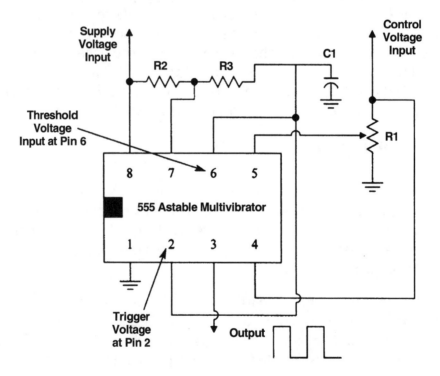

Figure 12-7

In some instances, the voltage-control oscillator (vco) portion of the tuning control circuit will consist of two emitter follower transistors combined with a differential amplifier, a fixed crystal that resonates at approximately 4 MHz, and a frequency adjust capacitor. Most tuner designs, however, use a 555-based astable multivibrator such as the one depicted in Figure 12-7 as a vco.

In Figure 12-7, a decrease in the control voltage causes the difference between the oscillator threshold and trigger voltages to decrease. The threshold voltage is a value that switches the multivibrator on, while the trigger voltage is a value that causes oscillation to occur. Varying R1 can either increase or decrease the control voltage at pin 4 of the multivibrator, while the internal circuitry of the IC controls the charge/discharge of C1. Thus, reducing the difference between the trigger and threshhold voltages also reduces the time needed to charge and discharge the capacitor. Since C1 connects to both the trigger input and the threshhold input, the output is a steady stream of pulses. With the decreased discharge time, the circuit cycle time also decreases and causes the output frequency to increase.

Frequency Division and Multiplication

Frequency division involves producing an output signal that has a fractional relationship—such as 1/2, 1/3, or 1/10—to the input signal. A frequency multiplier consists of:

- a time-varying circuit that introduces harmonics at the output along with the fundamental frequency
- a resonant circuit tuned to the desired output frequency

The resonant circuit passes only the desired output frequency to the load, while rejecting other frequencies including the fundamental frequency. For example, a frequency tripler uses a 1 MHz oscillator to convert dc power from a power supply line into a 1 MHz sine wave. When the sine wave feeds a non-linear amplifier, the amplifier symmetrically distorts the signal so that the positive and negative peaks flatten. With this flattening, the amplifier introduces odd harmonics into the signal.

As a result, the output signal consists of the 1 MHz fundamental frequency along with a sequence of odd harmonic frequencies. Starting with the third harmonic, each harmonic is progressively less than the fundamental. At the output, an LC tank circuit tuned to 3 MHz passes the 3 MHz signal, while rejecting the fundamental and all other harmonic frequencies.

Frequency Synthesis

Frequency synthesis is a method of digitally generating a single desired, highly accurate, sinusoidal frequency from the range of a highly stable master reference oscillator. The desired frequency corresponds with a precise function of subharmonic and/or harmonic relationships found in the reference oscillator frequency. With this, a frequency synthesizer translates the performance of the reference oscillator into useful frequencies. When designs employ several reference oscillators, the possible number of output frequencies exceeds the number of oscillators.

Most low-cost frequency synthesis circuits use frequency division to produce the desired frequency. The frequency division occurs through the use of a counter, because of the ability of the device to function over a wide bandwidth. Frequency synthesis accomplished through this method can only produce an output frequency that has a lower value than the input frequency. Since crystal oscillators have a top frequency of 200 MHz, frequency synthesizers using frequency division are capable of working at frequencies less than 100 MHz.

Other frequency synthesizer circuits rely on frequency multiplication. With this technique, an oscillating signal passes through a diode, transistor, or varactor diode. Then, the nonlinear semiconductor elements produce harmonics of the original signal. After that, the harmonically rich signal passes through a sharp, narrow-band filter that attenuates any undesired harmonics.

Another frequency synthesis method involves the mixing of frequencies. A mixer multiplies frequencies and generates a signal that contains both the sum and the difference of the two input frequencies. The circuit uses one frequency as the desired frequency and discards the other through filtering.

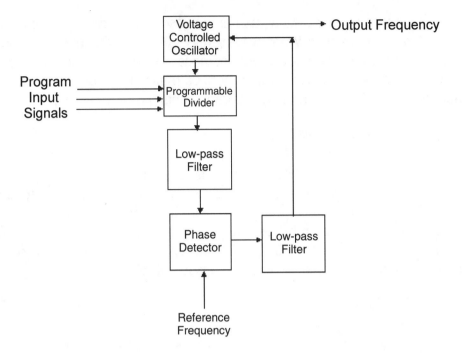

Figure 12-8

Frequency Synthesizer Operation

Figure 12-8 shows the operation of a basic frequency synthesizer. In the figure, the master reference oscillator has two outputs. Two divide-by-10 circuits divide the oscillator frequency by 10 and then subdivide those dividends by 10. As a result, two accurate subharmonics—a tenth and a hundredth—of the master oscillator frequency exist.

Within this frequency synthesis system, the output of a stable reference oscillator divides into precise subharmonics. Then, some type of discrete or integrated switching arrangement would select the proper harmonics, add the frequencies, and output the signal through a bandpass filter. The filter would allow only the desired frequency to pass and has an extremely precise frequency at the output.

The locking portion of a frequency synthesis circuit depends on the precise measurement, division, and comparison of two input frequencies. While the tuner oscillator supplies an input signal, a reference oscillator provides a known and stable reference frequency. When we begin to look at the frequency synthesis circuit as a whole, dividers and a prescaler measure the input pulses as a series of binary numbers and divide the numbers so that the output is a usable low frequency. Each off and on of the pulse represents a binary number.

Voltage-Controlled Oscillators

Indirect frequency synthesis circuits usually rely on a voltage-controlled oscillator to generate a frequency. With the vco, a square-wave output frequency has an inversely proportional relationship with the input voltage. Therefore, a low input control voltage produces a high output frequency, and a high input control voltage produces a low output frequency. Most vco designs rely on the precise frequency relationships given by a 555 astable timer.

Phase-Locked Loops

As mentioned in Chapter 10, a phase-locked loop (PLL) contains a volt-age-controlled oscillator, prescaler and divider circuits, a comparator, and a quartz crystal, while providing a low-cost alternative to frequency synthesis. The design of the phase-locked loop provides the most stable operating conditions. As Figure 12-9 shows, the PLL receives an input signal and then compares that signal with the feedback of an internal clock signal generated by the vco. Given the tuning provided by the phase-locked loop, the vco oscillates at a frequency where the two divided signals are equal and adjusts the feed-

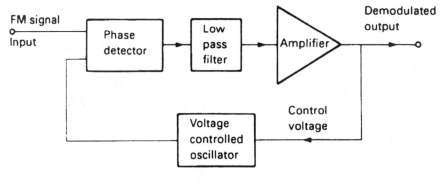

Figure 12-9

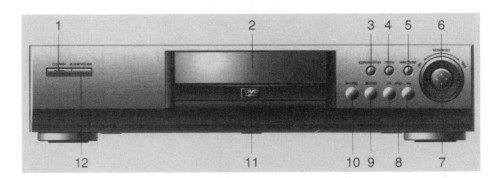

Figure 12-10

back signal so that it matches the reference signal applied to the phase detector in both frequency and phase. As a result, the internal and external clock signals synchronize.

Many PLL designs rely on a "charge pump" consisting of inverters, switches, and a passive RC low-pass filter. As shown in Figure 12-9, the input signal from the first frequency divider clock enters a phase detector. In this example, the phase detector consists of a set of buffers and D-type flip-flops. The phase detector compares the clock input with a feedback signal from the vco. The frequency divider portion of the PLL may use a basic digital counter or something as complex as a single-sideband modulator and translates the input and output frequencies to usable levels.

Zenith DVD Video Player Customer Controls

As Figure 12-10 shows, the Zenith DVC2200 DVD video player offers customer control through front panel controls, as well as through a remote control. Figure 12-11 (on Page 224) provides a block diagram of the circuit operation. The front panel controls provide access to the following functions.

- power
- play
- skip/scan
- select/enter

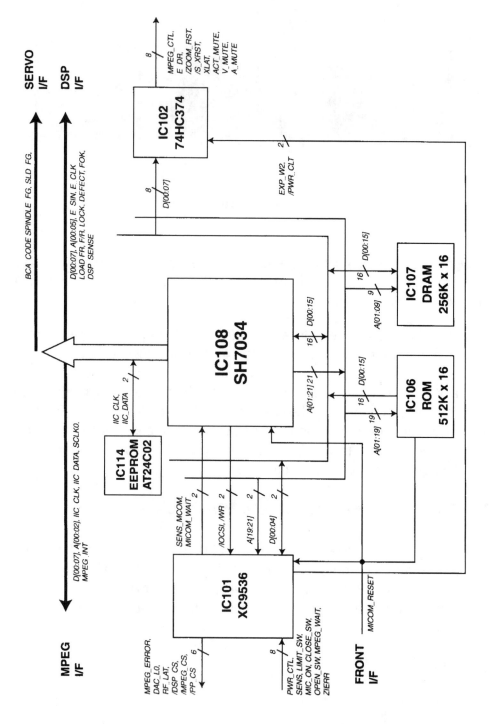

Figure 12-11

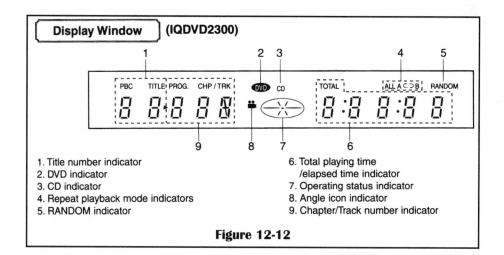

1. Title number indicator
2. DVD indicator
3. CD indicator
4. Repeat playback mode indicators
5. RANDOM indicator

6. Total playing time
   /elapsed time indicator
7. Operating status indicator
8. Angle icon indicator
9. Chapter/Track number indicator

Figure 12-12

- pause/step
- menu
- stop
- disc tray open and close

In addition, the DVD video player offers both an on-screen display and the LCD display illustrated in Figure 12-12. As the figure shows, the LCD display matches each of the DVD-Video functions described in Chapter 4 with an indicator. The display indicators include:

- operating status
- compact disc or DVD disc
- angle icon
- title number
- program
- chapter/track
- random playback mode
- total playing time/elapsed playing time.

Figure 12-13 (on Page 226) is a schematic diagram of the timer and key circuits that interface between the viewer and the control circuits found within the player. As shown in the diagram, IC500 establishes the processes required for each function. At the middle left of the diagram, the Remocon Receiver

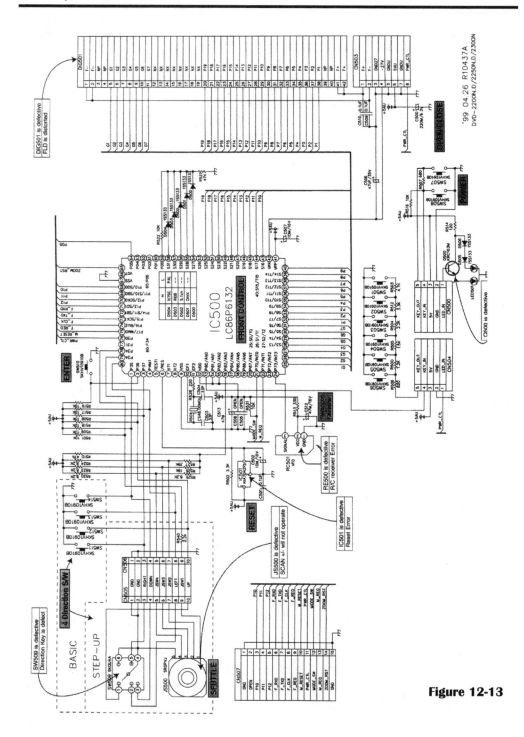

Figure 12-13

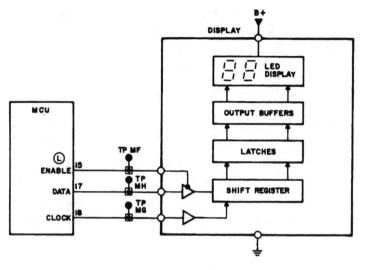

Figure 12-14

interfaces with the remote control. The interface connector found at the far right of Figure 12-13 connects the timer and key circuits to the microcontroller.

Customer Display Technologies

Figure 12-14 shows a block diagram for a channel display using light-emitting diodes and data from a microprocessor. When the customer selects a function using the remote control, the microprocessor senses the key closure. Then, the processor sends data, clock, and enable signals to the channel display circuit through three output lines. The display circuitry—which includes a combination of latches, buffers, and a shift register—decodes and stores the serial data. The proper segments of the channel display are driven to light by the data. In addition, three voltage sources — +5.4V dc for the display circuitry, +3.2V dc for the LED, and +4.3V dc for the LED segment brightness—power the display assembly.

On-Screen Channel and Menu Displays

Many DVD video players use on-screen displays to show everything from the time, volume settings, channels, and current channel to customer preferences and menu selections. In all cases, a character generator—enclosed in an integrated circuit—produces alphanumeric characters that can be positioned in different areas of the screen. Generally, however, the current channel number will display in the upper right screen and the time will display in the lower left corner.

The display circuit takes advantage of the red, blue, and green output signals found at the chrominance/luminance control integrated circuit. For example, the selection of a new channel causes the on-screen display integrated circuit to send a blanking signal to the character blanking transistor Q1. The transistor shorts the output signals from the chroma/luminance IC to ground, while the data from the on-screen display IC output goes to the RGB buffer transistors.

Zenith DVD Video Player LCD Display Circuit Operation

As shown in Figure 12-15, the LCD display controller drives liquid crystal displays with up to 32 segments directly or 64 segments in a duplex

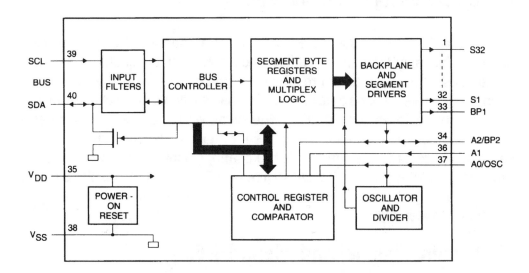

Figure 12-15

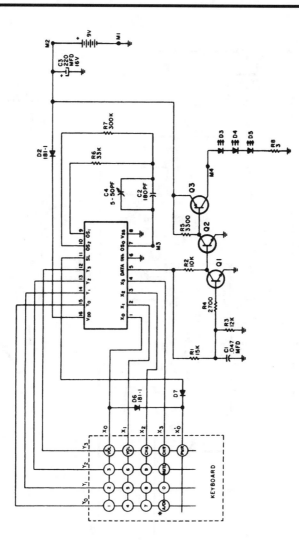

Figure 12-16

configuration. In the direct drive mode, the A2/BP2 pin becomes the exclusive A2 input. When operating in the duplex drive mode, the controller requires the second backplane signal found at BP2, and the A2 signal becomes undefined. In this mode, device selection occurs from lines A0 and A1.

The display controller relies on a single-pin, built-in oscillator that provides the modulation for the LCD segment-driver outputs. One external resistor and

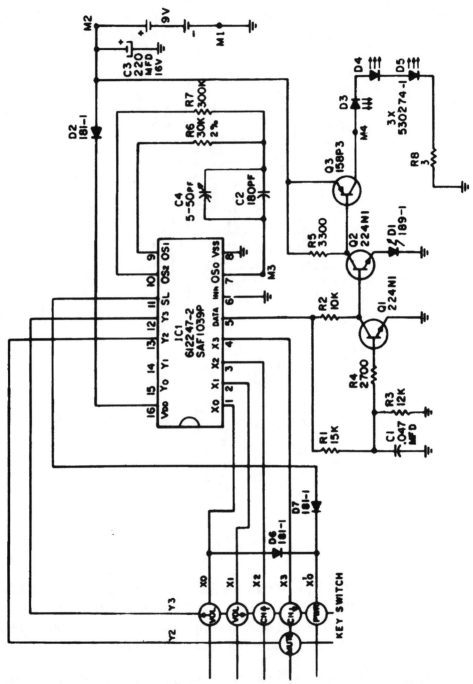

Figure 12-17

one external capacitor connect to the AO/OSC pin to form the oscillator. In addition, the circuit also uses nine user-accessible 1-byte registers. While the first register controls the loading of data into the segment byte registers used to select display options, the remaining eight registers split into two banks of storage and store the segment data.

Remote Controls and Remote Receivers

Figure 12-16 (on Page 229) shows a schematic for an infrared remote transmitter. The transmitter sends a 14-bit signal containing viewer selection information to the remote preamplifier circuit shown in Figure 12-17. During operation, the remote preamplifier applies the 14-bit signal to the microcontroller. When the first bit of the data string reaches the input pin, the digital level at the pin goes high and the microcontroller releases digital low enable pulses. The presence of the enable pulses allows the remote preamplifier to send the remainder of the data to the microcontroller.

Volume Control

The volume control circuit shown in Figure 12-18 receives serial data from the microcontroller and converts the data into a variable dc voltage that controls an audio IC. Going back to the keyboard for a moment, the

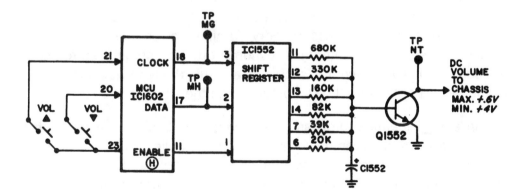

Figure 12-18

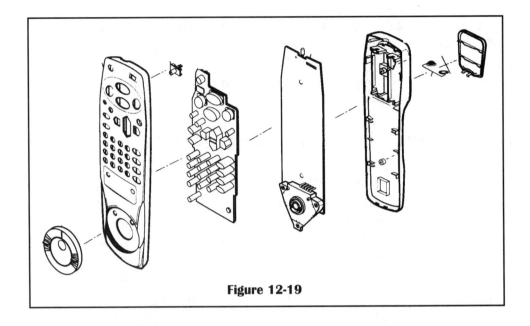

Figure 12-19

microcontroller senses the closing of either the volume-up or volume-down control. If the customer pushes the volume-up key, the microcontroller internal circuitry sends a logic high signal to pin 11 of the microprocessor. From there, an enable signal travels to pin 2 of a shift register, which is an integrated circuit that accepts and holds the serial data until the customer changes the volume.

When the customer turns the receiver off, the microcontroller uses an instruction set to store the serial data that represents the current volume level into the system random-access memory. Turning the receiver on causes the microcontroller to issue another instruction set that outputs the stored serial data back to the volume-control circuit. As a result, the receiver has the same volume level heard before the customer turned the power off.

An almost identical process occurs when the customer uses another function with the remote control. Again, the microcontroller issues an instruction set that stores serial data representing a volume level into the system RAM. But the microcontroller also sends a string of serial data 1s that cause the

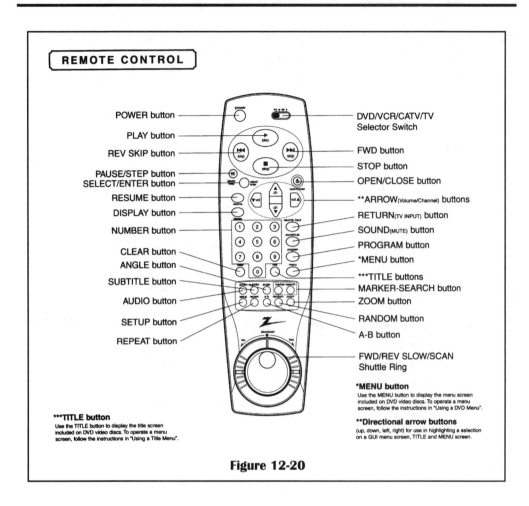

REMOTE CONTROL

POWER button

PLAY button

REV SKIP button

PAUSE/STEP button
SELECT/ENTER button

RESUME button

DISPLAY button

NUMBER button

CLEAR button

ANGLE button

SUBTITLE button

AUDIO button

SETUP button

REPEAT button

DVD/VCR/CATV/TV
Selector Switch

FWD button

STOP button

OPEN/CLOSE button

**ARROW(Volume/Channel) buttons

RETURN(TV INPUT) button

SOUND(MUTE) button

PROGRAM button

*MENU button

***TITLE buttons

MARKER-SEARCH button

ZOOM button

RANDOM button

A-B button

FWD/REV SLOW/SCAN
Shuttle Ring

*MENU button
Use the MENU button to display the menu screen
included on DVD video discs. To operate a menu
screen, follow the instructions in "Using a DVD Menu".

***TITLE button
Use the TITLE button to display the title screen
included on DVD video discs. To operate a menu
screen, follow the instructions in "Using a Title Menu".

**Directional arrow buttons
(up, down, left, right) for use in highlighting a selection
on a GUI menu screen, TITLE and MENU screen.

Figure 12-20

volume-control circuit to reduce the volume level to its lowest level during the operation. When the customer completes the operation, the microcontroller uses an instruction set to replace the serial data 1s with the stored data from the system RAM, and the volume returns to the original setting.

Zenith DVD Video Player Remote-Control Functions

Figure 12-19 provides an exploded drawing of the Zenith DVD video player remote control. As Figure 12-20 shows, the remote control provides all functions needed to operate the video player, as well as a variety of special effects functions. When comparing the remote-control functions with the key functions found at the front panel of the video player, the remote control adds:

- setup
- subtitle
- audio
- repeat
- marker search
- zoom

Remote-Control Transmitter Integrated Circuit

Figure 12-21 (on Page 235) shows a schematic diagram for a DVD video player remote-control integrated circuit. The circuit can generate 2,048 different commands and could address 32 different systems. In turn, each system contains 64 different commands. When operating in the single-system mode, the X inputs go high and the Z inputs remain disabled. Only legal key operations latch the oscillator enable signal and allow communication between the device and the remote receiver located in the video player.

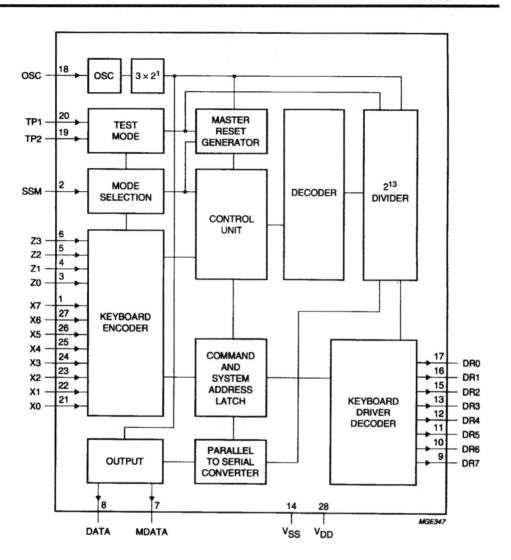

Figure 12-21

13

DVD and Computers

Introduction

Applications that utilize video and audio streaming have grown in popularity and importance. As Table 13-1 indicates, the many uses for video and audio streaming have placed additional burdens on personal computer hardware and software resources. With each streaming application, the hardware and software process a constant, sequential load of large amounts of data. With DVD applications the handling of the data becomes even more complicated, because of the need to manage and decode video, audio, subpicture, and navigation streams.

Table 13-1: Multimedia Bandwidth Requirements

Image Type	Bandwidth Requirement
640 x 480 Digital Video Image (30 frames per second, 24-bit color)	221 megabits per second
640 x 480 Digital Video Image (15 frames per second, 16-bit color)	74 megabits per second
320 x 240 Digital Video Image (30 frames per second, 24-bit color)	55 megabits per second
320 x 240 Digital Video Image (15 frames per second, 16-bit color)	18 megabits per second
High Quality Audio	18 megabits per second
Digital Audio Data (44,100 audio samples per second) (16-bit audio samples) (2 audio channels for stereo)	1.4 megabits per second
Reduced Quality Audio Digital Data (11,050 audio samples per second) (8-bit audio samples) (1 audio channel for monaural)	0.1 megabits per second

Managing and decoding the data is only part of the computing problem. Delivering the DVD application in a satisfactory manner involves precise synchronization that includes load balancing and processing. All this may saturate the processing capabilities of a personal computer and require an alternative to the traditional bus as a path for the data.

Computing System Basics

Computing systems function through the seamless integration of hardware and software. In the personal computing systems of today, installation of a hardware device involves not only the fastening of cables and mounting screws, but also the configuration of the operating system and applications software. The implementation of the latest Windows and Macintosh operating systems include plug-and-play capabilities that sense the installation of a DVD drive and automatically reconfigure the operating system.

Hardware

As the block diagram of a personal computer system in Figure 13-1 shows, every computer system contains a central processing unit (CPU). Performing operations and communicating with other parts of the system, a CPU contains an arithmetic logic unit (alu) that performs mathematical and logical operations. The CPU also contains a processor that pulls instructions from memory, decodes the instructions, and then executes the commands. Along with the CPU, other integrated circuits operate as controllers and manage the transfer of data between components, between devices, and between components and devices.

Memory in a computer stores data either on a permanent or temporary basis. The integrated circuit devices are classified as random-access memory (RAM) devices and as read-only memory (ROM) devices. All random-access memory devices are volatile. Once the power is turned off for the system, the memory loses its contents. The read-only memory of a computer system is nonvolatile. With this, the ROM retains its contents even with the system powered down. After data has been written onto a ROM chip, the data cannot be removed and, as the name implies, can only be read.

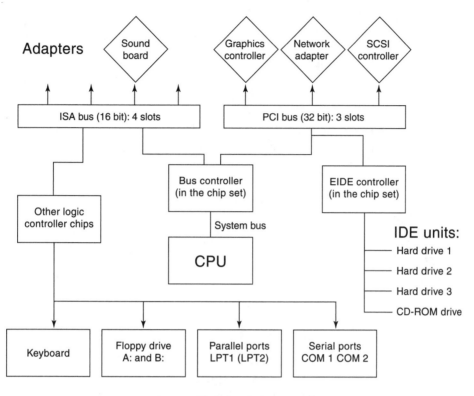

System bus

Figure 13-1

As shown in Figure 13-2 (on Page 240), computers use a highway-like set of internal circuit connectors called a bus for communication between the processor and the remainder of the system. The number of data paths found on a bus determines the data-transfer capacity of the system. Thirty-two-bit systems use 32 data paths, while 64-bit systems use 64 data paths. Most personal computers use a local bus, or data bus that connects directly—or almost directly—to the microprocessor.

While local buses have limited capability to support a large number of devices, the direct bus architecture offers very fast data traffic speeds, or throughput. As an example of local bus applications, a personal computer may use a local bus for video data and a general bus for other microprocessor data processes. Originally designed for adding memory to portable computers, the PCMCIA expansion standard also functions well for desktop applications.

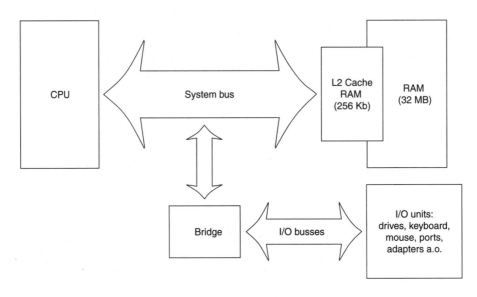

Figure 13-2

Data travels from one component to another, or from a component to either the CPU or RAM along the input/output (i/o) buses. In all systems, an i/o bus provides lower data-transfer speeds than the system bus. The i/o bus consists of:

- Data paths that move one bit at a time.
- Address paths that identify the destination for data.
- System paths that carry clock, voltage, and verification information.

When a component or device sends data along a bus, a binary address code matches with the destination component or device. Each device on the bus has an address. For example, the RAM divides into sections with each section owning an address.

Operating Systems Software

Operating systems software recognizes input from the keyboard, sends output to the monitor, keeps track of files and directories on the disk, and controls peripheral devices such as disk drives and printers. In addition, the operating systems software ensures that different programs and users running at the same time don't interfere with each other. Operating systems software includes compilers, loaders, linkers, debuggers, and drivers.

Operating systems are classified as multiuser, multiprocessing, and multitasking. A multiuser operating system allows two or more users to run programs simultaneously. A multiprocessing operating system—sometimes called a parallel processing system—allows more than one program to run concurrently. Both Unix and OS/2 are examples of multiprocessing operating systems. Multiprocessing operating systems involve more than one CPU and are much more complicated than single-process systems, because they allocate resources to different processes occurring within the computer.

With a multitasking operating system, only one CPU is involved. During operation, the CPU switches from one program to another so quickly that it gives the appearance of executing all of the programs at the same time. Windows and the Macintosh operating system are examples of multitasking operating systems.

Device Drivers

The integration of software and hardware often relies on small sets of software called device drivers. Operating systems and other applications use device drivers to communicate with network interface cards, disk drives, optical drives, and other peripheral devices. Along with controlling the operation of hardware devices, device drivers also establish communication between network interface cards and the network.

Hardware Requirements and Support for DVD Technologies

Given the versatility of DVD technologies, personal computers must support the playback, authoring, and storage capabilities of DVD-Video, DVD-ROM, DVD-RAM, DVD-Audio, and DVD-RW. Much of this support begins with a bus that can handle high-speed transfer of multiple data types. In addition, the system must include processing power and either hardware or software decoding for the video and audio streams.

In addition, DVD drives must support the functionality of compact disc technologies and include some type of defect management. To ensure backwards compatibility, DVD devices must conform to logical and physical format standards listed in the Red, Yellow, White, Orange, and Blue books. Along with meeting those standards, DVD devices must support the ECMA-272, 273, 274, 267, and 268 standards.

Bus Mastering Requirements

Bus mastering decreases the bandwidth required to move video and audio information from a DVD player or drive to the computer and then to the decoder. Each video, audio, navigation, or subpicture stream requires a set of 16 logical buffers. Consisting of physical data segments, each logical buffer can begin or end on any byte position in physical memory. Consequently, the first and last physical data segment may have smaller sizes than a physical memory page. All other segments, however, must remain as contiguous multiples of the physical memory page size.

ATA/ATAPI Standards

The abbreviation "ATA" signifies "AT attachment," while "ATAPI" represents "ATA packet interface." Originally developed in 1989 by a division of Control Data Corporation called Imprimus, the Western Digital Corporation, and Compaq Computer, ATA/ATAPI served as an interface for only Compaq computers. Since the ATA/ATAPI standard uses a command execution protocol that allows the operation of compact disc and DVD drives and players on the same interface cable as hard disk drives, the ATA/ATAPI standard has become the most popular storage-device interface.

Although most computer manufacturers designate Enhanced IDE (EIDE) as the current standard for the inexpensive, high-performance hard disk drives used in personal computers, EIDE and ATA/ATAPI represent the same standard. Registered as a trademark of the Western Digital Corporation, the EIDE host controller can accommodate four attached logical drives. Since the controller connects directly to the PCI bus, it allows personal computer systems to incorporate large-capacity disk drives and higher data-transfer rates.

SCSI Standard

Pronounced "scuzzy," the term "SCSI" represents the "small computer system interface" and allows the connection of a variety of devices to a personal computer. With the connection made through a SCSI card installed within the computer, the SCSI standard offers the fastest available i/o connection, supports high-speed mass storage devices, and transfers data at rates ranging from 10 megabytes per second to 160 megabytes per second.

Using a unique identification number for each device connected to the SCSI chain, a SCSI controller card offers connectivity for internal and external peripherals and can connect from seven to 15 devices per channel. As a result, SCSI-connected devices can multitask and accept simultaneous read/write operations. The first and last devices on a SCSI bus terminate and stop the data signal. Table 13-2 provides a listing of SCSI interface types and specifications.

Table 13-2: SCSI Types, Speeds, Connectors, and Applications

TYPE	SPEED	BUS WIDTH	CONNECTOR	MAXIMUM # OF DEVICES	APPLICATION
SCSI-1	5 MB/s	8-bit Narrow	50-pin Centronics	8	Scanners and tape drives.
SCSI-1	5 MB/s	8-bit Narrow	DB-25	8	Zip Drives
SCSI-2	10 MB/s	8-bit Narrow	50-pin High-Density (mini 50, micro 50)	16	CD-R, DVD, and Jaz Drives
Ultra SCSI	20 MB/s	16-bit Wide	50-pin High Density (mini 50, micro 50)	8	CD-R, DVD, and Jaz Drives
Wide SCSI	20 MB/s	16-bit Wide	68-pin High-Density	4	Hard Disk Drive Connections
Ultra Wide SCSI	40 MB/s	16-bit Wide	68-pin High-Density	16	Hard Disk Drive Connections
Ultra2 SCSI	80 MB/s	16-bit Wide	68-pin High-Density	8	Hard Disk Drive Connections
Ultra160 SCSI	160 MB/s	16-bit Wide	68-pin High-Density	16	Hard Disk Drive Connections
Ultra2 LVD (Low Voltage Differential)	160 MB/s		68-pin High-Density, 12' Length	16	Peripheral and Hard Disk Drive Connections
Single-ended SCSI	40 MB/s	16-bit Wide	68-pin High-Density, 3 Meter Length	16	Peripheral and Hard Disk Drive Connections
Ultra2 HVD (High Voltage Differential)	40 MB/s		68-pin High-Density, 25 Meter Length	16	Peripheral and Hard Disk Drive Connections

IEEE-1394

Currently, IEEE-1394 establishes high-performance multimedia connections for business and consumer electronic devices such as digital camcorders, televisions, stereos, digital videodiscs, set-top boxes, mixing consoles, and music keyboards, along with hard-disk drives, printers and scanners, and docking stations for portable computers.

In addition to superior bandwidth capabilities, IEEE-1394 provides a completely digital interface that allows devices to process the digital information without the expense and degradation caused by digital-to-analog conversion. The use of a digital interface eliminates devices such as video-capture cards and provides an entire digital data path. As a result, a monitor, computer, or digital VCR could accept the digital data and either display it or store when appropriate. From a video-editing point of view, a digital video camera applying the IEEE-1394 standard doesn't require the use of analog video computer frame buffers for the capture of digital video.

IEEE-1394 Operation

From a technical perspective, the serial bus management found with IEEE-1394 combines low-cost connectivity with:

- arbitration timing.
- assignment of a device as the cycle master.
- assignment of a channel identification number.
- error checking.
- to provide configuration control of the serial bus.

Although IEEE-1394 may seem to operate as a network interface, the standard relies on the use of a serial bus to establish a simple point-to-point connection that allows scalable capability with technology improvements. The bus can connect a large number of peripherals easily and inexpensively. In addition, serial bus management data-transmission commands consist of simple, straightforward functions such as a write to the address of the peripheral or a read from its address.

Arbitration timing occurs with a bus configuration that sends a 125-microsecond start-of-frame timing indicator that takes the form of a timing gap. With the timing indicator in place, time slots for isochronous channels one and two take the next place in the frame. User applications determine the number of required isochronous channels and the required bandwidth for each channel.

Low-cost connectivity occurs through the use of isochronous—or just-in-time—delivery that allows the implementation of time-critical multimedia interfaces and serial bus management. Even with the high data-transport speeds seen with IEEE-1394, just-in-time delivery ensures that multimedia data receives the appropriate bandwidth when needed. Once arbitration timing establishes the isochronous channel slots, the bus can ensure the delivery of the channels and sufficient bandwidth for the application requirements.

Then, the bus establishes the isochronous channel IDs that precede the sending of the packet data. During the data-transport process, the receiver monitors the incoming channel ID of the data and accepts only data with the specified ID. The channel IDs contain the addressing information for both the sending and receiving stations. Given the operating characteristics of isochronous data transmissions, even low-speed transmissions support two simultaneous channels of broadcast-quality video and CD-grade stereo audio.

IEEE-1394 also offers asynchronous data transfer so that interoperability with existing printers and modems can exist, as well as command and control for new devices. IEEE-1394 devices that rely on different data-transfer rates may interconnect. As a result, backward compatibility with devices having slower transport rates exists, and current 100 Mbps devices can operate properly with bus configurations that involve 200 Mbps and 400 Mbps devices. Arbitrary timing allocates any time that remains from the isochronous data transfer for asynchronous purposes.

With asynchronous data transfer, equipment sends data in one direction. In turn, equipment on the receiving end responds with an acknowledgment after receiving the packet. The IEEE-1394 standard improves throughput by allowing the sender to continue transmitting data until 64 outstanding transactions exist. If the sending station receives a negative acknowledgment, IEEE-1394 error correction and recovery begins.

The isochronous channels provide a direct path for the actual video data from the camera to other IEEE-1394-connected devices. Due to the just-in-time qualities of isochronous data transfer, the devices do not require collision detection. Control data used for tasks such as powering on the video camera transmits in the asynchronous mode.

IEEE-1394 Media

All this causes IEEE-1394 to appear as a complex set of devices and rules. But the user has a much simpler view of the interface. The IEEE-1394 serial bus uses thin serial cable to replace the typical large and more expensive interface cables. Going back to its Game Boy origins, IEEE-1394 cable con-

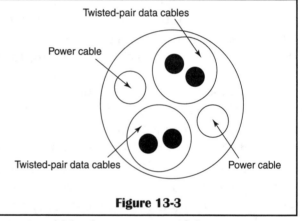

Figure 13-3

nectors place the electrical contacts within the structure of the connector to minimize any shock hazard and to protect the contacts from deterioration. As shown in Figure 13-3, the standard IEEE-1394 shielded cable contains six wires with data traveling through two shielded, twisted pair, 28 AWG transmission lines. To establish a transmit/receive connection, the two twisted pairs cross in each cable assembly.

The remaining two 22 AWG wires apply voltage to remote devices. With this, the IEEE-1394 standard specifies the application of 8V dc to 40V dc at a maximum of 1.5A when shut down to

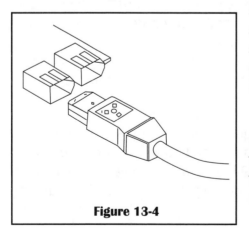

Figure 13-4

maintain physical layer continuity and provide power for any device connected to the bus. The voltages may come from the controlling device such as a computer, VCR, or audio receiver.

Unlike SCSI devices, IEEE-1394 devices don't require terminators, device IDs, or extensive configuration. The use of universal Nintendo Game Boy connectors such as those shown in Figure 13-4 makes IEEE-1394 much easier to connect a number of devices. Given "hot-pluggable" capabilities, IEEE-1394 allows the user to add or remove devices with an active bus.

For the purposes of allowing daisy chaining and establishing tree topologies, IEEE-1394 devices can accommodate multiple connectors. The application of plug-and-play eliminates the need for address switches or other methods used to reconfigure the bus. Typically, the phrase "plug-and-play" takes us to the world of microcomputing, in which the operating system recognizes the installation of a new device. With IEEE-1394, plug and play extends beyond the computer to the interface cabling. IEEE-1394 automatically recognizes and configures for any new device attached to the cable. Disconnecting the device causes the software/hardware standard to automatically reconfigure.

Hardware Decoders

During operation, hardware decoders use a video overlay to insert the video information into the computer display. In most cases, manufacturers place the decoder on the graphics adapter or within the graphics processor. The video overlay may take the form of either an analog VGA output signal from the graphics card and keys found in the video signal or a direct digital connection called the video port extension.

Software Support For DVD Technologies

With the addition of DVD drives and players to the computing environment, operating system and applications software must support the regional codes defined by the DVD standards. In addition, application software must include methods to maintain the licensing to descramble copy-protected movies. Either the operating system, application software, or add-on drivers must support the copy protection of movies through the implementation of CSS, Macrovision, and regional codes. In addition, the software must remain compatible with the universal disk format (UDF) and ISO-9660 file structures used with the DVD and compact disc standards.

Moreover, the operating system must support the interactive features found with the DVD standards. For example, the software must support subpicture compositing and closed captioning. With this, software drivers must have the capability to set subpicture properties and set parameters.

Software Decoders

Software decoders require a minimum of a 233 MHz Pentium II processor and a DVD-ROM drive that features bus-mastering DMA. With DMA, data transfers from a device to RAM through the device controller card without using the CPU. A DMA data transfer provides the fastest method for multitasking operating systems. As a result, the DVD drive can achieve 24-frames-per-second film or 30-frames-per-second video rates. For most applications, a video accelerator improves the performance of the software decoder software. The accelerator card improves the decoder performance by processing MPEG-2 decoding tasks.

Windows Driver Model Streaming Class Driver

The Windows Driver Model (WDM) streaming class driver operates with encoding and decoding devices that use streamed data. In brief, the WDM driver interconnects series of device drives and optimizes data flow in Windows 98 and Windows 2000 environments. The compatibility given through WDM occurs through binary-source coding that supports the use of minidrivers for interfaces such as the Universal Serial Bus, plug-and-play, IEEE-1394 FireWire, graphics cards, and DVD decoders.

Implementation of WDM support becomes possible through the distribution of class drivers by Microsoft. Each class driver establishes a device abstraction for a targeted class of devices. In addition, the class drivers utilize direct memory access, plug-and-play, and other system-wide functions to provide a standard interface for device drivers.

As a result, implementation of the WDM streaming class driver creates a single driver model for multifunction streaming hardware. With Microsoft providing WDM with the Windows 98 and Windows 2000 operating systems, hardware vendors can reduce the amount of interface code used for supporting a device under Windows. A minidriver ensures that features operate consistently in the Windows environment.

DirectShow

The WDM streaming class driver supports MPEG-2 and AC-3 hardware decoders in Windows 98 and Windows 2000. Given vendor support for WDM, most existing DVD decoders should operate with Windows without requiring any user intervention. Combined with WDM, DirectShow separates individual DVD program streams into audio, video, subpicture, and navigation component streams. Then, DirectShow feeds the individual streams in parallel to the WDM driver.

Created by Microsoft, DirectShow provides a software platform that allows the playback of compressed video and audio content regardless of the original compression source. As a result, DirectShow provides cross-platform compatibility with the MPEG, Apple Quicktime, AVI, WAV, Video for Windows, and Windows Driver Model. To accomplish this capability, DirectShow uses pluggable filters.

Regardless of the source, DirectShow selects and demultiplexes MPEG transport streams and program streams. Using a combination of filters and application level interfaces, DirectShow feeds the appropriate video stream to the MPEG decoder. Given the need for system-wide compatibility, and because the encoded streams may have different sources, the decoder must have the capability to support the MPEG without packet sequence numbering.

Configured in a filter graph, the filters follow the instructions given by a software component called a filter graph manager. In turn, application software communicates with the filter graph manager and controls the instructions flowing through the filter graph. With this, both the application

Table 13-3: DirectShow Filters

Filter Type	Filter Application
DVD Navigator/Splitter	Handles the playback of DVD-Video movies by interpreting programming codes embedded within the DVD video stream. The DVD Navigator/Splitter processes DVD data structures and responds to user commands.
Proxy	Converts DirectShow interface to the WDM connection and streaming architecture format and creates a device object for each data type used for decoding.
Closed-Caption Decoding	Converts text images into closed-caption data and includes the data in the DVD video stream.
Overlay Mixer	Uses hardware video ports to allow the playback of video stream, while overlaying low-bandwidth content onto the stream.

Table 13-4: DVD Application-Level Interfaces

Application-Level Interface Type	ALI Function
IAMLine21Decoder	Provides access to closed captioning information and settings.
IDvdControl	Enables an application to control playback and search mechanisms of a DVD-Video disc. Functions with DVD Navigator/Splitter filter.
IDvdGraphBuilder	Provides a method for the DVD application writer to build a filter graph for DVD-Video playback.
IDvdInfo	Enables an application to query for attributes of a DVD-Video disc. Functions with the DVD Navigator/Splitter filter.
IMixerPinConfig	Includes methods for manipulating video streams.
IMixerPinConfig2	Manipulates color controls when supported by graphics adapter.

and the filter-graph manager monitor the connection of the filters and control the video and audio streams. For example, a DirectShow interface can allow any application to control the playback of a DVD disc and establish interactive functions. Table 13-3 provides a listing of the DirectShow filters and filter applications.

DirectShow and DVD Application-Level Interfaces

DirectShow establishes a framework that facilitates the decoding and display of MPEG-2 video and Dolby Digital AC-3 audio streams by hardware or software DVD decoders. Along with the use of the filters, filter graph, and filter-

Table 13-5: DVD Decoder Filter Interfaces

Decoder Filter Interface Type	Decoder Filter Interface Function
IksPropertySet	Sets and retrieves device properties.
DVD Copy Protection Property Set	Authenticates copy protection information from hardware or software decrypters.
DVD Subpicture Property Set	Controls the color, contrast, and output of the subpicture display.
DVD Time Stamp Rate Change Property Set	Changes the DVD playback rate by modifying time stamps between input and output pins on two filters.
VIDEOINFOHEADER2 structure	Describes the bitmap and color information for a video image. The structure includes interlace, copy protection, and pixel aspect ratio information.
MPEG2VIDEOINFO structure	Describes an MPEG-2 video stream.
DVD Media Types and Formats	Diagrams a DVD filter graph and outlines the media types and data formats used in each connection.
DVD Event Notification Codes	Describes DirectShow system-defined events and lists filters that the filter graph should pass to the filter graph manager
DVD for Title Vendors	Describes DVD structures, DirectShow-supported features, and DirectShow-supported methods.
IVPConfig	Sets and retrieves configuration information by enabling communication between a video port mixer filter and a video port driver.

graph manager, the framework also becomes possible through the implementation of DVD Application-Level Interfaces and DVD Decoder Filter Interfaces. While Table 13-4 (on Page 250) provides a listing of the Application-Level Interfaces and the ALI functions, Table 13-5 (on Page 251) lists Decoder Filter Interface types and functions.

DVD-ROM/RAM Drives

While all computer manufacturers offer systems that include DVD-ROM drives, many also offer the availability of DVD-ROM/RAM drives. As we have already seen, the DVD format offers greater capacity and multimedia capability. When considering that capacity in terms of computing, a 1x DVD-ROM drive provides a 90-millisecond to 200-millisecond seek time and a 100-millisecond to 250-millisecond access time. Data transfers at a rate of 1.321 megabytes per second, with burst transfer rates that can exceed 12 megabytes per second.

But DVD-ROM drives spin the disc at a slower rate than comparable CD-ROM drives. The dramatically higher throughput seen with DVD-ROM drives occurs because of the data density seen with the DVD disc. As a result, a 1x DVD-ROM drive that has a data transfer rate of 1,350 Kbps yields the same data transfer speed as a 9x CD-ROM drive.

Newer 2x DVD-ROM drives transfer data at a rate of 22.2 megabits per second and read CD-ROMs at 20x speeds. The faster 6x, 8x, and 10x DVD-ROM drives read CD-ROMs at 32x speed and provide the potential of transferring data at a rate of 55.4 megabits per second. Enlarging the memory cache in the DVD-ROM increases the capability of the drive to transfer data at a faster rate. The higher speeds apply to the transfer of data, rather than the ability to reproduce a video image.

In addition, the data-transfer ratings of CD-ROM and DVD-ROM drives depend on the method for reading the data. Constant linear velocity (CLV) drives spin the disc at a lower slower rate when reading data located near the outside of the disc. Tracks located near the edge of the disk have a greater physical surface than tracks located near the center of the disc. Faster drives

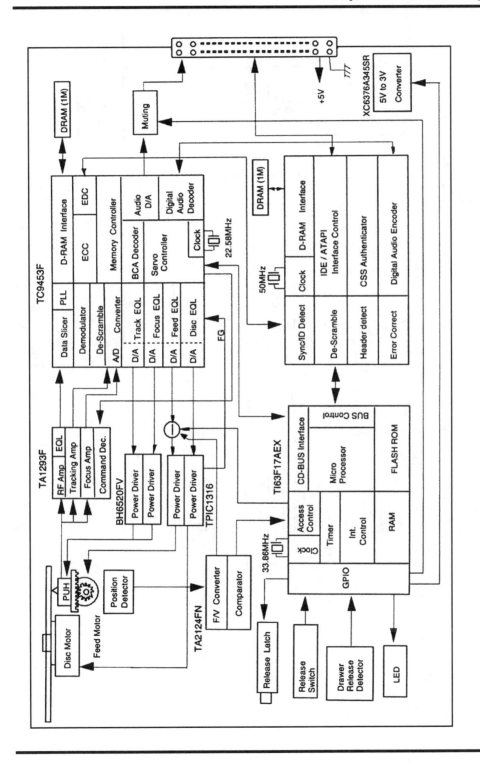

Figure 13-5A

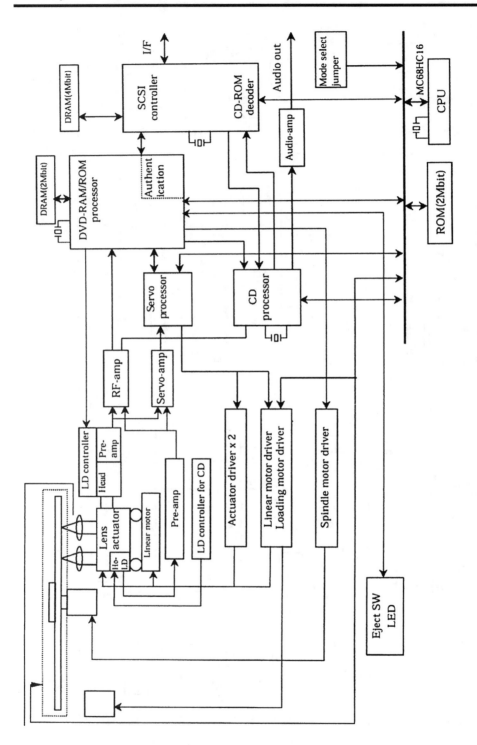

Figure 13-5B

rely on constant angular velocity (CAV), in which the rotational speed remains constant and a buffer compensates for differences in the data-transfer speed. As opposed to CLV drives, CAV drives have the fastest speed when reading data at the outside edge of the disc.

Figures 13-5A (on Page 253) and 13-5B compare block diagrams of DVD-ROM and DVD-ROM/RAM drives. Both drives offer both backward and forward compatibility through the use of a dual laser optical pickup unit.

As we saw in Chapter 9, the dual laser OPU ensures compatibility with CD-ROM and CD-Audio discs by incorporating dedicated lenses and semiconductor laser diodes that allow the reading of all compact disc and DVD disc formats. When the drive checks the inserted disc, it automatically selects the appropriate lens and laser by rotating the assembly.

Along with the dual lens OPU, the servo-control circuits also ensure compatibility with both optical disc formats. For DVD discs, the drive achieves an access time of 200 milliseconds and a random seek time of 130 milliseconds.

The transfer mode includes both the programmed i/o (PIO) mode and the direct memory access mode. Data transfers occur at a rate of 13.3 megabytes per second in burst mode. When operating with a CD-ROM, the drive offers the performance of an eight-times rotational speed CD-ROM drive.

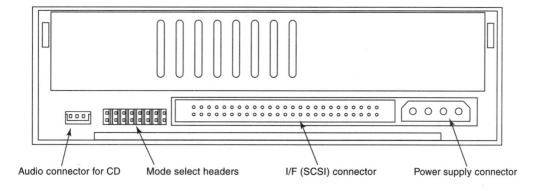

Audio connector for CD   Mode select headers   I/F (SCSI) connector   Power supply connector

Figure 13-6

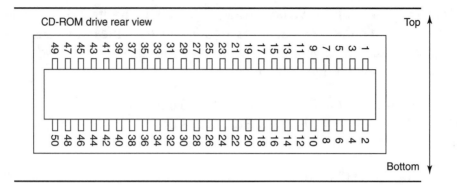

CD-ROM drive rear view

Top

Bottom

Figure 13-7

Drive Interface Cable Connections

Figure 13-6 (on Page 255) shows the back portion of a typical DVD-ROM reader and the locations of the interface connectors. Since manufacturers provide DVD-ROM drives that support either EIDE and SCSI-2 connections, connectivity remains the same with both CD-ROM and DVD-ROM drives. While the EIDE interface cable attaches directly from the drive to the computer motherboard, a SCSI-2 connection requires the installation of a SCSI controller card and different interface connectors and cable. Figure 13-7 shows the pinout connections for the EIDE connector.

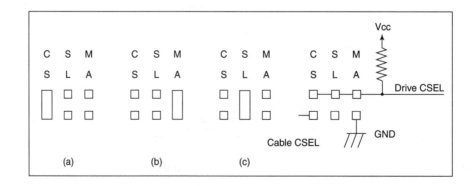

Figure 13-8

Device-Configuration Jumpers

Figure 13-8 shows several possibilities for using device-configuration jumpers to set master and slave drives. The six-pin device-configuration jumper has three marked positions. With CSEL placement, the device shall use the host interface signal CSEL to configure the device. While the MA position sets the device as a master unit, the SL position sets the device as a slave unit.

DVD-ROM Drive ATAPI Host Circuit

Figure 13-9 shows a schematic of the ATAPI Host circuit used in the DVD-ROM drive. The device operates as a block decoder/encoder and buffer for high-speed DVD-ROM functions. During operation, the ATAPI Host circuit integrates real-time error correction and detection, along with ATAPI

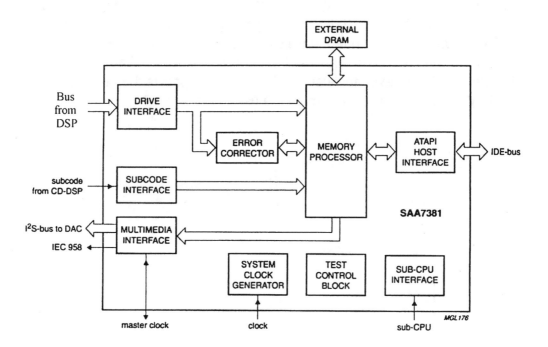

Figure 13-9

bidirectional transfer functions within one integrated circuit. The device attaches directly to the ATAPI bus and allows automated data transfers to and from the host through the use of PIO, DMA, and ultra-DMA circuits.

Cirrus DVD Drive Manager

With the CR3700 drive manager, Cirrus Logic integrates most of the necessary components for a DVD-ROM drive. The CR3700 combines an rf amplifier, data-read channel, servo controller, content scramble system, DVD error-correction code, and a decoder with an ATAPI interface. With the high level of integration, the drive manager delivers capabilities typically provided through several integrated circuits and provides a means for adding DVD-ROM drive functions to a DVD video player.

Supporting both single-layer and dual-layer disc technologies, the CR3700 drive manager incorporates an asynchronous ECC algorithm that can correct faulty sectors while continuing to read other sectors. The drive manager can connect with an audio digital-to-analog converter, external buffer memory, a local microcontroller, and power drivers to create a complete DVD-ROM solution. In addition, the CR3700 provides a direct interface to MPEG-2 audio and video decoders for DVD player applications. The device supports 4.5X DVD and 27X CD-ROM data transfer rates through the use of the ultra-ATA interface.

Index

N

O

P

U

UDF 25, 38
UDF file system 51, 122
ultraviolet light 44
universal disk format 25, 38
Universal Serial Bus 248

V

varactor diode 220
variable bit-rate (VBR) encoding
    105
VAT 25
VBR 105
VBR encoding 105
vco 222
Verbiti error-correction code 15
vertical lines 29
video decoder 202
Video for Windows 249
video stream 59, 63
video zone 52
video-capture card 244
video-decoder hardware 81
video-frequency bandwidth 189
video-object set 53
video-storage capacity 50
video-title set 52, 59
violet laser 157
virtual allocation table 25
virtual sector number 25
visible laser diode 152

VLD 152
VOB 61
VOB playback 61
VOBS 53
volt 128
voltage amplifier 177
voltage divider 137
voltage divider circuit 139
voltage gain 175
voltage regulator 136
voltage-control oscillator 219
voltage-controlled oscillator 222
VTS 53

W

WAV 249
wave, direct 172
wave, ground 172
wave, radio 172
wave, rectangular 8
wave, sawtooth 8
wave, sine 8
wave, sky 172
wave, triangle 8
wavelength 43
WDM 248
White Book 32
white raster 191
wide-screen video 63
Windows Driver Model 248
wipe in color 60
WORM 23
write-once, read-many 23

X

Y

Z

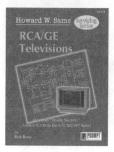

Exploring Solid-State Amplifiers

Joseph Carr

Modern Electronics Soldering Techniques

Andrew Singmin

Exploring Solid-State Amplifiers is a complete and authoritative guide to the world of amplifiers. If you're a professional technician or a hobbyist interested in learning more about amplifiers, this is the book for you.

Beginning with amplifier electronics: overcoming the effects of noise, this book covers many useful and interesting topics. It includes helpful, detailed schematics and diagrams to guide you through the circuitry and construction of solid-state amplifiers, such as: Transistor Amplifiers; Junction Field-Effect Transistors and MOSFET Transistors; Operational Amplifiers; Audio Small Signal and Power Amplifiers; Solid-State Parametric Amplifiers; and Monolithic Microwave Integrated Circuits (MMICs). Two bonus chapters are devoted to troubleshooting circuits and selecting solid-state replacement parts.

The traditional notion of soldering no longer applies in the quickly changing world of technology. Having the skills to solder electronics devices helps to advance your career.

Modern Electronics Soldering Techniques is designed as a total learning package, providing an extensive electronics foundation that enhances your electronics capabilities. This book covers how to solder wires and components as well as how to read schematics. Also learn how to apply your newly learned knowledge by following step-by-step instructions to take simple circuits and convert them into prototype breadboard designs. Other tospic covered include troubleshooting, basic math principles used in electronics, simple test meters and instruments, surface-mount technology, safety, and much more!

Electronics Technology
240 pages • paperback • 7-3/8" x 9-1/4"
ISBN: 0-7906-1192-9 • Sams: 61192
$29.95

Electronics Basics
304 pages • paperback • 6" x 9"
ISBN: 0-7906-1199-6 • Sams 61199
$24.95

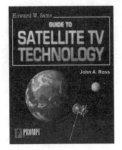

Audio Systems Technology, Level III

Handbook for Installers and Engineers
NSCA

Audio Systems Technology Level III is an essential for the library of the advanced technician who has several years of job experience and an associate's degree or the equivalent. While each book in this series contains its own unique information, there is overlap from one level to the next, providing repetition on the most important, fundamental points. This intentional dovetailing also allows the entire series to be used as a systematic, progressive course of study from the basics through intermediate and advanced topics.

Theory and Design of Loudspeaker Enclosures
J.E. Benson

Written for design engineers and technicians, students, and intermediate-to-advanced level acoustics enthusiasts, Theory & Design of Loudspeaker Enclosures presents a general theory of loudspeaker enclosure systems. Full of illustrated and numerical examples, this book examines diverse developments in enclosure design, and studies the various types of enclosures as well as varying parameter values and performance optimization.

Topics examined in Theory & Design of Loudspeaker Enclosures include: The Synthesis of Vented Systems, Infinite-Baffle and Closed-Box Systems, Electro-Acoustical Relations, Reflex Response Relationships, System Response Formulae, Input Impedance, Circuit Parameters, System Parameters, Driver Parameters, Analogous Circuits, Terminology, And More.

Audio
320 pages • paperback • 7-3/8 x 9-1/4"
ISBN: 0-7906-1178-3 • Sams 61178
$34.95

Audio
244 pages • paperback • 6 x 9"
ISBN: 0-7906-1093-0 • Sams: 61093
$24.95

To order today or locate your nearest Prompt® Publications distributor at 1-800-428-7267 or www.samswebsite.com

Prices subject to change.

Electronics for the Electrican
by Newton Braga

Guide to PIC Microcontrollers
by Carl Bergquist

Author Newton Braga takes an innovative approach to helping the electrician advance his or her career. Electronics have become more and more common in the world of the electrician, and this book will help the electrician become more comfortable and proficient at tackling the new tasks required of him or her. Projects and topics include:
- Circuits
- Components
- Fiber Optics
- Troubleshooting Tips

PICs, or peripheral interface controllers, easy to use and are the "chip of the '90s." Aimed at students and entry level technicians, Bergquist displays his expertise in the electronics field with this excellent guide on the use of PIC Microcontrollers. Projects and topics include:
- Electrical Structure
- Software Codes
- Prototype layout boards

Electrical Technology
320 pages • paperback • 7-3/8" x 9-1/4"
ISBN 0-7906-1218-6 • Sams 61218
$34.95

Electronics Technology
336 pages • paperback • 7-3/8" x 9-1/4"
ISBN 0-7906-1217-8 • Sams 61217
$39.95

To order today or locate your nearest Prompt® Publications distributor at 1-800-428-7267 or www.samswebsite.com

Prices subject to change.

PROMPT®
PUBLICATIONS

Computer Networking for Small Businesses

by John Ross

Small businesses, home offices, and satellite offices have flourished in recent years. These small and unique networks of two or more PCs can be a challenge for any technician. Topics include:
• Installation
• Troubleshooting and repair
• Common network applications

Telecommunications Technologies:

Voice, Data & Fiber Optic Applications

by John Ross

This book contains the information needed to develop a complete understanding of the technologies used within telephony, data and telecommunications networks. Projects and topics include:
• Equipment comparisons
• Business office applications
• Understanding the Technology

Communication
368 pages • paperback • 7-3/8" x 9-1/4"
ISBN 0-7906-1221-6 • Sams 61221
$39.95

Communications
368 pages • paperback • 7-3/8" x 9-1/4"
ISBN 0-7906-1225-9 • Sams 61225
$39.95